CW00641391

Squeeze

SONG BY SONG

Printed and bound in the United Kingdom by MPG Books Ltd, Bodmin

Distributed in the UK by Faber and Faber
Distributed in the US by Publishers Group West

Published by Sanctuary Publishing Limited, Sanctuary House
45–53 Sinclair Road
London W14 0NS
United Kingdom
www.sanctuarypublishing.com

Copyright © Chris Difford & Glenn Tillbrook 2004

Cover photo: courtesy of Redferns Music Picture Library
Cover design by Ash

Song credits: see page 319

All rights reserved. No part of this book may be reproduced in any form or by any electronic or mechanical means, including information storage or retrieval systems, without permission in writing from the publisher, except by a reviewer, who may quote brief passages.

While the publishers have made every reasonable effort to trace the copyright owners for any or all of the photographs in this book, there may be some omissions of credits, for which we apologise.

ISBN: 1-86074-604-7

Squeeze

SONG BY SONG

Chris Difford & Glenn Tilbrook

with Jim Drury

Sanctuary

Contents

Acknowledgements

Chris would like to thank Glenn for being my life long partner in writing, and by reading this book I now know that I love you more and thank you for being there for me at all times. All band members across the years, Lew Difford, all our managers past and present. My children Natalie Riley Grace and Cissy. Heidi Miller.

Thanks also to all of my friends in the rooms, far and wide. Big hugs to Clive Banks and Moira, Gordon, Les Difford, Cindy Difford, Suzanne Hunt, Colin Young, James Harman and to Jim Drury for spending all those hours with me on the book drinking water by the river.

And love to my M for being a new inspiration in my life. I think its time to pick up the pen again...

Glenn would like to thank:

Jim Drury for his patience, his tact, and his understanding;

Chris for sharing an incredible journey;

The 22 people who came in and out of Squeeze besides me and Chris;

Our managers Paul Lilley, Shep Gordon, and last but not least Suzanne Hunt for her tact, understanding, and love, for which I am forever grateful;

James Harman, Lew Difford, John Wood, John Cale, Elvis Costello, Roger Bechirian, Laurie Latham, Eric Thorngren, Tony Berg, Pete Smith, Alison Vernon-Smith, Bill Saurer, and Karyn Soroka;

Ted, Louis, and Leon for being lovely and providing ballast;

The fans for giving us support and keeping us going.

Introduction

THE SONGWRITING partnership of Chris Difford and Glenn Tilbrook is among the most respected in the world of pop music. During a 25-year association the pair enjoyed a working relationship that was almost telepathic in its nature and yet, at the same time, oddly distant.

Having met in south London as teenagers, the pair quickly established a strict demarcation of roles in their partnership; Chris taking responsibility for lyrics while Glenn created the accompanying music. That this neat division of labour was never formally discussed illustrates one of the most intriguing aspects of Chris and Glenn's relationship: their almost complete lack of verbal communication.

From their joyful exchanging of rock 'n' roll vows in 1973 to their painful divorce in 1998, the pair's union was never straightforward. Despite their immense respect for one another's undoubted talents, the pair were frequently at odds, be it over musical styles, perceived slights in the studio and even their choice in women. Yet full-scale rows were rare, the pair choosing to brood in silence, harbouring resentments that could lead to months without their exchanging a solitary word. One can only imagine what it must have been like for their bandmates on tour, being asked if Glenn or Chris could pass the salt.

Despite the fallouts and the feuds, and a distinct lack of common interests, Chris and Glenn shared a love of music and stuck together through thick and thin. Both men knew instinctively that their talents fitted hand in tailored glove and that their writing partnership was more than the sum of its – admittedly exceptional – parts.

Six years on from the dissolution of the Difford-Tilbrook partnership, the pair have decided to reveal once and for all the truth behind Squeeze and the minutiae of their quarter-century writing partnership. It has been my enormous privilege to help them take this journey.

The importance of the other 14 musicians who over the years filled the various berths in Squeeze should not be underestimated. In particular, the contributions of Gilson Lavis, Jools Holland and Keith Wilkinson were vital. Yet, despite the assorted attempts at band democracy over the years, Squeeze was at most times a duopoly, with Glenn and Chris maintaining a joint share of the power base.

Songwriting ideas from others within the band were viewed at best with pained acquiescence, and at worst disdain and outright hostility. It is perhaps no surprise, therefore, that from their third LP onwards, Squeeze's line-up would change with every album. Indeed, when Squeeze initially broke up in 1982, Chris and Glenn stuck resolutely together to form Difford And Tilbrook, despite their increasingly fractious personal relationship.

Both Chris and Glenn were nothing but honest and accommodating throughout their interviews with me. Neither shirked what must at times have been difficult questions and did their best to give a balanced view of life in Squeeze. Much of the interviewing took place separately, for reasons of expediency, and to enable both men to be more open without the other's presence.

What I hope shines through in this book is the enormous respect and affection, even love, that Glenn and Chris feel towards one another. You will lose count of the occasions when one praises the other's contribution to a song, with expressions like 'genius' and 'brilliant' commonplace.

When it comes to discussing the details of the band's catalogue it is uncanny how much the two men agree on a track's relative merits. With the passage of time both feel an enormous sense of pride in their consistently high-quality output, particularly during the 1987–95 period when creatively they could barely do wrong. On other occasions, for instance the surprising success of the lightweight '853-5937' in the US, the pair are filled with a sense of embarrassment.

Although they never quite reached their full commercial potential, Squeeze sold an impressive number of records and recorded a total of 12 studio albums (plus 1984's dual effort *Difford And Tilbrook*), a figure that most bands can only dream of. Although reluctant to adopt the monikers of 'The new Lennon and McCartney' and the 'Godfathers Of Britpop' that were foisted upon them, the Difford-Tilbrook partnership has been an inspiration to countless artists over the years.

In addition, many of the band's songs have seeped into the British public's consciousness. Who on this sceptred isle would fail to recognise 'Cool For Cats' or 'Up The Junction' if they heard them on the radio? Indeed, just last month, as my train passed through Clapham Junction recently, a middle-aged man turned to his children and quoted the first two lines of the latter: 'I never thought it would happen/ With me and the girl from Clapham'. This scene probably happens every day at what is England's busiest railway station.

This book is rather unconventional in its style, incorporating two distinct genres. It is written in the narrative form when dealing with the overall history of Squeeze, reverting to dialogue format for the detailed track-by-track analyses. The book is in fact a mixture of the two styles employed in my first two books in Sanctuary's ongoing 'Song By Song' series. *The Stranglers – Song by Song* was constructed entirely as a dialogue between myself and co-author Hugh Cornwell, the band's original lead singer, while *Ian Dury And The Blockheads – Song by Song* was written in biographical style. I can only hope that the reader will agree with me that in this instance, *Squeeze – Song by Song* is a hybrid breed, rather than a mongrel.

If Glenn and Chris have enjoyed working on this book even half as much as I have, I shall be heartened. At the risk of browning my nostrils, I have been left with a host of terrific memories from working with two great blokes. Chris and Glenn really are the most witty and down-to-earth pop stars you could ever hope to meet. I had a ball, guys.

The interviews were conducted in a variety of settings, including Chris's trendy flat overlooking the Thames, BBC dressing rooms, campsites in the West Country and on board Glenn's enormous RV touring bus. I can only imagine what I must have looked like when waking up face down on the floor of Glenn's RV as he drove his band down the motorway the morning after I'd helped empty his fridge of lager in Cardiff. Fortunately, Glenn and his terrific backing band The Fluffers found the episode hilarious and allowed me to stay on board…so long as I bought the next round.

The last time I'd been that drunk after watching Mr Tilbrook perform, I was propelled off the stage and onto a polished wooden floor by an over-enthusiastic roadie at a show my sister Cathy had organised in Oxford back in 1991. In spite of the fulsome apologies from Messrs Difford and

Tilbrook 13 years later, I'm still considering making a phone call to one of those 'no win no fee' ambulance chasers advertised on daytime telly.

There are a few people I'd like to thank, in addition to Glenn and Chris, for their help with this book: Suzanne Hunt for skilfully and sympathetically fitting me into Glenn's hectic schedule in May in the build-up to his US tour; Glenn's backing band, namely Simon Hanson, Stephen Large and Lucy Shaw, and tour manager Alison Vernon Smith, for making my stay on the road such a barrel of laughs; Hugh Cornwell, Mick Gallagher and my comedy writing partner Graeme Chesters for their encouragement. Sue Nicholls, Mitzi Bagpuss, Lawrence Impey, Kristen Marzec and David Bailey at packetofthree.com for their photographs; Ken Drury for his Herculean work on transcriptions; Dorothy Howe and Diana Bell for their brilliant PR work; and last but by no means least, my first-class commissioning editors at Sanctuary, Albert DePetrillo and Iain MacGregor.

Jim Drury
Malaga, Spain
August 2004

1 A Couple of Likely Lads

'GUITARIST WANTED for band with record deal and tour.' The advert in the sweet shop in Blackheath village looked appealing to the 15-year-old hippy walking barefoot along the pavement. Glenn Tilbrook, a keen guitar player, had been desperate for rock stardom since the age of five, when his mother took him to the pictures to watch Cliff Richard in *Summer Holiday*. Spotting the handwritten card in the south London shop window, alongside ads for second-hand divans, cookers and Tomahawk bicycles, it seemed to offer the long-haired schoolboy instant access to the big time.

Arriving home, Glenn was in two minds about ringing the number on the card, but after some persuading by girlfriend Maxine, he made the call. The deep voice on the other end of the line had almost given up hope of a reply. Chris Difford, a shy and self-conscious 18-year-old, had placed the ad many weeks earlier, without receiving a single reply. Arranging to meet at the Three Tuns pub in Blackheath, it was difficult to judge which of the two budding musicians was the more delighted.

Chris had been playing guitar since he was 15 and writing lyrics from the age of 12. 'My elder brother had moved to the country and when I went there to stay I got this flair for writing lyrics about the countryside and my imagination would go off in all sorts of odd ways. If you don't have many friends it's good to create them in your imagination. I know that sounds sad, because I did have friends, but you could never be alone when you were writing. There was always somebody with you.'

During his final year at West Greenwich Boys School, Chris decided that despite his evident intelligence he would eschew the chance of higher education and dedicate his life to the lofty aim of being a successful songwriter. His parents, with whom he lived on a Blackheath council estate, were appalled. 'My folks were not at all keen on my being in a band and at that time I was taking sulphate and all manner of other drugs, which they didn't approve of.'

His first attempt at performing, in a makeshift band of schoolmates, was inauspicious: 'We reckoned we were like The Velvet Underground and because we were all on drugs thought our music sounded great, but we weren't making a very interesting sound at all.' Perhaps fortunately, the band never performed live.

Having left school at 16, Chris began work as a clerk for a local solicitor. Originally his plan was to involve part-time law studies as a fall-back position in the likely event his songwriting career failed. But the plan was scuppered by an incident characteristic of Chris's out-of-kilter moral compass at that time.

Working for an attractive young solicitor, Miss Valerie Morrance, Chris was frustrated at his low salary and decided upon drastic measures to supplement his wages. 'I've lived with delusions of grandeur all my life and at that time I thought because I was working in the Law Courts I should be getting more money. I was also developing a sulphate habit, so one night, when everyone had gone, I raided the safe. Of course, I was found out and got the sack. My dad was so pissed off and had to pay the money back. I was in a terrible mess at that time.'

Despite Miss Morrance kindly agreeing not to involve the police, Chris was forced to abandon any hope of a career in law. 'Who knows, if I hadn't been sacked I could have ended up working in the local solicitor's office doing probate, God help us.'

Not content with heavy drug-taking and theft, Chris also began hanging out with a gang of skinheads, getting into numerous scrapes with other local mobs. 'It became quite violent and I got involved in some sticky situations, which I now regret, but I was young. Then one day something clicked and overnight I turned into a hippy. I was completely changed and at that point I thought I really should take the idea of getting a band together seriously.'

Chris's stint as a skinhead was not entirely wasted, his shaven-headed pals encouraging him to listen to a wide range of music, from reggae to Tamla Motown and soul. The gang's unlikely friendships with some black youths also helped develop his interest in dance music.

By the spring of 1973 Chris had composed a vast swathe of lyrics in his bedroom and was anxious to find a like-minded companion with whom to share his songs. The scale of his desperation was clear from the outlandish claims contained in the scrawled ad in the sweet shop window. 'I thought if I was going to get people interested I should say I was in a band and that we had a record deal and a tour lined up. In fact, none of it was true. It was just me and my songs. No one answered for weeks and I was getting increasingly despondent until Glenn rang.'

Sitting inside the Three Tuns with a pint of lager Chris was bemused by his first sighting of the lad with whom he would form one of the best-known writing partnerships of the following 30 years. 'I looked out of the window and saw this boy who looked very young and didn't have any shoes or socks on. He was wearing pink satin flares and a T-shirt, and had a mandolin under his arm. I was a bit freaked out by that, because it wasn't what I was expecting.'

Chris's choice of venue was certainly in keeping with his new acquaintance. 'The Three Tuns was a notorious pub for potheads to go and drink. It was a dreamy binge parlour with fruit gums glued on the wall.'

Accompanying Glenn to the pub on that fateful day in April 1973 was his girlfriend Maxine Barker. According to Chris, 'Maxine had long flowing blondish hair and was wearing a long kaftan. The two of them together were angelic. They were almost identical, both with long hair, and had a glow of youth and beauty around them. I was immediately attracted to their energy.'

Like his crop-haired companion, Glenn was a working-class product of Blackheath, albeit with a more independent and bohemian upbringing. His parents, Peter and Margaret, split up when he was just five years old, leaving his mother to raise Glenn and his brother Roger, seven years his senior, on her own.

Glenn recalls, 'My brother left home when I was eight, and from then on it was just me and my mum. I recognise now that we were quite poor, but I had no idea at the time. Because there was just me and my mum I was always happy to be self-absorbed and that took its form in my love of music. I pestered my parents into getting me a guitar, and I then got a piano off an aunt. From the age of seven I taught myself music and could play chords by the time I was eleven.'

The break-up of her marriage shattered Margaret and it wasn't long before her headstrong younger son became completely uncontrollable. 'Mum never really recovered her ground after her divorce. She loved me to bits but she was weak-willed, whereas I was very strong-minded.

'I was expelled from Eltham Green School when I was twelve or thirteen. I played truant for about six months and intercepted all the letters which were sent home and threw them in the bin. My mum didn't have a clue what was going on. It all came to a head when I refused to have my hair cut. The headmaster had a rule about hair not being below collar length and that affronted my personal sense of space. I was kept outside his office for three weeks and then expelled. The local paper ran a story with a picture of me standing outside the school gates looking forlorn, as instructed by the photographer.'

Moving to Crown Woods School, Glenn was exposed to a middle-class environment, and to families 'where people read books and had conversations at supper time. It was a bit of a mystery to me, but I liked it and began to resent my mum. I was terrible to her.'

Having fallen in love for the first time, with Maxine, Glenn moved out of his mother's house at the tender age of 14. Incredibly, the authorities never batted an eyelid when he moved into his girlfriend's home. 'Social Services would be straight in there now,' he jokes.

'Quite a lot of the time when I was growing up I supported my mum in an emotional way without my being aware of that fact. I couldn't wait to leave home because it had simply got too claustrophobic.'

Maxine's family life, into which Glenn was hesitantly accepted, was a world away from his own working-class upbringing. Her father was a critic for *The Evening News* and her mother an actress. Glenn looks back on his time *en famille* with the Barkers with great affection. 'Maxine's parents were lovely. Her mum was very dramatic and thespian, although her dad put up with me with a veneer of thinly disguised disgust. I lived there on and off for a couple of years. Looking back on it, the whole situation was bizarre. My eldest son is 13 and when I think about me losing my virginity at Glastonbury at that age and taking drugs, I'm horrified.

'I had far too much freedom and fell in with a crowd of paedophiles who would invite kids round to their flat in Woolwich. Me and a bunch of other boys would bunk off school to go round there and these men would light up bongs and try to seduce us. Although potentially easily manipulated, I always had a sense of what was right and wrong, so they never got anywhere with me.'

Chris and Glenn gelled instantly and were soon invited into each other's homes to rifle through their very different record collections. Chris was fascinated by Glenn's catholic taste in music, including such luminaries as Amon Duul, Fats Domino, Jimi Hendrix and Elvis Presley. 'It was very attractive to find a mate who had a new stack of records to look through. At home I still had all my ska records and Motown and here was a bloke who had Tonto's Expanding Headband and Hendrix albums.'

Glenn was equally inspired. 'Chris's taste was a tad more sophisticated than mine. He was listening to stuff like The Velvet Underground and I really liked what he played me. Also there was the age gap, with me looking up to this 18-year-old.'

Within weeks Glenn and Maxine had visited Chris's bedroom to witness the gauche teenager's first public performance. 'I played them about ten of my songs, which was the first time I'd ever performed to anybody. It gave me a real buzz, just to have two people in my bedroom and play to them. They really liked what I'd written. Then I heard a couple of Glenn's songs and from that point we spent nearly every evening writing or playing at each other's houses.'

As their partnership blossomed, the pair soon struck upon the writing formula that was to serve them so well, namely for Chris to write all the lyrics while Glenn concentrated on the music. Chris explains, 'I was writing loads of lyrics and one day Glenn said, "Let me have one of your songs and I'll see if I can put a tune to it." I gave him a lyric and he wrote a tune and from that moment on I stopped writing music.'

Glenn regarded Chris's own ability to write music as more than adequate, but they had an unspoken agreement about their division of labour. 'Chris's own songs were way ahead of anything I was doing at the time,' says Glenn. 'Musically he was great, although I suppose that I was a little stronger in that regard. For our first song Chris handed me a lyric without saying anything, in that teenage, non-communicative way that we had of dealing with each other. In fact, that non-communication carried on throughout our writing partnership. We both liked the song, so we carried on writing in that fashion without ever formally saying it.'

The title of that fledgling collaboration was 'Hotel Woman', a recording of which Chris still possesses. Over the forthcoming months the duo churned out dozens of songs, which they honed in their bedrooms during the evenings.

Chris was intrigued by life chez Barker, beginning a lasting fascination with the chattering classes. 'Maxine's house was a wonderful community of friends, with people dropping by unannounced all the time. It was a different world, and one that I found incredible. Her parents were very liberal and loved us being there playing music upstairs. Her mother used to say, "Oh darling, when you're famous we'll put a blue plaque on the wall saying this is where Glenn and Chris wrote their first songs."'

By the summer of 1973 the young duo were playing at the bottom of the bill at festivals, looked after by celebrated photographer Ron Reid, who had befriended Glenn. 'He adopted us as sons,' says Chris. 'We went around in his van and played gigs like the Windsor Free Festival at two o' clock in the afternoon. Ron was producing a book of music photographs and included some of us playing. There's one of us at Windsor that's hilarious. We look so young in it and you can see that no one is taking much notice, especially the Hell's Angels. At one festival, the Trentashoe in Devon, we went on just before a group of Hare Krishnas.'

Over the next two years Glenn and Chris would continue to write songs and hone their craft as a double act. At one stage a short-term manager booked them into a studio where they recorded one track, but the project was abandoned.

Without any hope of a record deal the budding songwriters decided to look for work to subsidise their attempt to become pop megastars. A committed vegetarian, Glenn took a job working in a health food shop in Blackheath village, while Chris opted for a rather less genteel, though far more lucrative, occupation.

Chris's brother Les had worked for some years at the docks in Charlton and wangled his sibling a job for the same firm, a shady export business. 'As I was young I got the job of checking the lorry loads in and out. The drivers were carrying 45 gallon drums of engine oil, so they'd go out with pallets loaded up, and when they'd return their truck would be empty, after they had sold a couple of the pallets to their mates. People would bung me money to tick off the wrong boxes. If they made £100 I'd get £20. All that money, plus my wages, would go to buy us amplifiers and equipment, and pay for rehearsal time.'

In addition to the financial rewards of the job, Chris received life lessons that would help shape much of his writing on the early Squeeze albums. Popular with his workmates, the young lad would be taken during his lunch hour to the local pub and stand goggle-eyed as a succession of strippers paraded their wares to hordes of leering, cheering dockers.

'That job was such an education,' insists Chris. 'All the people who worked there were really tough. One of the owners was an alcoholic and I'd arrive at work in the morning and he would literally be below a barrel of rum, drunk out of his mind. The other owner was a complete villain and the company went down the tubes because so much stuff was going missing. One day we had a delivery of nuts for Safeway, so I took half a pallet to Glenn and he flogged them in the health food shop.

'It was a fascinating time when I got to meet a lot of interesting people and, thanks to my brother Les, I always had a few quid.'

Although delighted to have met his musical soulmate, Glenn continued to jam separately with his friend Julian Holland, known to his pals as Jools. The pair had met when they were 13, when Jools was attempting to sell a guitar to another boy. As the resident guitar expert among his peers Glenn was roped in to judge the quality of the instrument. 'The guitar was rubbish and I recommended very strongly that it wasn't worth a quid, let alone the fiver Jools wanted,' laughs Glenn.

Despite being foiled at his attempt to make a quick buck Jools, a talented boogie-woogie piano player, rapidly became friends with Glenn and the pair started rehearsing together regularly. Glenn recalls, 'Jools was a really gifted piano player, even then. The basis of the way he plays today was all present and correct at that point, although perhaps with not as much refinement as now.'

Glenn and Jools briefly attempted to co-write some songs, but quickly abandoned the experiment, deciding instead to concentrate on practising their craft together.

As Glenn and Chris's burgeoning writing partnership gathered pace, the former decided it was time to introduce his colleague to Jools. Chris's first impressions of Jools were decidedly mixed. 'Jools was quite scruffy. He was wearing a battered leather jacket and trousers with holes, he hadn't washed his hair for weeks, and he stunk of piss. He had really dirty hands and fingernails. He was a real Hell's Angel hangabout, totally unrecognisable to how he is now. He has gone from that to David Jacobs, two opposite ends of the spectrum.

'In fact, when I was a skinhead my gang had a fight outside the Dover Patrol pub with a load of greasers, as we called them. Jools could well have been part of that mob at that time.'

In spite of his disdain for Jools's unkempt appearance, Chris was mightily impressed by his ability on the piano. 'We were at Maxine's house, where there was a piano, and Jools played some boogie-woogie. I was stunned by what I heard.' Chris's master plan of forming a band to take on the world seemed to be coming together. 'I was excited to be playing with two musicians who were so talented. Glenn was dedicated to his instrument and played his guitar in such a fluent manner, and Jools played piano masterfully.'

Next to join the fledgling band was Harry Kakoulli, who had met Chris and Glenn in 1974 whilst playing with Pete Perrett in a group called England's Glory. A school friend of Glenn's, Paul Gunn, was appointed as drummer, although his erratic time-keeping on the sticks led to his departure before their recording career got off the ground.

The quintet began getting regular gigs under the moniker Squeeze, a name picked out of a hat by Maxine's mother. As the alternatives included such instantly forgettable names as Cum, The Hubcaps and Skyco, the band must have subsequently counted their blessings at Mrs Barker's fortuitous movement of hand. 'Squeeze' had been thrown into the hat as a mark of respect to Chris's favourite band The Velvet Underground, who had recorded an album called *Squeeze*, albeit after the departures of both Lou Reed and John Cale.

Throughout 1975 the band built up a sizeable south London following, securing residences at the Bricklayers Arms in Greenwich and the Oxford Arms in Deptford. 'We were playing mainly to our mates,' recalls Chris. 'We used to rehearse at Greenwich Swimming Baths, and then push our gear along the street to the Bricklayers Arms, where we'd often do two sets.'

Emboldened by their loyal army of friends, Squeeze decided from their very first gig to play their own material, with only a handful of covers thrown in, unlike most of their contemporaries, who did the reverse. The few non-original numbers included songs by The Beatles and Todd Rundgren.

'It was a wonderful time,' says Chris. 'After a while we had such a following that people could not get into the pub because it was so packed. Sitting here now I can still feel that atmosphere, even though there were probably only 50 or 60 people there. It felt like we were playing Madison Square Garden.'

After the break-up of Glenn's relationship with Maxine the young singer moved in with Perrett, who was by now frontman in The Only Ones, and played on some of the band's recordings. Paying his rent by moonlighting with Perrett's band, Glenn remembers the experience of living with the singer, who supplemented his income by selling large quantities of narcotics, as 'bizarre'. He adds: 'It was great being in The Only Ones because the whole unit was tight musically, and Pete's songs were fantastic, but it was weird living with a major drug dealer when I was 16.'

Chris was less enthusiastic about his partner working with another band and sunk into deep melancholy, convinced that Glenn no longer wished to work with him. 'It was the first time I thought I was going to lose Glenn and I got frustrated and upset that he'd gone to work with somebody else. I sulked for weeks.'

Glenn had no such plans and continued to devote the majority of his time to Squeeze. The band's big break into the wider London circuit came via a fortuitous encounter with the now legendary manager and promoter Miles Copeland. The man who subsequently launched the career of The Police, which included his brother Stewart on drums, Copeland was a confident, brash American with the gift of the gab and a full contacts book.

It was Glenn's association with Pete Perrett that brought them to Copeland's attention. As Glenn explains, 'Pete had a friend called Laurence Impey, who desperately wanted to manage him. Harry's sister Zena managed Pete, so it was out of the question, but Squeeze were next in line, so he managed us instead. Laurence had been to school with Stewart Copeland and through him got Miles down to see us play. It must have been early 1975.'

Miles was bowled over by what he saw, telling his brother, 'I think I've just found the new Beatles.' He quickly impressed the band with the promise of larger-scale gigs and a record deal, and persuaded them to sign a contract with him. Eventually the marriage would turn sour, which led Squeeze to undertake three years of expensive litigation. According to

Chris, 'We thought it was fantastic that this impressive guy from America wanted to sign us. We signed a contract with him, which we hardly even read. It was for £15 a week and if you saw that deal now you would weep. It wasn't a pretty sight, but we were young and excited.'

The deal involved signing 50 per cent of Squeeze's publishing rights over to Copeland for the entirety of their career. 'We still don't own them,' sighs Chris. 'We really shot ourselves in the foot.'

Despite their annoyance at the deal, both Chris and Glenn credit Copeland with getting their career off the ground, and indeed reluctantly re-signed to his management in 1985 after the cessation of hostilities between the two parties. Chris says, 'I'm not really disappointed or upset by that first deal because we did the right thing signing to Miles. Without that contract we wouldn't have got to support other bands at bigger venues and of course when the New Wave thing came along Miles was at the forefront of it and pushed us forward. We may very easily have got left behind otherwise.'

Copeland secured the band support slots with '70s rock acts like Renaissance, The Climax Blues Band, and Curved Air, although Squeeze's performances frequently confused its new audience. Chris explains: 'Some of the bands we supported would play these really self-indulgent songs that would go on for 20 minutes. We'd go on beforehand and knock out our three-minute tunes and the audiences would be sitting cross-legged on the floor not knowing what had hit them. As soon as New Wave came along these bands were buried in the dust and we just snuck straight in.'

Harry (Kakoulli), a married Greek Cypriot from Catford, quickly became the band's visual focal point, his mop of dark hair and Mediterranean good looks attracting the attention of female fans, up until his departure from Squeeze in 1979. He also specialised in theatrics, performing back flips whilst holding his bass and dancing energetically across the stage. His bass playing, though, was rather more basic. 'He was a bit of a fumbler on the bass,' admits Chris. 'He had one or two riffs that he repeatedly used in every song. I don't know how he got away with it. But he had a good head of hair and all the girls seemed to like him.'

Glenn agrees with Chris's description of their colleague's musical abilities, but cites Harry as crucial to the band's success. 'Harry was a forward-looking chap and important in the development of Squeeze. His bass playing was quite limited but that made him occasionally do things quite brilliantly, sometimes by accident, and sometimes by design. He was into reggae, which was exotic to people like me who listened to rock 'n' roll. He was influential in our development and he was also brilliant onstage.'

Having established Squeeze on the burgeoning London scene, Copeland decided it was time to get his young charges into the studio. His company, British Talent Management (BTM), had a distribution deal with RCA Records and Copeland persuaded them to finance some recordings in Rockfield Studios in Wales. An orchestra was hired for the occasion and a producer whose main success had been with glam-rockers Mud enrolled. Four tracks were recorded, none of which bore resemblance to the sound that was to become synonymous with Squeeze nor, in fact, to the sound that the band had at the time. Fortunately for Squeeze, if not Copeland, BTM went bankrupt within a week of the recordings being made and they were left to gather dust in RCA's vaults.

Another false start occurred in 1976 when the band went to Island Records and recorded a track with Fritz Fryer, whose brief was to make Squeeze sound as much like The Bay City Rollers as possible, and he strong-armed the bemused musicians into playing in the Scottish group's style. Again, the resulting recordings were abandoned. Had either of the recordings been released, Squeeze's career might have been over before it began. Punk was just around the corner and a debut record that sounded like the dying gods of glam rock would surely have been a fatal blow.

The collaboration with Fryer and Island's head honcho Muff Winwood also led to Paul Gunn's departure from Squeeze's ranks. The producer had no patience with the drummer's inability to keep time and insisted the band axe him forthwith. Despite his evident failings, Glenn and Chris still feel guilty about Gunn's dismissal, almost 30 years later. 'Paul was somewhat unfairly dismissed,' claims Glenn. 'He was one of the many unfair casualties of the Squeeze world.'

Chris is more forthcoming and claims the musical perfectionist Glenn found Gunn's playing difficult to accept. 'Paul was a really nice guy, but when you're a drummer one of the benefits of keeping time is keeping your job in the group. Paul could not keep time and this would invariably niggle Glenn, who was the fastidious musician out of us all. Glenn has always been able to see the musical flaws in people very quickly, whereas it takes me ages to discover who's good and who's bad.'

The band responded to the situation by putting an advert in *Melody Maker*, asking drummers to come for audition. 'Being inexperienced, we gave each drummer an hour to play, which was ridiculous,' laughs Glenn. 'We had two weeks of sitting through hour after hour of drumming. Some people would play for three seconds and we'd know immediately that we had 59 minutes of torment ahead.

'One guy brought his dad along, who sat in the corner motioning to his son when to go on to the tom-toms and when to hit the cymbals. Being young we found it difficult to contain our smirking sometimes. It must have been horrible for those who played to us.'

One candidate stood head and shoulders above the others. Gilson Lavis was 25 and had played his first gig at the age of 13 in Luton. Having performed with an impressive variety of artists, he had been working on a building site and looking for a route back into the music business. As Glenn explains, 'Gilson came along and was so obviously the one we should choose. He was experienced, he was brilliant, and above all he was really up for it, so he got the job. We were really excited because Gilson had played with Chuck Berry and Jerry Lee Lewis, whereas we'd mainly been playing in pubs in Greenwich.'

Chris was equally impressed. 'Gilson turned up with this massive drum kit, bigger than the rehearsal room. He was a larger-than-life character, a huge hairy bear, and very passionate about music.'

With a line-up that both band and management were finally happy with, Squeeze recorded a set of demos in Pathway Studios, in north London, at the end of 1976. For the first time Squeeze's exciting live sound was successfully recreated in a studio environment. 'We recorded about 18 songs in there,' says Chris. 'We just topped and tailed them without too much effort and they sounded amazing.'

Towards the end of the recordings Copeland surprised his band by bringing along Velvet Underground legend John Cale to watch, with a view to recording an EP with them. Sensing the changing dynamics of the rock scene, Copeland had pulled off a fantastic coup by bringing the dark-edged guitarist-songwriter in to produce three of the acts in his stable, the others being The Police and The Models.

Cale liked what he saw and agreed to produce the three-track EP. Chris, in particular, was delighted to be playing for a man he had worshipped since he was at school. 'It was so exciting working with someone I had idolised, especially to see him up close and find that he was actually taking as many drugs as people thought and that he was very ill and incoherent. He was everything I had imagined.

'We all knew that the myth around the people in The Velvet Underground was laced with illness, sickness and witnessing it so close felt like walking into a horror show. But it was inspirational at the same time. I thought to myself, "I want to get as stoned as that."'

Cale's major influence on the recording was to make the band sound tougher and less poppy and he helped bring out their more aggressive side. Glenn is full of admiration for his work. 'The EP was successful in highlighting that side of us, which we'd never shown before. He did a great job on "Cat On The Wall", making me sing in a way that I had never done, either before or since. He made us slot into the punk era.'

The resulting EP, which had the cheeky title *Packet Of Three*, contained 'Cat On The Wall', 'Night Ride' and 'Backtrack'. Released in July 1977 it sold a very respectable 25,000 copies, despite being on the little-known Fun City label, receiving significant radio airplay and helping to establish the band's name nationally.

With their recording career up and running Copeland's next task was to find Squeeze an album deal with a major label, and A&M were targeted as a priority. The success of *Packet Of Three*, the band's live profile and radio accessibility, and the fact that John Cale was undertaking production duties no doubt helped assuage any doubts that A&M may have entertained. A deal was quickly agreed upon, and Squeeze returned to the studio determined to make their mark.

But if Messrs Tilbrook, Difford, Holland, Kakoulli and Lavis were under any illusions that they were in for a smooth continuation of their journey, then John Cale was about to shatter their illusions. He wanted a roller-coaster ride.

2 *Squeeze*

WITH THEIR youth, streetwise cockney charm and 'a huge hairy bear' behind the drum kit, it was perhaps inevitable that Squeeze would see how far they could push their new master. Cale would be no physical match for the youthful south London upstarts, but what he lacked in violent promise he more than made up for in sheer psychological menace.

Squeeze's one and only practical joke at Cale's expense was a belter, but his subsequent regaining of control in the studio soon wiped the grins off the band's faces and put the cocky musicians firmly in their place.

Shortly before recording was to proceed, Squeeze were sent by Copeland to some studios in Chelsea to rehearse in front of Cale, who would then choose which segments of their vast repertoire was to go on the LP.

Cale spent much of the time in a drunken haze, swigging liberally from a bottle of brandy, and one day he passed out, to the delight of his charges. Jools's reaction was to hulk two PA stacks next to the comatose producer's head; yet when the giggling band burst into their set as loud as they could, Cale still could not be roused from his slumber. The piano player then took a pen and in a magnificently juvenile act wrote 'I am a cunt' on Cale's forehead before ordering him a taxi back to his hotel.

The next day Cale arrived for work hung-over and with the slogan still emblazoned proudly on his head. When he eventually discovered why the group had spent the morning alternating between sniggers and fully-blown hysterics the former Velvet Underground man was incandescent with rage.

From that point onwards Cale vowed to impose his rule with an iron fist, without even the hint of a velvet glove. At one stage during the album's recording he locked the band in the studio and forced them to play the American standard 'Amazing Grace'. He informed the gob-smacked musicians curtly that until they had perfected a note-for-note rendition with which he was satisfied, they would not be allowed to leave the studio that night.

Cale added that if their rendition was inferior he would also refuse to continue working on their record. One might have expected the five terrified young lads to have seen the latter threat as a bonus, considering their precarious imprisonment, but they were anxious to please this overbearing monster for whom they had enormous respect, and meekly agreed to knuckle down.

Cale's extraordinary request wasn't yet complete. The fact that the band never before had played 'Amazing Grace' had already made their chances of leaving the studio for a cup of bedtime cocoa rather slim. Cale's further insistence that they swap instruments with each other made the task positively anemic. The band members gingerly picked up the alien instruments and did their best to earn their ticket home.

According to Chris, 'Glenn was the only one of us who could remotely play another instrument, the drum kit. It was very embarrassing and John made us feel very stupid.'

Having provided the young musicians with a salutary lesson in knowing their place, the chastened band were released and sent home, with their tails between their legs.

Cale's odd approach also resulted in a decision that left his pupils stunned. Assembling at Surrey Sound Studios for the first day of recording, Cale declared that the songs Squeeze had spent four years writing were inadequate and demanded that they write replacements on the spot in the studio.

Cale told songwriters Difford and Tilbrook that the new tracks must be completely different in style from their predecessors, demanding that they write aggressive, suggestive songs with little melody and absolutely no vocal harmonies for the listener to sing along to.

The result was a patchy first album which, as you will see, neither Chris nor Glenn hold close to their hearts.

***

'Sex Master'

Jim Drury: This is totally unrecognisable from the Squeeze sound we came to know and love. Was this John Cale's influence?

Chris Difford: It was completely down to John. He instigated the punky, attacking music that we played on this album and the lyrics were heavily influenced by him. You can hear our excitement on this track, though. We're obviously enjoying it.

The lyrics are about sexual domination. Why did you write a song like that?

Glenn Tilbrook: I didn't know what the fuck Chris was on about here. It was a different world to me, but I was quite happy to pretend that I knew all about the things he was singing about. I don't know if there's any basis of truth in that lyric. Perhaps Chris could answer.

CD: John told me to write a song about sex fetishes, which at that stage I knew nothing about. The closest I had come to wearing rubber was a pair of marigolds at the kitchen sink. We went with whatever concept John threw at us. He was educating us in all of these things, which was pretty surreal.

Listening now I'm struck by just how powerful Gilson's drums are. His playing and timing was so brilliant and he brought a maturity to the band which previously wasn't there.

GT: Gilson was using his Octoplus kit, which he got in at every available opportunity, willingly spurred on by us. He used every drum on every song, which became Gilson's trademark. Just like on 'Cat On The Wall', from *Packet Of Three*, 'Sex Master' was tremendously propelled by Gilson and without him it would have sounded very ordinary.

CD: No other band at the time had a drummer as good, not of our age anyway. Gilson really kept us on our toes because he'd make us question arrangements and even if he was wrong, it was great to have a drummer who was interested. If you listen to the drumming on this album it's very inventive.

'BANG BANG'

'Bang Bang' was one of two songs on this album that was produced by Squeeze rather than John Cale. Why wasn't he involved?

CD: John was too ill to work by this stage, so we thought if he wasn't going to come in we might as well do it ourselves. Glenn led the way, to be fair, rolling up his sleeves and getting on with the lion's share of the work.

GT: We recorded both this and 'Take Me I'm Yours' when John was ill and they ended up as the two singles from the album, which tells you all you need to know about the record really.

CD: This was written after a heavy weekend of sulphate abuse when all I could hear was my heart going bang-bang, bang-bang. It was a strange feeling. You can hear the heart beating throughout the song. It was written in a small café in Greenwich near to where Glenn and I lived in a house together.

GT: I think the song's rubbish. Like all novelty songs, it had its moment. I think we thought it tremendously funny at the time but I have to say I don't laugh anymore.

Chris, I've read an interview with you in which you said 'Bang Bang' was the song you'd most like to disown.

CD: I don't feel like that now. I used to disown tracks like 'Cool For Cats' as well, which is odd. It was all to do with my fragile ego, but now it's in the past I look at this as part of my education in life. Recently I have been archiving these songs, and going back through the history book, and I can respect each piece for its own merit. I listen to 'Bang Bang' now and respect it because it sums up the attitude of us as at the time. We were a bunch of excited young men who had just got a record deal and were flying. It was terribly exciting.

'STRONG IN REASON'

This song has another unusual subject matter.

CD: John decided I should write a song about a muscle man, so that night I went away, thought about what it would be like, and wrote the lyric. Glenn wrote a sort of Velvet Underground backing track for it. Then it was suggested that I should sing it, which was frightening for me in those days. I hated being at the front and had this huge fear that I was singing out of tune. Glenn was a better singer so I couldn't understand why he didn't do all the singing. I gave it a go and because it sounded a bit like The Velvet Underground I managed to get away with it.

What do you think of the song lyrically?

CD: I'm very proud of it because I took a subject I knew nothing about and managed to make sense of it. I still like playing it, actually. If I was doing an acoustic show tomorrow I'd play 'Strong In Reason'.

The imagery in the lyric is very funny. The muscle man getting his 'trunks out of the drawer' and putting away his sun lamp. It's quite patronising.

CD: That's just the juvenile young writer not understanding the sensitivity of the situation. I wrote the lyric very quickly to impress John Cale. For the first three years of my writing, the only person I wanted to impress was Glenn and suddenly there was this other man in my life and I had to please him as well as Glenn. Fortunately he loved this track.

We went to Los Angeles and did a convention for A&M Records and we came out onstage with two muscle men. The song started and these two men would come on and do their stuff. It was freaky.

'WILD SEWERAGE TICKLES BRAZIL'

This one's an instrumental. A bizarre title for a bizarre song.

CD: I was really pissed off because it didn't have a lyric to it. My job in the band was as lyric writer, so I was completely sidelined. It was frustrating to have written all these songs with good lyrics, but John was just being John and feeding us to the lions.

John wanted half the album to be instrumental, didn't he?

GT: I don't remember that, but it could well be true because it's just the kind of thing John would have come up with. The band all got a credit for writing this. It consists of two chords and a lot of atmosphere. I think that it took a lot from dub reggae in the sense that John had us play all the way through, and at certain points he'd have flag posts where he wanted some of us to stop. It was very dubby in its approach, and when the sound effects and atmospherics were overdubbed it worked pretty well.

It's certainly not easy listening, is it?

CD: Not at all. John got the girl in from the studio restaurant to do the screaming on it. This poor young girl was petrified, having been summoned in from pouring the tea to scream into a microphone. John said to her, 'Imagine you're being raped.' He was probably getting off on it.

Was she frightened?

CD: I'm sure she was frightened. I would have been. I was certainly scared of being with John. He was an intimidating man and came with this huge reputation and ego, but he had a real assertiveness that we needed at that time.

'OUT OF CONTROL'

The rhythm section dictates the groove on this, doesn't it?

GT: Yes, particularly Gilson. His playing is really sophisticated and dictates the way the rest of us play. His grasp of dynamics was excellent. Jools's playing on this is pretty good as well, but it's a poor song.

This was the first of many songs where you got stick for being a misogynist. It's certainly got that element, singing about leering at schoolgirls.

CD: All men leer at schoolgirls. Glenn and I lived around the corner to a girls' school and I have some photographs of us taken by Ron Reid, with our flat rammed full of about 30 schoolgirls. Me and Glenn are drinking bottles of whisky, holding our guitars, and surrounded by these girls. The lyric is pretty sexist. It's all over the place. There's no real story to it, just lists of what men like looking at. It's not an in-depth lyric. Excuse the pun, but it was just tossed off at the time.

GT: When we went to America for the first time we did a record shop signing in San Francisco, which about six people came to. One of them was dressed up as a schoolgirl, pouting at us. We had this particularly enthusiastic A&M rep who'd obviously got her to come along and pout at us. It was a bit embarrassing.

Were the accusations of misogyny levelled at you difficult to cope with?

GT: These were very different times and initially we were probably unaware of what misogyny meant, let alone be conscious of it. In the environment we'd grown up in, that kind of view wouldn't have been out of place, so for people to draw attention to it was hurtful, firstly because they were right and secondly because we hadn't realised it.

I think the criticism helped Chris turn round his whole perception of women in his songwriting. Although most criticism written about you is rubbish, this advice was very helpful to us and drew attention to something we hadn't really thought about.

I speak as a person who, in 1983, attacked my first wife, so I had a long journey to travel in order to shape the person that I am now. I didn't think that was wrong at that time but now it shocks me that I could be so barbaric.

Chris, your vocal backing on this becomes more prominent as the song reaches its climax, and is pretty sinister.

CD: There was definitely a sinister side to us at that time, although it was brought to the fore by John. We used to do a song called 'Deep Cuts' in our set, which was about a dirty phone call. During the song we'd take turns in shagging a blow-up doll onstage. People were quite disturbed by this young band getting off in that way.

As you say, 'Deep Cuts' is even more sinister, especially the ending when you're shouting, 'Please don't hang up.'

CD: When I played that to my son he was really freaked out. He said, 'Dad, for God's sake. What were you doing?'

'TAKE ME I'M YOURS'

This is one of the most popular songs from your catalogue. I understand that it went through a number of changes until you got to a version you were happy with.

CD: That's right. We first recorded this for RCA in Wales and by the time we recorded it for this album it had been completely changed. 'Take Me' is probably the song we've played more than any other in our live set and the one with the most variations and versions recorded.

GT: We recorded a version of this with Fritz Fryer, from The Four Pennies, who told us that he wrote 'Juliet' whilst sitting on the toilet. We weren't happy with the version he produced because it had a bit of a poncy tune, with a falsetto part. We flattened that out for the record and it sounded much better. 'Take Me' was far more of an expression of how we were as a band than the other songs on this album. It was perfectly innocent, simple pop music.

John Cale, of course, wasn't present for this recording. Were you left to your own devices to record it?

GT: The engineer John Wood was very helpful. Before the band had developed a clearly defined role of what we did and who we are, we were more willing to experiment, so we got a synth in and recorded it in a day. It was great fun but John Wood knew how to rein in what we were producing and gave us some structure.

The song has a great psychedelic ending. Whose idea was that?

CD: That was down to Glenn. We were both into psychedelics of some kind but Glenn was always more inclined to take risks musically than I was. He's always been good at pushing the boundaries, whereas I err on the side of conservatism.

This is the first time the listener is made aware of the Difford-Tilbrook octave-apart harmonies, which became such a trademark.

GT: We arrived at that accidentally. My register is quite high and Chris's is much lower, so we naturally approach the same tune an octave apart. I wish it was more conscious, but it just worked that way. It meant that Chris and I could sing together without encroaching on each other's territory. I don't think we could have harmonised if we tried, so it was lucky.

What can you tell me about the lyrics, Chris?

CD: I stayed at Miles Copeland's house in Maida Vale for a week because I'd fallen out with Glenn. Miles's mother is an archaeologist and his family had been based in the Middle East, so the house was covered in Middle

Eastern artefacts, stone sculptures and pyramids. It was fascinating. One night there I sat up in bed and wrote the whole lyric.

The lyric describes the journey through mystic Middle Eastern venues, although looking at it now it's really about the journey of a rock 'n' roll musician. It conjures up images of going across the desert in a tour bus. There are lots of lines and signposts which are autobiographical to me in some way now.

One example would be the line about the Golden Eagle. When we went to America we used Golden Eagles tour buses. It's bizarre the way the song has matured into its own storyline. It's almost mystical in itself.

'THE CALL'

CD: Christ. This is such a weird song.

It starts off with a bell ringing and a voice saying, 'Bring out your dead.'

CD: That's Gilson. What can I say about this song? It's another John Cale moment. This is a ludicrous song. I was never enthusiastic about it.

It sounds very much like The Velvet Underground, especially Glenn's jagged guitar, which makes you sound like Lou Reed.

GT: Yes, it does sound like the Velvets. There are many things that don't work on this album, but of this period, 'The Call' is the song I'm most fond of. That 'off the wallness' was part of John's genius. If we'd been different sorts of people it might have brought out something better in us. John exposed my dark side on 'The Call'. It's a powerful and dark song in a way that we never visited again.

CD: The one thing which is astounding is the drum track. Gilson's drum riff is so intricate, yet simple. But I almost can't listen to this song. It's like punk theatre. I imagine people running around in leotards and leaping about under mauve lights.

GT: 'The Call' also contains one of my many misreadings of Chris's lyrics. Right up until we recorded it I was singing 'don't be mighsled' instead of 'misled'. I felt a bit silly about that.

The lyric concerned suicide. Was this John's idea?

CD: Yes.

So you had to try and imagine what it was like.

CD: Well, I'd had an attempt at it myself. Glenn was going out with Maxine and I was single and spending my time writing loads of lyrics and taking too many drugs. I was very depressed one night, so I took a bottle of gin up to my room and some sleeping tablets. I put the wardrobe against the door and had a little attempt at saying goodnight to the world.

Then I realised that nobody would be able to hear me so I moved the wardrobe away from the door. I was grovelling around on the floor being sick but all I could hear from downstairs was the television. Glenn and Maxine were watching a black and white film, and I thought, 'Fucking hell, man, I'm up here dying and they're not paying any attention.' So I opened the door and fell down the stairs. I cried out, 'Can't you hear me up here trying to kill myself?' At this point I was cradled in somebody's arms and looked after. I was young and looking for some attention. It's amusing in retrospect.

Did this experience stay with you for a long time?

CD: I guess so. Being a young man and that desperate was weird but it went with the territory of where I was in my life. I don't ponder on it anymore.

'MODEL'

This song is quite upbeat, although, I suspect, influenced heavily by John Cale.

GT: Yes, it was John Cale-influenced in that the line 'She's so lovely' became 'She's so ugly'. John was desperately trying to 'de-pop' everything we did and 'Model' actually has quite a poppy tune. It was made darker by that one change of word and the more aggressive approach, which I do think benefited the song. Musically, it was influenced directly by Roxy Music, although you probably wouldn't hear it like that.

CD: When John asked me to write about models, it was at the back of my tiny mind that we might get some models coming to our gigs and I'd be able to get off with them. It never happened. When we went to New York for the first time it was a song that went down really well in the small clubs, along with 'Strong In Reason'. It had a cabaret feel to it.

Lou Reed came to see us at the Hurrah Club in New York, with an entourage of gay men who loved the whole muscle man concept. In fact, John Cale wanted to call the album 'Gay Guys'. We were horrified at the time, but now I think it would have been hilarious. The record company wouldn't accept it, though, and we couldn't think of a title, so it was just called *Squeeze*.

'REMEMBER WHAT'

This is a simple two-chord thrash, with a hint of the '60s about it.

CD: It reminds me of The Kinks a bit. I like the line 'I was out with what's her name.'

GT: This was the first of our drink songs, but I have to say thoroughly representative of our lives at the time. It was great being in a band at that point, drinking in dodgy pubs with criminals, which was quite exciting, and being paid a reasonable amount of money. When we recorded this album we were still on the tail end of playing locally, so we were being paid by local boozers to play, and being well rewarded. We'd been getting about 200 quid a week, which was a relative fortune, but as soon as we started making records we went back to 15 quid a week.

Why was that?

GT: As soon as we signed to Miles's production company, we went on a £15 a week retainer, with minimal royalties. Not that we sat bemoaning our fate. We were just happy to be playing and be successful.

You became a connoisseur of alcohol songs, didn't you, Chris?

CD: You could say that. The songs about alcohol grew and grew right through my career as a lyricist. There have always been songs about how much I, or the character, enjoyed drinking, although they took on a more negative element towards the end of Squeeze.

Unfortunately, we became associated with sexism and beer for a while and it was a hard image to shrug off. None of us wanted to be labelled sexist. It wasn't helping us pick up women, for a start.

I like the image of the character in the song finding his suit 'all over the hall'. I'm sure a lot of men can empathise with that.

CD: It's perfect for adolescents, a song I have good memories of, although I don't remember doing it live much.

'FIRST THING WRONG'

GT: This had been left over from the *Packet Of Three* sessions, and showed the slightly tougher side of Squeeze that existed even before John Cale came into the equation. It was one of the few places when Jools had the opportunity to shine with his keyboard playing. Some of the poppy stuff left him without too much to do, which must have been very frustrating for him.

CD: What Jools brought to our chemistry was his natural ability to play boogie-woogie and blues and rock 'n' roll. We couldn't help but lean in that direction because of the spirit in which he played the piano. You couldn't get Jools to play any other way. That was a powerful energy to have in the band and we may have overlooked his assets sometimes because Glenn and I were just interested in becoming good songwriters. Perhaps we could have homed in more on what Jools did. Having said that, he wasn't very tamed on the songs on the early albums. He's all over them like a rash.

GT: Jools's playing on 'First Thing Wrong' was terrific. When we played songs like this live I didn't think any of our contemporaries could touch us. We were really powerful.

Did Jools express any dissatisfaction at his marginalisation in the band?

CD: Jools never gave it too much thought. He'd do one take and whether we liked it or not he'd just go to the pub. I don't fault him for that, though.

If there had been three of you competing for control of the band's sound it might have sounded cramped.

CD: That's a fair point.

Did Glenn and yourself have the most input of the band members in the studio?

CD: Definitely. Glenn would be in the studio all the time, while I'd be there until I got pissed off, and Jools would only be there when he was needed. As for the others, Harry would just float around and do what was required while Gilson would turn up like a wolf, play the drums really loudly, and then bugger off.

'HESITATION (ROOL BRITANNIA)'

CD: This is just us jamming. John Cale stuck us in the studio and said, 'Jam around these chords and Chris, come up with a lyric.' There's no meat to this song. I was making up the lyric as I went along. There was no real thought put into it.

It's not something I'd want played at my funeral and I don't know how we got away with having this on a record. Imagine a record company being given a track like that now. They'd be totally bemused.

GT: This was another song written just to please John. In spite of the fact that *Squeeze* was our debut album, I feel that *Cool For Cats* was our first album really. It was certainly more representative of our songwriting and the direction that we naturally gravitated towards.

'GET SMART'

This is another thrash.

CD: Yeah. We were good at that. It's rubbish really, but it has that '50s rock 'n' roll influence that Glenn and Jools brought to the band. It has a sound of spunky, adolescent boys making music. To use a John Cale phrase we were just 'jerking off'. That's what you do at that age when you haven't developed your own ego and are looking for it. You keep banging against all four walls until you find who you are. 'Bang Bang' is exactly the same.

GT: Please don't ask me about 'Get Smart'. It's crap.

Are you glad you went through that whole experience of working with John Cale?

CD: We had no option, but I'm not unhappy that we worked with him. Successes and failures all happen for a reason and are all stepping stones to where we ended up as a band.

The positive side of making this album was that it meant we didn't end up running out of steam. A lot of bands spend their formative years writing their first album and by their second they're worn out and have got nothing left to give. We'd spent all those years writing our first album but hadn't been allowed to record most of it, so it was all saved up for the second album.

***

AFTER THE extraordinary experience of making their first album, Squeeze hit the road in early 1978 for their first nationwide tour, supporting punk/pub-rock combo Eddie And The Hot Rods. 'When we first started playing around Britain, I thought everywhere was going to be like a Hovis advert,' admits Glenn. 'We were pretty parochial.'

The success of 'Take Me I'm Yours' as a single midway through the tour meant that Squeeze quickly established a sizeable following across the country. The record reached an impressive Number 19, and gave the band their first appearance on *Top Of The Pops*. Chris remembers this first taste of national stardom with great affection. 'A Rolls Royce came and picked me up from my mum's house and it felt like being the local mayor. All the neighbours were looking out of their windows.'

Revelling in the attention, the band decided to play a trick on their new public, swapping instruments as they mimed on *Top Of The Pops*, recalling their day of terror at the hands of John Cale a few months beforehand.

Despite the national success of 'Take Me', and the knock-on sales enjoyed by Squeeze, the band were in no hurry to lose their local hero status in south London. For some time they had been championed by a gang of notorious villains, who invited them to never-ending 'lock-ins' in the local pubs and plied them with drink in exchange for the glory of associated celebrity. The band were initially flattered by the interest and continued to revel in the association with both minor- and major-league criminals for the next two years. Indeed, many of the lyrics on the following album were directly influenced by many of these friendships.

'It was a lovely feeling being a local celeb,' admits Chris. 'We'd go into the local café for tea and toast and all the girls would know us. I used to sit in the corner there and write lyrics. After the album came out A&M spent a lot of money putting posters around Deptford to develop the local interest. I'd drive down Jamaica Road and see a huge billboard with Squeeze on it. It was fantastic.'

Although the band were happy to bask in their status as Deptford's favourite sons, Miles Copeland could see the bigger picture and used his burgeoning contacts book to secure a tour of the United States. The album had already been released in the US under the moniker *UK Squeeze* to avoid a legal dispute with an American group of the same name, and Copeland was convinced that despite their quintessential Englishness, his band could be a success across the Atlantic.

The band were full of trepidation at the prospect of a long tour stateside, but excited in equal measure. 'It was incredible, to actually be in America,' says Glenn. 'I hadn't been abroad until I was 13 and that was only to Holland, so this was mind-blowing.'

Copeland bought a blue Chevy van and drove the band around the country, to minimise costs. Both Glenn and Chris recall travelling around the US in great physical discomfort, and that friction among the cramped band members was never far from the surface. The tour was originally planned to be three weeks long but as the band began successfully wooing the American public it was gradually extended, stretching the group's patience to the breaking point.

'It was my first taste of psychological torture,' claims Glenn. 'The goalposts were constantly being shifted on that tour. It was a hard tour, travelling in a van with our suitcases piled up at the back. We were all living on top of each other. We'd toured in similar conditions in the UK but always been able to go home, whereas in the States there was no "going home" and we spent two months in each other's pockets.'

Squeeze's debut US tour was groundbreaking, with Copeland booking them to play in towns and cities that were not accustomed to foreign visitors. At the Bull Horn Bar in Dallas, Texas, Squeeze were forced to play behind chicken wire to prevent local rednecks from throwing bottles at the stage. The band were bemused by this state of affairs, although they acknowledge that the decision to dress Glenn in a ballerina outfit while Jools donned a priest's garb might have been a trifle misconceived given the reputation of the ultra-conservative state.

Chris, who spent the first two weeks of the tour wearing yellow pyjamas, believed Copeland's straight-talking New York persona helped open doors across America, both for Squeeze and subsequently for The Police. 'When we got to a town Miles would take us straight to the local radio station, give them our record, and say "Get that ELO crap off of here and start playing Squeeze." He did that on the whole tour and it paid dividends because later on when The Police came around all the record stations knew Miles and would play whatever he had in his hand. So we did all the groundwork for The Police, but it also worked out well for us because we ended up getting a big American following.'

Despite Copeland's undoubted nous and ability to get things done, one decision was to slightly sour relations with A&M America. The cocksure manager thought it would be a hoot to buy Chris a T-shirt emblazoned with the memorable line 'I can see your tits, now show us your cunt.' Playing to a roomful of A&M movers and shakers in Los Angeles was not the best venue to premier the shirt, as Chris explains. 'Miles told me to wear the shirt, and literally standing five feet in front of me was the wife of the head of A&M, Jerry Moss. She didn't take kindly to it and it caused a bit of a furore.'

Despite their obvious tiredness, the band's return to Blighty heralded yet another long stint on the road, although the opportunity of occasional home comforts was some succour. As 1978 drew to a close, the band's hard work was paying off and a core audience had been built on both sides of the Atlantic. With their newly-formed army of fans eager to hear new material, attention now turned to recording their second album.

3 *Cool For Cats*

WITH A successful album behind them and a string of unused songs from their extensive catalogue waiting to be laid down, Squeeze expected the recording of their follow-up LP to be straightfor ward. Learning from their folly of hiring John Cale, Copeland and A&M agreed to hand over production duties to Brian Humphries, who had engineered the early Pink Floyd and Black Sabbath albums.

The band decamped to Britannia Row Studios, part-owned by Pink Floyd, in London's Wandsworth and got to work in late 1978. But passing the likes of Roger Waters and Dave Gilmour in the studio failed to be a source of inspiration. Summoned by A&M, the band were startled by the record company's insistence that they scrap their recordings and begin work with another producer.

Aware of the need to make the band feel comfortable in their surroundings, Copeland wisely agreed to Squeeze's request that they co-produce the second batch of recordings themselves with John Wood, who had engineered their debut album. An avuncular figure and brilliant engineer, Wood had helped soothe the tensions between the band and the eccentric Cale and had helped them flourish on both 'Take Me, I'm Yours' and 'Bang Bang,' when the producer had been indisposed.

Chris remembers Wood fondly, describing him as 'like a geography teacher who always wore a nice woolly jumper and corduroy trousers, but had a sense of authority. He was a father figure to Glenn and let him experiment musically in a way other producers wouldn't have allowed. Experimentation was very much part of the Squeeze songwriting process, inspired mostly by the way Glenn saw the song, and John was really good at seeing Glenn's vision. He also facilitated the brilliance of Jools on the piano.'

Wood had an impressive track record, and had worked with folk acts like Fairport Convention and Nick Drake but possessed pop sensibility in abundance. Glenn, in particular, found him a joy to work with. 'John had great ears, as well as tact and diplomacy. He needed all these things to be able to deal with me, who had none of them. It was great to be in a studio where I had more control, not in the power sense, but with regard to getting things to sound the way I wanted. When we finished that album I felt we'd made a proper record, and one that sounded like us.'

The band had not been happy in the industrial-like confines of Britannia Row and were delighted to be moved to Sound Technology Studios, just off the Kings Road. The recordings were a revelation and with the band still writing prolifically, a number of new songs were added during proceedings. In fact, had it not been for A&M's insistence that the entire Britannia Row recordings be scrapped, the two biggest hits of Squeeze's career would never have happened.

The initial recording of 'Up The Junction' was a pedestrian, folk number, influenced by Bob Dylan And The Band, with strumming guitars and minimal organ. A&M could see the song's potential and demanded that it be restructured with a poppier sound. The rest, as they say, is history.

As for the song 'Cool For Cats', this almost certainly wouldn't have existed at all without the pressure to augment the songs that A&M liked with fresh material.

Although initially heartbroken at A&M's insistence that they scrap their first effort, Squeeze ended up deep in gratitude for their record company's insistence. The decision helped push the band into the rock 'n' roll stratosphere.

***

'SLAP AND TICKLE'

CD: A lot of this album was inspired lyrically by being courted by publicans and hanging out in the Deptford Arms and The Bell in Greenwich. We were mixing with a very seedy crew and I couldn't help but absorb the language of those characters. I loved being with them because they were the kind of people I'd shied away from at school. Now I had the authority of being in a successful band, I was hanging out with them.

From a lyrical point of view, I was becoming inspired by the pub rock scene that had been around and was listening to Ian Dury, Elvis Costello and Brinsley Schwarz. The metre of some of their lyrics inspired me to write in that rap fashion. I remember playing 'Slap And Tickle' in a club in New York and realising that no one understood what the hell was going on.

I saw Glenn play this recently at a gig and although the instrumentation was lacking in some ways, it was interesting to hear 'Slap And Tickle' being played again because it stands up as a great song.

It's an accomplished arrangement on the record. It has those shuddering synthesisers at the start that were a few years ahead of their time.

GT: I'd been listening to Kraftwerk and Giorgio Moroder at the time. I didn't know about sequences then, so I played it all by hand. There's a clip of me on the *Old Grey Whistle Test* prodding away manfully at the keyboard.

It probably sounded more organic like that.

GT: That's true. It does give it a sort of charm all of its own, but I would have liked it to have sounded perfect. I felt slightly uncomfortable about playing keyboards because I was encroaching on Jools's territory, but it didn't stop me. I don't know to this day how Jools felt about it but I think that must have been the start of the crowding out of Jools to a certain extent.

CD: 'Slap And Tickle' heralded the start of the set where Glenn switched to playing a Mini Moog and I was playing Cabassa instead of guitar. When you're starting out in a band you hold on to a guitar like a teddy bear that you can't bear to let go of. Replacing it with a Cabassa was scary, but I got the hang of it. It was great fun dancing around like we were in a ska band but the sight of Glenn playing the Mini Moog was more frightening than anything.

The sight and sound of it was pretty weird and because of the different voltage settings in America it would never sound like the original. It was very touch and go.

The section towards the end of 'Slap And Tickle' is fantastic, where the music slows down.

GT: A lot of those breaks were really down to Gilson. He understood instinctively that it could be powerful to drop away from the pace of a song midway through and then come back, to build tension.

'REVUE'

CD: 'Revue' was written a long time beforehand.

Was it one of those rejected by John Cale?

CD: Yes. It was one of a whole bunch of songs written around that time that all began with the letter R for some reason.

The lyric is quite adolescent. Andrew Lloyd Webber's musical *Jesus Christ Superstar* had just taken off in London, so this lyric was based on looking around at the world of theatre. It wasn't deep or thought out, like most things I wrote at that time. Dare I say it, this is an album filler, whereas 'Slap And Tickle' was similar to Ian Dury And The Blockheads. Chaz Jankel could have written a tune to that and Ian Dury could have sung it. It was almost a rap.

GT: This was very much a band arrangement, with Jools coming out with the keyboard line and me fitting round it on guitar. There was an element of 'Like Clockwork', the Boomtown Rats song, which they'd recently released. Despite what Chris says, I like the song lyrically. It's one of Chris's talents to go outside his own life and imagine another circumstance, in this case an actor down on his luck. This lyric immediately conjured up a vivid picture when Chris gave it to me, which shows what a natural talent he has.

'TOUCHING ME TOUCHING YOU'

This is a very cheeky little song about masturbation.

GT: I'd like to apply to the *Guinness Book of Records* for being the person involved in writing the most songs about masturbation over the longest period. I have one on my album now, called 'Reinventing The Wheel'.

CD: There aren't many songs about masturbation. Prince has got a few but I bet Cliff Richard hasn't. 'Touching Me' became one of the first of many masturbation songs in our repertoire, but this was from quite a sad teenage perspective.

GT: I remember reading this lyric for the first time and thinking, 'This is a bit weird, isn't it?' But I looked at it again and thought it was great to write something like that. I thought masturbation must at least be something Chris and I got up to, even if other people didn't.

I wrote it as a wistful ballad first of all but we sped it up and made it more chirpy. There was part of the tune that we cut out that was very complicated. At first it was a bit prissy, but we turned it into a punk song and it worked just as well.

CD: The original demo is beautiful. It's just Glenn and I on acoustic guitars, sounding like Nick Drake. It's so passionate and sounds like the singer really understands what he's singing about and is in touch with that young feeling of enjoying masturbation. When the band got hold of it they sped it up and made it more street- or punk-like. I prefer the demo. To write a tune around the lyric in the way Glenn did was sublime.

Is there any chance this version might appear on an album of out-takes?

CD: Possibly. The album I would love to do is the *Chris Sings Glenn* album. I'd record this with a string quartet and sing it in the wholesome way Glenn originally did on the demo.

'It's Not Cricket'

This is in the same vein as 'Touching Me Touching You'.

GT: Exactly the same vein. It's a brilliant lyric that again directly reflects our social life at the time. We were hanging out with a lot of geezers. We were also influenced again by Ian Dury and musically a certain amount of that shone through.

It does have a sense of the music hall that Ian loved.

GT: It does, although my delivery of the vocals as a geezer wasn't entirely successful.

CD: I've got a soft spot for this. Musically it's interesting, because it has a cabaret sound, which is a bizarre way of looking at this kind of lyric, but inspired. It must have been difficult for Glenn to weave a tune around these lyrics.

The lyric is terribly Deptford and sums up when I was working with my brother and we went to the pub to see the topless dancers. It mentions Deptford, the beano to Southend, 40 crates of lager under the bus and holidays in Bognor. All the characters we'd met were coming out in my lyric writing.

I eventually moved away from that storytelling, which was prevalent on the early albums. As you get older you become more personal and stop telling so many tales about other people's lives. I kind of miss that now because you can write great songs by describing other people's situations.

'It's So Dirty'

Glenn's love of 1960s music is evident here.

CD: It does have a sort of Kinks vibe about it.

GT: It's also influenced by Elvis Costello, although he never did guitar breaks like that. I must say I was very proud of those guitar breaks.

Your solo is absolutely manic.

GT: Yes, although it's quite lucid, I think, and a part of the song that took it away from being an Elvis Costello And The Attractions number. The song itself is very influenced by 'This Year's Model'-era Elvis but the musical breaks were not that at all and took it to a different place. That's my analysis of it now but at the time I didn't realise this. What I was writing was a product of what I was listening to, without my necessarily being aware of it.

So what about the lyric, Chris?

CD: It's absolutely disgraceful. This is a top shelf album which really ought to be sold in a plastic bag. I was only reflecting the time and my own situation, which was virtually living in a pub where everyone spoke like that. The girl I was going out with at the time had a sister who was a prostitute in the West End. Her and her mates saw themselves as being 'it'. There was no liberation involved. It was just a job they did. They would have preferred to have been treated better, but they were lucky if they got a cherry in their tequila sunrise.

That was the way women were treated at that time. I guess I couldn't help getting swept up in it and probably behaved badly because of it. But I was young and impressionable and it's quite nice to be courted by men of a certain nature.

GT: There were a lot of songs on this album which reflect our lowlife socialising and our hanging out with the wrong sort of people. They were good to us, though.

And they loved their mum.

GT: They certainly did. We enjoyed that whole period. It was only when I saw one man hit another with a fire extinguisher that I thought perhaps I shouldn't be hanging around with these people. It was horrible, but at that time we were writing about the lighter side of lowlife.

Were these people aware that you were writing about them?

GT: Absolutely, and they loved it. They would say, 'Is that about me?' and it usually was.

How did you react when you got stick for writing sexist lyrics?

CD: I ducked. We didn't include this in the set very often and by the time the record had run its course these songs were being pushed further and further back in the catalogue.

When you were asked about these songs by journalists did you try to be arty and say you were just reflecting society?

CD: I suppose I could have said that I was Oscar Wilde, that I picked up the emotions of the time and that the lyrics were nothing to do with my life. But I would have been a bloody liar.

'THE KNACK'

GT: This was another track that we'd written a couple of years earlier.

The song marks quite a change of pace, with Chris singing. Pardon me for bringing up another influence but the music could be by Kraftwerk.

CD: That was Glenn's influence. He really enjoyed listening to German bands at that time, such as Can and Kraftwerk. It was a bit industrial for my taste but I remember going to see Kraftwerk play in New York. The whole stage was littered with electronic gear and the band were like robots on the stage. It was an amazing gig, but it's funny to think that all the technology on that stage could probably be fitted into a mobile phone now. They were well ahead of their time, though.

What was the lyric about?

CD: 'The Knack' leans towards the theatrical side of Glenn and I. Prior to getting a record deal we'd written a musical called Trixie, which was about a nightclub and the characters who lived there. It was very vaudeville, with tangos and waltzes, and bizarre burlesque arrangements.

Lyrically the musical was about these characters that lived in the back of my mind, like characters in a James Cagney or Humphrey Bogart film. It never saw the light of day, but one of the offshoots was 'The Knack', where I was trying to tell the story about a black and white film, inventing a scenario with actors.

It wasn't until after this that I started to read Damon Runyon, who wrote a lot of short stories. He wrote this fantastic story called 'Little Pinks', which I always wanted to turn into a musical or a play.

GT: The music is quite evocative. There was a celeste in the studio, which was a kind of keyboard that made a sound like a chime. In those days studios had a lot more instruments of that order lying around and I was keen to get as many of them on to the record.

How did Jools take to playing a song like 'The Knack'? It's not the kind of music I would normally associate with him.

CD: To be honest Jools may not have even played on it. Glenn did all the donkey work on these songs, and played keyboards and most of the Moog parts on this album. It's probably fair to say that I didn't play on the first three albums.

I find that astonishing.

CD: I may have played the odd thing but I'm talking about playing on a song through its entirety. As a guitar player I wasn't that precise and Glenn was always looking for perfection. Unless you were working with a very patient Glenn, or a patient John Wood, there was no point. Glenn was so great at guitar, I'd say, 'Why don't you play it rather than keep giving me grief?'

'HOP SKIP AND JUMP'

We go from 'The Knack', where Jools was sidelined, to a song that's got his influence stamped all over it. It's a nice juxtaposition of styles.

CD: All over the place is another way of putting it.

Personally I love albums that have a certain mood that flows from one song to the next, but I also enjoy albums like this which contain a mixture of styles.

CD: I'd agree with that, and I think it sums up the band. We were five individuals going in five different directions. The only common ground was that Glenn and I used to write all the songs, so it's not surprising that we didn't all sound the same, like The Ramones.

All the band had completely different personalities. The only thing that made us come together was being onstage in front of people. At the time I found it frustrating. Having been brought up on The Velvet Underground and The Beatles I wanted it to be one image and one particular style. That was my vision but all the time I was being talked out of it by what Glenn wrote or Jools brought to the table. It was always a compromise. At rehearsals we would have a vote on whether we liked songs or not and if we didn't have complete agreement then we would try another way.

Did Jools often come up with song ideas?

GT: Not that often, although he had another song we recorded called 'Cars And Trucks', which was great but Jools wasn't that keen on doing it. I liked working on Jools's songs because it put me into a different spot of thinking what I should do as a guitarist. On anything I wrote, the song as a whole took preference over my guitar parts whereas I was forced to think more as a guitarist when working on tracks that Jools had written.

'Up The Junction'

CD: I never thought that would happen.

With you and the girl from Clapham. You wrote this on a US tour, didn't you?

CD: I don't remember that.

GT: I remember exactly where Chris was. We were staying in a motel 15 miles outside New Orleans, and feeling totally marooned. It was a frustrating place to be, so near to New Orleans but stuck in a motel on a freeway in the middle of nowhere.

CD: When I wrote this it was Dylanesque and was much longer, with about 16 verses. Our old manager Laurence Impey was a massive Bob Dylan fan and he introduced me to the obscurities that he'd recorded, like 'Who Killed Davey Moore?' That was a stunning lyric about a boxer who died in the ring, written from the point of view of a ringside journalist. It inspired me to write in a seamless way, like I was narrating a story, with no chorus.

I was going to mention the fact that 'Up The Junction' has no chorus. It's quite unusual to have a hit single without a chorus.

GT: The lyric was a story that had no obvious repeats, and I thought it read perfectly well as it was. I was thinking of something like Dylan's 'Positively Fourth Street' as a template when I wrote the music. I sat down to write the music one lunchtime when someone had gone to get our traditional ham or cheese rolls.

CD: There were lots of our lyrics at that time which had a similar flavour and made their way on to the next album. The characters in this song reappeared on Squeeze's last album, *Domino*, in a song called 'Moving Story', when they've all come of age.

I was brought up on Wednesday night plays on the BBC. I loved those short stories, with lives condensed into half an hour. I was intrigued to see if I could tell a similar story in three minutes.

GT: This is the also first instance of reviewers using the dreaded phrase 'kitchen sink drama' to describe our songs.

The record company had already seen this as a possible single, hadn't they?

CD: Well, Miles Copeland hadn't. After we recorded it in the Kings Road I recall Miles coming down to hear it and saying, 'That'll never be a hit, it hasn't got a bloody chorus. Why don't you write a chorus and stick it in there? It'll be massive.' Glenn and I dug our heels and said, 'If you don't like it as it is then it will just be an album track,' to which Miles replied, 'OK, it's just an album track then.' Lo and behold, it was released and got to Number Two in the charts. Incidentally, there aren't many songs that end with the title as the last line. Two spring to mind: one is 'Up The Junction'. The other is 'Virginia Plain'.

You were unlucky not to have a Number One here, considering the fact that it sold 500,000 copies.

CD: That's true.

GT: It was lovely to have huge hits, with both 'Up The Junction' and 'Cool For Cats', which we felt immensely proud of. Later on we experienced the horrible feeling of having hits with songs that we didn't think were any good, like '853-5937'.

CD: The video we recorded was hysterical. We went down to John Lennon's old house, where *Imagine* was filmed. There was a chapel at the side of the house and we filmed the 'Cool For Cats' video there between about two and four o'clock with Derek Burbridge, who went on to produce all The Police videos. We were wrapping up for the day and someone suggested that as we had the place booked for another two hours we should shoot a video for 'Up The Junction'. We sat on the kitchen wall, played it twice, and it was finished. Two videos in one day.

'HARD TO FIND'

GT: I was still as baffled by Chris's sexual lyrics as I had been on 'Sex Master', never having experienced that sort of thing at the time.

CD: This is me influenced by John Cale. It's almost as if I'm bowing to his madness and I think it could have fitted on the first album. I guess it's the bridge between the two albums. It has that sort of Germanic rhythm, which is not sexy at all. It's just horrific. I didn't have the confidence to do much singing in those days and this was the closest I got to it, but it sounds more like barking.

Did the lyrics come from personal experience? I'm particularly interested to know if you dressed up as a girl.

CD: No, I didn't. Well, I say that now. All Englishmen like getting dressed up as women. Christ, this country has had the best collection of gay men in the world, people like Quentin Crisp, Oscar Wilde, Noel Coward and Elton John. There's a campness about this song, but at the time I didn't know what campness was. I certainly do now because I've got quite a few friends who lean towards the lavender.

What a lovely turn of phrase. You should put that in a lyric.

CD: It's in there. It says, 'Enchant you with some lavender but this was my mistake.' I have to say I'm not too fond of this track. Lyrically it doesn't do an awful lot for me.

GT: We'd written a version of this before we started the recordings, but then I came up with a very different one in the studio. So the song ended up as a mixture of the two, which was good because it took it to somewhere different. It reminded me in my fevered imagination of The Doors, something much simpler than my normal style of a ten-chord progression followed by 12 bars of something else. It was nice to occasionally write something very simple, but I always had to trick myself into it by writing on the spot.

'Slightly Drunk'

GT: This is pretty self-explanatory. There was no darkness in our drinking songs at this point. There was a great evolution of our drinking songs that charted Chris's life as a drinker, from when he was totally carefree, then his being concerned at what alcohol was doing to him, to when he'd given up drink and come through the other side. But this song was about having a laugh. There's nothing serious in it.

CD: I really like this song. All that testosterone going off in this little lad. The title sums up where I was at that time, being successful and on TV, wandering around Deptford High Street being recognised.

There is an element of sadness in the verse, though, especially lines like 'I'm pretty sad but so what?/ I should be glad but I'm not.' Overall, because of the way the music is, it has a laddish quality. When I visualise us playing it now I see lots of men in the audience jumping up and down, shaking their heads in different directions. But the lyric is sad, about a lonely person talking to himself. It comes from a dark place.

Gilson's drumming is brilliant. There are some great little drum breaks in this song which nailed the whole thing to the floor.

'Goodbye Girl'

I'd always considered 'Goodbye Girl' as being a hit single. I was amazed when I looked it up and found it only got to Number 63 in the charts.

CD: It was the first single off this album and our last release had been 'Bang Bang', which was another miserable failure. It was only when 'Cool For Cats' came out four months later that we started to walk like Egyptians.

A lot of people would regard Squeeze as a great singles band.

CD: That was one of the things about Squeeze. We gave the illusion that we were massive everywhere and had all these hit singles, but it was a mirage.

Funnily enough, 'Goodbye Girl' was the song from this album that really took off in America. We recorded an American version with a slightly different lyric to get us radio play there. We changed 'My wife has moved to Guernsey' to 'My wife has moved to Boston'. It got huge radio play and got us moving in Boston, New York, and all down the East Coast. One line we kept in was 'Sunlight on the lino', which the Americans didn't understand at all.

It has a very upbeat arrangement, despite the laconic mood of the lyric.

GT: You're right. Gilson's influence in the arrangement was massive, not bringing the drums in until the third verse. How weird is that? Gilson had four percussion parts that he overdubbed one after the other that went throughout the song. It had a jolly tune, which later to my horror someone pointed out sounded like The Muppets theme tune. And I have to agree with them.

CD: Gilson constructed a washing line of bottles and bits of metal and tin and played them instead of a drum kit. It was a very inventive thing to do, slightly surreal, but it worked a treat. Our trademark octave apart vocal is all over it. We recorded another rock 'n' roll version, more the way Jools would play it, which was released as a B-side. When we went on tour we played it in that style rather than as on the record, because we'd had such an awful time rehearsing it.

'Cool For Cats'

GT: We'd recorded the track some time earlier with a completely different lyric. It had a tune that was a lot slower and not that exciting. Both John Wood and I suggested Chris take the track home without the vocal and come up with a different lyric.

CD: I went back to my flat in Greenwich and sat on the sofa, but my mind just went blank. So I gave up, turned on the telly, and started watching *The*

Benny Hill Show. He always used to have a couple of songs on his show and the metre of his songs was very flat. Each verse would be about a different character, which was quite an interesting idea.

I know it's bizarre, but I was inspired by listening to Benny Hill's song that night, so I turned the telly off and within a few minutes I'd written twelve verses. I had a tape machine in the flat, so I switched it on and sang my idea into it, and the next day I went back to the studio and we cut it straight away.

I got the title from a 1960s Canadian TV show of the same name. I thought 'Cool For Cats' was a great song title. The lyric isn't about anything in particular, just a stream of consciousness. We had to change one line for *Top Of The Pops*, though, otherwise they weren't going to let us on.

Which line?

'I'm invited in for a coffee/ And I give the dog a bone.' It was the BBC at its worst at that time.

What did you think when Chris came to the studio with the new lyric?

GT: As soon as Chris played what he'd recorded on to tape, we all knew it was going to be a great song. Chris's delivery was so good. He sounded unbelievably cool. Then I got my girlfriend and a couple of her mates in to sing the backing vocals on it and it slotted into place easily.

What makes me cringe about the song is the video, where I look really idiotic. I was devastated when I first saw it. There's a bit where I burst through a group of girls, panther-like and super-sexy I thought, but when I saw it I realised that I just look pissed. It's a high comedy moment for me now that I've got over my super-sensitivity, but to discover that I didn't have the feline-like movements I thought I had was quite hard on the ego.

CD: We actually recorded two 'Cool For Cats' videos. There's a straight one with me singing to the camera and the band playing behind, and another where the band are constantly changing their hats. It was much more visual than the other video and includes a great shot of Gilson picking up a pint of beer and downing it in two seconds flat. The video was never shown on TV because of that.

That's a bit harsh. Len Fairclough was always shown downing pints in the Rovers Return.

CD: Yes, but we were playing on *Top Of The Pops* for kids, so the BBC thought we were being irresponsible. We were right to fit in with what they wanted because 'Cool For Cats' was another Number Two hit.

And sold another 500,000 copies. Do you mind when people who aren't Squeeze fans equate your entire career with 'Cool For Cats' and 'Up The Junction'?

CD: No, but I did for a while. Around the time we recorded *East Side Story*, Glenn and I were dubbed 'the new Lennon and McCartney' in America, and we deliberately binned stuff like 'Up The Junction' and 'Cool For Cats'. We got precious about what we were writing and ignoring what had made us successful.

We'd go onstage in some mega dome and when people shouted out for 'Up The Junction' we'd ignore them and play something else. It's incredible, in retrospect. We were shooting ourselves in the foot every time. Now I look back on those songs with great affection because without them I wouldn't be where I am today.

***

AFTER THE disappointment of their debut LP, Squeeze had now proved to A&M they were worth the multi-album deal skilfully negotiated by Miles Copeland. The band had produced an accomplished, mature follow-up far superior and commercially accessible to its successor. Not only that, but the album had spawned a pair of smash hits which together sold a million copies and cemented the band in the public's consciousness.

Another hectic round of touring followed, with the now-obligatory stay in America causing tension among the troops. 'Miles kept slinging dates at us, which was exhausting,' complains Chris. 'We got to the end of what had been a very long tour, in Boston, and I remember packing my bag and thinking, "Great. I'm going back to London. I can have some cheese on toast and a proper pint of beer." Then Miles flew in, gathered us round and said, "Right guys, we've just been offered another six weeks here in the States. If we do it we'll get on MTV and if we don't we'll have to come back later in the year when it will be harder. We're already here now, so we can save on air flights." He managed to talk us into it, but I've never forgotten that feeling of deflation.'

One by-product of the ever-lengthening US tour was that Chris met his first wife Cindy while playing pinball in New York club CBGBs with The Ramones and Blondie. Cindy was a bubbly counterpart to the quieter, more serious songwriter, who fell in love instantly and began dividing his time between London and his new partner's home in New York.

The back end of 1979 also saw the first major change in Squeeze's personnel, when Glenn finally lost patience with bassist Harry Kakoulli's limited playing ability. 'I was at the centre of getting rid of him,' admits Glenn. 'I felt musically frustrated at what we couldn't do because of the way Harry played. It was terribly unfair on him in many ways but we moved forward without Harry in a way we couldn't have done had he stayed.'

Although not at the forefront of the decision, Chris is equally convinced that Kakoulli's sacking was inevitable. 'He was wooden on the bass and he used to do mad things onstage, running in different directions like a headless chicken in order to attract girls. One time he did it and fell off the stage, breaking his leg. He spent most of the tour with his leg in plaster. It was a ridiculous way of behaving.'

Using the time-honoured tradition of advertising in *Melody Maker*, Squeeze plucked John Bentley out of an incredible round of 83 auditions. 'It was absurd,' laughs Chris. 'Imagine 83 plumbers coming round to change a tap.' Bentley was a more accomplished musician than Kakoulli, far more rock-oriented in style, and with a good sense of melody.

He was also an instant hit with Squeeze's legion of female fans, which caused some consternation among his new colleagues. Chris was further worried by Bentley's songwriting ambitions, but found his ally Glenn in full agreement that the Difford-Tilbrook writing partnership should remain exclusive. 'I did have an underlying fear that John wanted to bring in his songs to the band,' confesses Chris. 'Glenn and I were careful that only our songs would get on our records and we'd only grudgingly begun allowing Jools one song per album. I would have been very unhappy if John had started bringing stuff into the pot.'

The first song recorded by the new line-up was the festive single 'Christmas Day', released in November 1979. Now long-forgotten by Squeeze aficionados, the track had an arrangement that was practically impossible for Christmas revellers to dance to, and despite a fine video in which the band enacted a nativity scene, it sank without trace.

The single's fate was not helped by yet another run-in with the BBC, who refused to play it on the grounds that the lyrics were deemed to be blasphemous. 'The lyric was shot through with Chris's sense of humour, dovetailing the story of Mary and Jesus with Morecambe and Wise,' explains Glenn. 'It was about all those things that Christmas had become in the '70s for the majority of non-believers, as we were. I think it was a brilliant lyric and very adventurous musically. We even used a harp on it.'

The release of 'Christmas Day' also resulted in an extraordinary outburst of pique from legendary TV presenter Chris Tarrant, then a host on the anarchic ITV children's show *Tiswas*. The show was recorded live on Saturday mornings in Birmingham and when the band's hired harpist turned up late a huffy Tarrant marched over to Squeeze and announced, 'Mark my words. You will never work on television again.'

'It was a complete over-reaction,' says Chris. 'And Jools Holland is the living testament to the fact that he was totally wrong.'

4 *Argybargy*

THE SUCCESS of *Cool For Cats* had made Squeeze an internationally recognised act. In addition to their growing following in America and mainland Europe, a lengthy tour of Australia had been booked for the start of 1980. The band's rapid leap into the pop big time also transformed their lifestyles and put an end to the band's association with the south London criminal fraternity.

Glenn recalls the difficulty that he and Chris faced in cutting themselves off from their shady benefactors. 'These guys were the type who were good to their own but fucking horrible to be on the wrong side of. After the incident with the fire extinguisher I knew I didn't want to be with them anymore, but equally I felt threatened that I didn't want to be seen to withdraw from them. At that point our career was beginning to take off so it made it easier to distance ourselves.'

Initially delighted by his local celebrity status, the pressure of fame was beginning to take its toll on Glenn. One incident at this time summed up his growing sense of unease. 'I was standing in the Princess of Wales in Blackheath with my mates when I became conscious of the fact that a lot of people were looking at me. I'd been on telly a reasonable amount by then, so lots of people knew who I was. I remember that the room started spinning and I had to get out. I'd never experienced anything like it before and it was a horrible feeling. As much as I wanted to be successful and famous, I wasn't as comfortable with fame as I'd thought.'

For the first time the 22-year-old singer had also become aware of feelings of jealousy among his peers. 'People started perceiving us in a different way. I was aware of people with what I'd describe as a "chip on the shoulder" reaction to our success. We had people saying we were too big for our boots, which I didn't think we were. At that time I also started playing down what we were doing to my friends. It seemed impossible to convey the vastness of what we'd been doing compared to what had been going on in south London.'

After the temporary cessation of the band's extensive touring marathon, Chris had spent much of the summer of 1979 living with his new wife in America and writing songs. Blissfully in love and finding life in New York's Greenwich Village exhilarating, the songwriter went through the most productive stage of his career, and in one purple patch produced an incredible 45 lyrics in five days.

'It was a very intense experience. Greenwich Village was quite a heavy neighbourhood. Going to clubs like CBGBs every night was frightening for a young man from south London. It made Deptford seem like Trumpton.

'I would sit in the flat all day while Cindy went to work and this fluidity of lyricism came gushing forth. The whole of the *Argybargy* album came in one fell swoop and lots more besides that never saw the light of day.'

When A&M demanded a third album the following spring, it was only a question of which of Chris's expansive list of songs would make it on to the LP.

After Glenn had composed music to the best of the batch, the band went into the studio that autumn to record the new material. Sticking to the adage 'If it ain't broke, don't fix it,' the band and John Wood shared production duties and the final months of 1979 were spent recording and mixing Squeeze's all-important third album.

***

'Pulling Mussels (From The Shell)'

The lyric evokes a picture-postcard image of an English holiday.

CD: It was inspired by a holiday taken when I was 12 with a friend of mine, who lived opposite me on the estate. His father had an Austin A40, which was new to me because I'd never been in a car before. The family also had a caravan, which was something else I'd never experienced.

My friend was an only child and his parents suggested I go along with them to Margate for a weekend. We stayed in the caravan at a holiday camp. There was a club there where bands played and the song reflects that atmosphere of the traditional working class 'get away from it all' weekend holiday.

It was the first time I had really looked up into the sky to see what it was like. It was a beautiful dark sky and it felt amazing to be away from London.

I wrote the song with Steve Marriott and The Small Faces in mind.

Musically there is a lovely mood to this song, alternating between the bliss of the verses and the tension of the chorus.

GT: I have to thank Chris for that because the lyric made it easy. I was influenced by two things. I was smoking a lot of dope at this time, so everything I wrote was very slow. Also, the year beforehand we had supported The Tubes, who I thought had a wonderfully theatrical element to them and a grandiosity to their songs.

The section at the end of the chorus is definitely influenced by The Tubes. Even though the song is quite straightforward, the chorus adds a little twist. This was at a time when the band worked together on our arrangements. Everyone was chipping in with suggestions and almost all the liveliness and invention on *Argybargy* came from having that band approach.

CD: It's a great arrangement, with a fantastic selection of chords, although that made it quite difficult to play. It has a lot of angst about it at times, which sums up the story well.

'ANOTHER NAIL IN MY HEART'

CD: I don't think the lyric is much cop, but the guitar solo after the first verse is stunning. It's really thought through and bristlingly played. It was unheard of at the time to have a solo that early in a song.

GT: Yes, but there are only two verses and I couldn't put it at the end. So it was either after the first verse or nowhere. It was a purely practical reason.

It took a whole afternoon to get the solo right and John Wood was very patient with me. I had a definite idea of how I wanted it to sound and he could see what I was after, although there was a lot of groping around in the dark.

This was another slow number. I had the melody line to start with and the band fleshed it out. It would have been very ordinary without their input.

Were you playing Moog on this?

GT: I was playing Jools's Polyphonic Moog on this song and quite a few others, like 'Here Comes That Feeling'.

CD: Jools doesn't appear on 'Another Nail' until the very end when he plays arpeggio on piano. On the video the band are performing and all the way through Jools is pushing a piano towards the building. Right at the end he's inside the building and starts playing. Again, it's a skilful way of putting music to a simple lyric. I've never been able to play it properly, I must say. There's always two chords I get wrong.

You mentioned the fact that Jools doesn't appear until the end. Was his musical style becoming less incorporated in the band?

CD: He was becoming less and less involved at this time. I think he was getting frustrated that he wasn't getting more of a shout in the band, but by then he was spending less time thinking about being in the band and more about his career.

He always had his sights on bigger things. When I first met him he used to carry round a diary and draw pictures of Rolls Royces and princesses on it. He married a princess and he now has three Rolls Royces, so all those little pictures he drew have now been coloured in for him, and I think that's wonderful. He even owns a castle. I went down there to see him last summer and said, 'This is amazing. You've got the things you used to draw and talk about.'

Do you think he's content?

CD: Jools is very driven. He's a really sharp person who is driven by his own success. His diary is always full.

'Separate Beds'

CD: I really like this song. It's one we played in America a lot and reminds me of a time when I was dating a particular young girl. The first time I went to stay at her parents' house I had that awkward feeling you always get in those situations, that you're trespassing on someone else's land. When you wake up in the morning you have to creep to the bathroom, and you're really polite the first time you have breakfast with them, sitting there wondering what they're thinking.

I always found that situation fascinating, the time when you are allowed to sleep in the same bed as someone's daughter. It's a very special moment in a young man's life, when you are finally marking your ground as a young man. Then you take her back to meet your parents and the shoe is on the other foot. Your girlfriend is trying to impress your parents and you're looking for your mum and dad to give you the thumbs-up. It's a very animal thing and an interesting idea for a lyric.

There are some killer lines in this.

GT: 'Her mother didn't like me/ She thought I was on drugs/ My mother didn't like her/ She'd never peel the spuds.' That's pure genius. It still makes me laugh now. Myself, Chris and Jools fell in with a group of middle-class people and there were plenty of girlfriends' mums who disapproved of us. You just sensed it and they were perfectly right to frown on us, I have to say.

CD: The first time I went to stay at this girl's house in north London she said to her parents, 'Do you mind if Chris stays the night? It's such a long way back to Greenwich.' They said that was fine. Later they toddled off to bed in this big house, so I thought, 'Right. I'll get down to a bit of business here, under her mum and dad's nose.'

We started having a bit of fun and after we'd finished she screamed out and I was horrified because her parents were in the next room. The next morning we went downstairs and her mother said brightly, 'Would you like some breakfast, Chris?' I went straight out of the house and on to the bus home.

Did you ever go back?

CD: No. We didn't see much of each other after that, but not because of that incident. This lyric sums up that whole atmosphere and I'm very attached to it.

'MISADVENTURE'

GT: This was a bit of a throwback to 'Cool For Cats' really. A great live song.

CD: It was about lorry drivers who were importing rugs from Turkey and the Middle East, people I'd met at the docks.

What fascinated you about their lives?

CD: What a great job they had, getting in their truck and driving across Europe to bring back rugs. It wasn't just rugs they were carrying. They were bringing dope wrapped up in them. The last verse sums it up. 'Then they discovered/ A shipment of Moroccan/ And said excuse me sir/ There's something you've forgotten.'

GT: It's also about the uncle of someone we knew who was involved in smuggling.

Whose uncle?

GT: I can't tell you that, I'm afraid. It wouldn't be right. The only other thing I remember about this song was Gilson putting a cow bell part in it.

I couldn't remember the part and he told me it went to the tempo of 'Fuck off, cunt. Fuck off.' Funnily enough, I always remembered it after that!

CD: It's not a great tune or lyric, but it filled up the album.

'I Think I'm Go Go'

GT: This was a step forward in our imaginations. It was influenced lyrically by the fact we had been whopped around the head and rendered bewildered by the amount of travelling we'd been doing. We all found it bewildering, but I had the sense that Chris probably felt this more so than the rest of us.

CD: This was a song about touring, which could be a very strange experience. It would get to the stage where I'd think 'I don't know where I am, I don't know which country I am in, what time we're onstage, or who I'm sleeping with.' 'I think I'm go go' was the turn of phrase in the band at the time.

GT: Going to America had a huge influence on us. People were different there, and they had another way of dealing with things. We judged things on the standards that we'd grown up with in Britain, which were very different. We found the directness of Americans weird and we felt dislocated.

CD: Interestingly, this song was very popular in America. The first verse is about being in Amsterdam because a lot of our early gigs were in Holland. Glenn's dad lived out there and he used to arrange gigs for us. It was always good fun playing there.

The second verse is about New York and mentions liquor stores, rodeos, and PIX, which was an American radio station. The last verse is about London.

When we toured the States that year the Americans did not understand the title *Argybargy* at all. Miles told us no one would know what it meant but we didn't give a shit and were in a belligerent, young Englishmen's mood, so we kept it. *Argybargy* sums up succinctly what our lives were like at the time. We were in each other's pockets, travelling in a minibus and on Freddie Laker planes. It was getting tiring, but we lived on the adrenalin of it.

Did you find being on tour addictive?

CD: I found everything addictive. As a self-confessed addict it's not surprising I was addicted to touring. It was great fun.

These days you don't tour so much, whereas Glenn is always on the road.

CD: Glenn is more of a performer than I am, whereas I'm more reflective. But that's a whole different conversation. The song has some lovely melodies that Glenn used to play on keyboards. It was a very delicate and peaceful song to play live. We split the vocals with Glenn and I alternating between verses, which at the time was unusual. We sang the last verse together. It was quite challenging.

Glenn, your ascending chord progression is a very strong part of the song.

GT: It's very Beatles-like and also has a similar sound to our song, 'The Knack'. There's a direct through line from 'The Knack' to 'I Think I'm Go Go', with that sense of other-worldness. The use of strings added to that feeling. I wanted to contrast real strings with synth strings and change the feel between the verses. This meant the listener got a sense of being jolted out of one mood into another.

'Farifisa Beat'

This is the song I least like on the album. The ultimate filler track.

GT: I can't disagree with you there, but I was particularly pleased with that guitar riff, which is a minor point in its favour.

CD: The song's crap. I don't have anything to say about the lyric. The music for me sums up a kind of B52s, American club sound. As you say, it's an album filler at best and one of the few which I don't remember recording at all. It was probably just stuck on the album because it was up-tempo.

'HERE COMES THAT FEELING'

Why are you laughing?

CD: Because I sing this in such a deadpan fashion. It leans towards the theatrical side of our work, like 'The Knack'. It's a story about an actor going to work, but it doesn't really do anything except take up three minutes of an album. I don't think we ever played it live. I was never happy with my vocal, which just sounds very stupid.

Do you think *Cool For Cats* was a better album than *Argybargy*?

CD: Only in the sense that it was the first time we'd been able to make a record that we wanted to, rather than what John Cale wanted. *Argybargy* was an extension of *Cool For Cats*. 'Another Nail', 'Pulling Mussels', and 'If I Didn't Love You' were the three outstanding songs on the album. Musically and lyrically we were growing, and we were going through a natural progression.

GT: For me *Argybargy* is the more complete brother of *Cool For Cats*. It's a step up in the songwriting subjects, and slightly more mature. We were beginning to lose our cheeky chappy style of writing as our circumstances changed. As we went up in the world so we started losing the low-life element to our songs.

'VICKY VERKY'

'Vicky Verky' concerns the same characters from 'Up The Junction', but five years earlier in their lives, doesn't it?

CD: Loosely. I really like the song because it's so cute. Again it has that Bob Dylan kind of lyrical spread about it. I used to feel sorry for Glenn when he had to sing it live because the lyric is so long. It was quite a lot to take on board when he was also playing guitar and having to keep the spirit of the band going onstage. Glenn does have a great capacity for remembering words and an ability to sing any song you care to mention, from Gilbert O' Sullivan to Gilbert and Sullivan. If I go onstage I have to take a book with me with the lyrics in.

It's one of your lyrics which has that ability to immerse the listener in the lives of characters in a short space of time. It's the small images that make the lyric. 'With her hair up in his fingers/ The fish and chips smell lingers' is one example.

CD: Yes. I don't get fish and chip fingers in my hair very often these days. They're quite a nice couple, the two main characters. 'Vicky Verky', like 'Argybargy', was a phrase the Americans didn't understand.

I don't understand it either. What does it mean?

CD: I don't know where it comes from in history but it means 'the opposite' of something.

Can you give an example?

CD: If that boat there was going backwards down the river you might say that it was going a bit 'Vicky Verky'. I rarely hear it these days. It's a south London phrase.

GT: This is a song which Jools really hated but when I do solo shows it's one of the most constantly requested songs. As affectionate as many people are of it, I think Jools was right. It's lyrically slightly twee in the way that 'Up The Junction' isn't, which makes it less interesting to me. Musically, I don't think it's very good either.

'If I Didn't Love You'

CD: I used to love playing this song live. Glenn and I sang it together as a duet, an octave apart. Lyrically it has to be my proudest moment from this album and it takes me back to New York when I was living there and writing lyrics. It's about the early cosy part of a relationship, which I call the nesting stage. It's a lovely place to be, somewhere where I think people only go two or three times in their life.

At the same time it has that juxtaposition of emotions, saying 'If I didn't love you I'd hate you,' because at the back of your mind you've got that insecurity about your inability to have a proper relationship with somebody.

I also love Glenn's slide guitar solo. When he first did it I thought 'This guy's out of his tree. What's he doing?,' but it's brilliant.

GT: This is a really storming lyric from Chris and was chosen as a different single in America. It was a massive radio hit there, particularly on the East Coast, whereas it was just an album track in Britain. The lyric caught a lot of people's imaginations because of that thing Chris does so well, picking up on small, almost irrelevant details. What he wrote here rang absolutely true to me and was all the more powerful for it.

The line 'The record jumps on a scratch' was such a gift that I had to use it, so we sang 'If I, If I, If I, If I, If I.'

CD: 'I'm playing your stereogram/ Singles remind me of kisses/ Albums remind me of plans.' They are my favourite lines on the whole album. When I used to have girls back to my flat I'd go through my record collection and find the album which had the longest side, be it Todd Rundgren or the Grateful Dead. I knew that by a certain point on the record if I didn't have my hand down her pants then it wasn't going to happen because I'd have to get up and change the record over. So it was all about timing.

The best album for that purpose would be *Something Anything* by Todd Rundgren, because it had one side that was 30 minutes long. I'd put it on and get down to business and knew that I had a couple of minutes at the end of the album to lie on my back and then I'd have the excuse to get up and change the record.

'Wrong Side Of The Moon'

CD: I don't remember writing this one and it doesn't do much for me lyrically. Musically, it's quite fun and we got some girlfriends in to do the backing vocals.

This was a Difford-Holland collaboration? Did you feel obliged to have a Jools track on this album?

CD: We'd reach that embarrassing moment while recording albums when we'd look at the clock and see that we had 20 minutes to go and think 'Oh my God. We've got to get one of Jools's tracks on. It might as well be this one.'

I always felt a bit odd writing with Jools because it took me out of my relationship with Glenn, although it meant that I'd written the lyrics for the entire album. That was, and still is, really important to me. I'd hate to perform on albums where I hadn't written all the lyrics. It wouldn't be my album.

Later on Keith Wilkinson wrote some lyrics for Squeeze. How did you feel about that?

CD: I felt so disengaged from those songs. I thought, 'Why the hell do we need another songwriter?'

Was that sort of thing ever spoken about?

CD: No. We were terrible at communicating. For years we went without communicating anything emotionally.

'There At The Top'

Having been accused of being misogynist, you sought to rescue your reputation with a song about a very strong female character.

CD: Yes, it's a very positive lyrics about a woman. In fact it's about Maxine.

GT: That's very interesting. I didn't know that.

CD: After Glenn and Maxine stopped going out, they went in different directions, and she became a very independent woman. From somebody who was a mate of ours she overnight became a very proper young lady and changed from wearing hippy jeans to a pencil skirt and driving a company car. Suddenly she'd grown up and it was an inspiration to see.

I saw for the first time that women could have independence and the skill to stand on their own two feet without being in the shadow of somebody else. The girls I was hanging out with at that time didn't have that. They weren't as studious as Maxine.

I was also influenced by what I saw in New York where women were very independent. Maybe subconsciously this lyric was my way of clawing back some Brownie points from my relationship with my wife.

***

THE MASTERING of *Argybargy* was completed on 2 January, 1980, but there was to be no time for either celebratory back-slapping or a well-earned rest. The very next day the disconsolate band had to pack their suitcases and get to Heathrow bright and early for a 24-hour flight to Australia.

Copeland had booked them on to a gruelling tour Down Under, and the grumpy mood of the tired musicians failed to lift for almost the entirety of the trip. The band members couldn't comprehend Australian culture and made little effort to disguise their contempt when interviewed.

According to Glenn, 'To us it just seemed like an inferior version of Britain. It was 1980 and yet there were loads of 1960s TV shows on prime time every evening. It was too much for our fragile little minds to take.'

Their visit to Brisbane was a particularly galling experience, with the state of Queensland in the iron grip of right-wing dictator Joh Bjelke Petersen. A Swedish national, Petersen had moved to Australia in the 1970s, having been refused access to Britain. Storming to power in Queensland on a no-nonsense manifesto, Petersen proceeded to install numerous draconian laws. One of the strangest regulations was to limit gatherings in public places to six people, unless a special permit had been sought in advance.

The omens for a successful tour were not good. Eighteen months earlier New Wave contemporaries The Stranglers, whose image and music were rather more menacing than those associated with Squeeze, had caused outrage on Australian television. During an interview on current affairs show *Willessee At Seven*, the four band members mercilessly goaded a young presenter, causing shock waves akin to The Sex Pistols' infamous interview with Bill Grundy in Britain. To top it all, a Stranglers show in Brisbane almost led to the band's arrest after jumped-up allegations of inciting violence.

The Stranglers' trip had hardly endeared Australia to British New Wave bands and Squeeze were treated with disdain by audiences, particularly in Broken Hill. Glenn recalls, 'We were laughing our heads off at the support band. They were this sub-Led Zeppelin band doing these really heavy riffs. We thought "We're the sound of the future. We're going to fucking show you who's boss." The support band went down brilliantly and the audience just stared at us when we came on and retreated gradually. They didn't like us at all.' Squeeze were never asked on an Australian tour again.

Weary and disheartened, the band returned to the UK, but were in for further disappointment. Shortly after their return Jools announced he was leaving Squeeze with immediate effect.

Sidelined by Glenn's musical dominance in the band and his limited songwriting opportunities, the pianist was already planning a solo career, and within a year released an album, *Jools Holland With The Millionaires*.

His colleagues were devastated by his departure. Chris recalls, 'I went off to Gambadellas, a greasy café in Blackheath, with Glenn. I was very upset and cried. It was sad because there was the fear of the unknown. We thought we wouldn't be able to replace him.

'Jools was an important artery in the band. The flow of blood came from Glenn to me to John and Gilson via Jools. He was such a comedic, easy-to-get-along-with-person, that if Glenn and I weren't speaking on tour, both of us could always talk to Jools. If there were any problems he'd be very helpful in getting things sorted out. He's quite diplomatic.'

Glenn describes his reaction to Jools's departure as one of 'absolute devastation.' He adds, 'I was convinced that we could be the biggest band in the world and I felt like we were a unit that was welded at each hip. It came as a complete surprise to me, but obviously I didn't have enough nous to know what other people were thinking. Perhaps I had my head too much up my own arse to do that.'

In addition to his desire to undertake a solo career, Jools had one eye on a career in the more lucrative field of TV presenting. In 1981 he presented a high-profile documentary on The Police and began to tout his name around for television shows. A year later he secured the plum job as co-presenter on Channel 4's live music show *The Tube*.

Jools's talent for connecting with an audience had become apparent towards the end of his time with Squeeze. Having been asked by Copeland to introduce the band halfway through their set, Jools's nightly performance at the microphone fast became a highlight of the show.

As Chris explains, 'It was often mentioned that we weren't very good at talking to the audience. Miles would say to us, "Why the hell don't you talk to them?," because we'd just go from one number to the next, with no banter. So in the middle of an American tour Miles suggested that Jools come out and introduce everybody. That night Jools came to the front, grabbed the microphone, and talked for about a minute and a half. By the end of the tour he was taking about 20 minutes.

'He really got off on it, going into this Southern preacher vibe and putting on a preacher's hat and a cloak. He was hysterically funny and it gave us all a breathing space to cool the set down. It became apparent that he had a real knack for it. So he took that skill to the audition for *The Tube* and, of course, got the job.'

Having said goodbye to the friends with whom he'd earned his musical stripes, Jools began his extraordinarily successful career on the small screen, one that has endured for a quarter of a century and shows no sign of ending. Yet 1980 did not mark the end of his association with Squeeze. Within five years he would be back in the band.

5 *East Side Story*

AFTER JOOLS'S dramatic departure, the Squeeze revolution continued at pace, with the acrimonious departure of Miles Copeland from the manager's chair. Glenn and Chris in particular had grown frustrated with Copeland's apparent waning of interest in Squeeze, while the other major act in his stable, The Police, were on their way to becoming rock megastars.

With the exception of Jools, who was close to Copeland, the band had been complaining internally for months about his decreasing commitment to their career. 'We didn't think we were achieving what we should be and we were growing frustrated with Miles,' claims Glenn. 'There was only one hit on *Argybargy* and it wasn't anywhere near as big as the two from the previous album. The whole situation had been drawing to a head. I think we were right to be concerned.'

The issue came to a head after a fortuitous meeting in a Derbyshire hotel with singer Elvis Costello and his manager Jake Riviera, a larger-than-life character who had risen to prominence after co-founding Stiff Records with Irish impresario Dave Robinson. Squeeze were playing in the town of Matlock, while Costello had also been appearing locally, so both bands embarked upon a five-hour drinking session amid much mutual back-slapping. Towards the end of the evening Chris found himself pinned against the wall by a foaming-mouthed Riviera.

Chris recalls, 'Jake was shouting that our career with Miles was going nowhere and that he was screwing us. He told me we needed to make a record that would change the world. I liked Jake instantly and realised he was primarily a music fan, who really enjoyed our music.' The following morning Glenn and Chris ate breakfast together in the hotel and decided over tea and toast that Riviera should replace Copeland with immediate effect.

When informed of the band's decision to join his company, Riviera Global, their new manager further delighted the pair by offering to work without a contract. 'He slapped down a pint on a bar and we agreed everything on a shake of hands,' says Chris. 'It was very inspirational.'

According to Chris, Copeland was 'distraught and very pissed off' by his axing. As the parting of the ways descended into acrimony, Chris and Glenn began legal proceedings against the American to reclaim his 50 per cent lease on their publishing royalties. Licking his wounds, Copeland renewed acquaintances with Jools and began working on making him into a TV star.

Buoyed by Riviera's faith in their ability, Squeeze's attention soon turned to recording the band's fourth album. Riviera originally suggested making a four-sided LP on ten-inch vinyl, with a different producer for each side. Elvis Costello was eager to be involved, as were Nick Lowe, Paul McCartney and rock 'n' roll singer/producer Dave Edmunds.

Unfortunately, McCartney quickly pulled out, to concentrate on writing his forthcoming LP *Tug Of War*. Next stop was Nick Lowe. A fun figure for the beer-swilling musicians to be with, most of their time with Lowe was spent in local hostelries and the recordings made with him were scrapped. Squeeze's stint with Edmunds was slightly more productive, although just one of the songs recorded with the pub rocker, 'In Quintessence', made it on to *East Side Story*.

Out of the four producers pencilled in for the record, this left Costello. The band could hardly contain their excitement at the opportunity to work alongside the Irish singer, who was coming from four years of sustained commercial success.

A busy man, Costello informed the band that the record would have to be made in a matter of weeks because he had a list of other projects on the back burner that would soon require his attention. To ensure that their deadline was met, Costello installed a strict regime of work, with recording taking place from 10am until 9pm from Monday to Friday. Trips to the pub were outlawed and a healthy-eating regime consisting mainly of salads was introduced. 'I baulked at it at first, but it did work for the most part,' admits Chris.

Working alongside Costello was Roger Bechirian, who had produced the early wave of hits for Irish punk combo The Undertones, including 'Teenage Kicks' and 'My Perfect Cousin.'

Before recording began there was the small matter of recruiting a keyboard player. On the advice of Riviera, Squeeze hired Paul Carrack, formerly of pub rock outfit Ace. Described by Glenn as 'one of the loveliest men ever in music,' Carrack brought his love of soul into the band, an influence that would have lasting effect on Squeeze's lead singer.

All 14 songs for the album had been written months earlier and the majority of lyrics had come out of Chris's lyrical outpouring in New York 18 months earlier. But it would be Costello and Bechirian's inspirational regime that would lick the songs into shape and move the band into new and exciting directions.

***

'IN QUINTESSENCE'

CD: The lyric is autobiographical in some ways, another song that mentions masturbation.

Yes. 'In a corner with his book and tissue/ All he can do is pretend to miss you.'

CD: I guess I was a bit of a wanker at the time. It reminds me of living with Glenn in a house in Crooms Hill. I had a room in the basement and Glenn was on the top floor. I used to leave lyrics on a tray outside and when Glenn came down to get the milk he would pick them up and go upstairs to write the music. I'd be able to hear him working on songs from the basement and then he'd come and fetch me to listen to what he'd done. It was a really inspiring time. There's a great *NME* cover of us working in one of the rooms there.

GT: The bloke who the lyric was about is now a very responsible teacher working just outside Liverpool. I saw him a couple of months ago and he said how perfectly this described his life at the time. Chris was spot on in analysing him as someone who liked smoking joints and shagging birds, but what's wrong with that?

CD: 'In Quintessence' was in our set for quite a while and we used to segue it into 'Time Is Tight', which was a Booker T And The MGs song.

GT: Musically it was my tip of the hat to Elvis. He'd borrowed the riff from 'Time Is Tight' and used it on a song called 'Temptation'. I thought it would be funny to use that riff again for 'In Quintessence' and expand it.

'SOMEONE ELSE'S HEART'

CD: I wrote the words on a notepad at a motorway service station between the M6 and Liverpool where we were driving for a gig. It was a little too high for me to sing but I quite like the sound of my voice on it.

Presumably Chris's high voice was necessitated by Glenn's arrangement.

GT: I can't remember whose idea it was but I thought he sounded great. Chris used to sing higher before we began making records. On the next album I tried to get him up there again but I think he felt I was trying to play a trick on him and make him sound silly, which I had no interest in. I just wanted him to sing a bit higher, because I'd heard him do it.

I think that if Chris really respected someone, as he did Elvis, he would do it for them. For whatever reason, he could never be like that with me.

Was that because you were too close?

GT: I can only think that in some way I must have been insensitive to him at some point. I certainly don't remember consciously trying to belittle him or doing anything except to encourage him.

Paul's vocals on this were also fantastic. No disrespect to Jools, but it was wonderful to have someone like Paul with whom I could harmonise. Vocally it opened up an entirely different set of windows. On this song Chris sang half the verses, while Paul and I sang the other half. We did this live and it was lovely to have that vocal spread.

CD: I also like Gilson's imaginative drumming, although John's bass playing sounds wooden and rather dated. I have a soft spot for this number because it was written quickly and songs written that way are quite important to me.

'Tempted'

CD: This was written on the back of a fag packet in a minicab on the way to Heathrow. We were going on tour.

The first verse does conjure up the image of going to the airport, buying all your toiletries, like the toothpaste and flannel.

CD: Yes, and in America, where it was a big radio hit, people used to throw toothbrushes, flannels and all those other things on to the stage. The first time it happened was in New York. Everything Glenn sang in the first verse was thrown at us. There were literally hundreds of toothbrushes around our feet, which was bizarre.

Is the lyric autobiographical?

CD: I think so. I was married by then but going on the road does mean that you are tempted. It's like being in the Merchant Navy. You're going to all the ports in the world and there are women of easy virtue there and you have to behave yourself or go home with a guilty conscience, or worse still the pox.

What did you go home with?

CD: A huge bunch of flowers and a guilty conscience.

Why did Paul Carrack sing this?

GT: That was down to Elvis, who recognised what a wonderful soulful voice Paul had.

Without Paul's vocal this would have been just another Squeeze song. He did a remarkable job and, even though my ego was bruised initially, I realised that the more different facets we could get across to people the more interesting we became.

CD: Having said that, the other night I was in a restaurant and a woman said 'Hey. Didn't you sing "Cool For Cats"?' I said to her, 'Yeah, but I bet you can't name another Squeeze song.' She sat there quietly and as I was getting up to leave I said, 'Up The Junction'. She said, 'Was that you?,' which sums up our career. We didn't have one singer right the way through that people could associate us with.

You had particular trouble writing a tune to this, didn't you, Glenn?

GT: It was such a fantastic lyric I was desperate not to get it wrong. I had the first two lines for days and couldn't get any further. It was like climbing a rock face and took me about a week, edging my way forward, then going back, and edging forward a little more. Bob Dylan once said to David Bowie that anything that takes more than ten minutes should just be binned, which is wrong in my eyes.

CD: 'Tempted' sounds so easy to play but it's actually quite complex and has some very difficult chord sequences. There's one guitar lick that goes all the way through the song, which Elvis picked out when we were recording, so when we went out on the road I stole that line because it was only two notes. I could bluff my way round the stage with two notes no problem and avoided having to play all the chords.

GT: The first version, which I was chiefly responsible for, sounded like fucking ELO. It was absolutely wrong but Elvis pulled us in a few different directions and helped us change it.

CD: Elvis had the idea of giving the song a Temptations arrangement, so that we all got a chance to sing. Except for me, that is. Elvis sang the lower lines which I would have otherwise sung.

I've heard Glenn sing some wonderful versions of 'Tempted' because he wrote the music and brought quite a lot of passion to it. I've heard Glenn sing it some nights and it makes you weep. I've done it in my set and it will make you weep as well, but for different reasons.

'PICCADILLY'

This lyric is quite similar to 'Separate Beds'.

CD: Yes, it's from the same corner of the song book, although it's not about anyone in particular. I especially like the line, 'She hooks up her cupcakes.'

GT: This is a lovely song. It's brilliant because it's a whole story of an evening out. It's one of Chris's lyrics where I see exactly the same pictures in my mind whenever I hear it. I find it incredible that he can write a lyric that gives such stunningly clear pictures in your mind, like a radio play. A lot of Chris's lyrics could take you on a journey and my job was to make it feel like a pleasant one.

The lyrics were apparently written on a napkin in a pub.

CD: It was the Rose and Crown, next to the Greenwich Theatre. It's a gay pub now. This is another storyboard song about characters who lived around my life at that time. Glenn's arrangement is top drawer. Each verse has a different feel to it: the tom-tom part followed by the stabbing guitar. It's a very inventive walk through the song and keeps the listener busy.

GT: The riff was plainly inspired by 'Another Nail'. I thought that it had worked before so I might as well use it again. Then I added the usual fistful of chords.

Paul's piano gives a nice lilt to this song. I can imagine Jools playing this.

CD: You're right. It has the same sort of expression in the piano. Paul is a very good piano player, as well as an extremely good Hammond player.

'There's No Tomorrow'

This sounds like it could have come from The Beatles' psychadelic period.

CD: It is very Beatles-esque. Very George Harrison, although listening to it makes me go cross-eyed. When I first heard Glenn's demo of this I was so scared that I wanted to jump out of the window. When we were rehearsing for the album Glenn kept pushing for this song. There's another called 'F-Hole' and every time that came on I had to find an excuse to go to the pub. It used to drive me up the wall because my vision was so impaired. I couldn't see how brilliant Glenn was at experimentation.

Why do you think your vision was impaired?

CD: Because I wanted all the songs to sound like 'In Quintessence' and have a flow from start to finish. I wanted the girls to be able to put their handbags on the floor and dance around it, but they didn't.

You couldn't dance to this.

CD: Unless you had your legs sawn off. Elvis was also big on experimentation so he and Glenn got on very well when it came to this arrangement. It was a real turning point in our songwriting relationship, but I wish I'd realised it at that time.

GT: I seem to remember 'There's No Tomorrow' was a song I'd written much earlier that no one else had liked. I tried to circumnavigate that by playing it to Elvis in the hope that he'd get enthused by it. Fortunately he did.

It was around this time that you were labelled the new Lennon and McCartney. Was that a millstone around your neck?

CD: It was for a while. On the following record it was quite a painful sack to carry, but at this time it was useful because it got us played on radio stations. When *Sweets From A Stranger* came out in America A&M put a sticker on the front saying, 'The new Lennon and McCartney.' All those radio stations in places like Texas, who would normally play Kansas, REO Speedwagon and Rush, would play us because of that label. It was a useful tool, although it was a ball and chain for us, especially for Glenn.

When I met Paul McCartney for the first time he said, 'Which one are you? Paul or John?' I said, 'I'm Ringo,' and he laughed.

GT: That label is something that's affected us to this day because people still ask us about it. The fact is that it's just something a couple of blokes wrote in magazine reviews, but the A&M press office wanted to milk it and threw out a barrage of press releases for *Sweets From A Stranger* with that slogan.

'HEAVEN'

The first thing I'd like to mention is the inspired Greek guitar at the end. I had to stop playing this at home before I started smashing up all my plates.

CD: I know what you mean. It makes me think of hummus and olives. It's actually played on a banjo and when Glenn first played that part to me I was appalled. I used to run a mile when Glenn brought out these weird instruments but now I realise it was inspired. What other bands were using a banjo?

Presumably the inspiration for its use was because the song concerned Cypriot sailors on their night out?

GT: I always favour the literal interpretation of everything! I definitely used a Moog on this. I don't remember much else about it, except that Chris hated the seasick Moog, warbling in and out of tune.

In the middle section Gilson does a fantastic fill, which no one else would have thought of. He stamped himself on it, but not in a way that's intrusive.

There is an element of 'Taxman' by The Beatles to this, but Chris's vocal carries it completely. He sounds totally at ease with himself.

What inspired the lyrics?

CD: I'd just discovered Jacques Brel and was intrigued by the translation of his lyrics. I was trying to describe characters in the same way. David Bowie had already recorded songs like 'Amsterdam' and 'My Death' and The Walker Brothers used to play some as well. Brel wrote filthy lyrics, influenced by opium and aniseed. He was absolutely off his face but brilliant.

Did you ever write like that?

CD: I never got close to it, although I don't think I was ever more than a couple of hours away from a drink. Most of my early writing was written on a bed of hangover. It was a lovely place to be, that fantastic place between death and the next drink.

'Woman's World'

Glenn, I've just read an interview with you in which you said you pretended to be Ray Davies on this song.

GT: The tune itself had nothing to do with Ray Davies but the chord structure is like The Kinks' 'Dead End Street'. It has the same progression on the guitar part. It's another drink song, isn't it? The woman getting fed up and going out to get smashed and the family being dismayed.

Chris was stunned by people saying his lyrics were sexist and he was trying to address that, but unlike 'There At The Top' he did it in a self-assured and unpatronising way.

CD: Around this time I was beginning to respect the female race more than I had done previously. I was trying to show in this lyric how hard it was to be a woman in a man's world. I was still slightly living under the illusion that men always had the last word. Of course, I've since learnt that isn't always the case.

I wrote this on a tour bus in America where I was influenced by seeing women treated like second-class citizens, except for in New York. English women seemed to be treated better, which was saying an awful lot.

It's a clever lyric with the lines about the female character having her domestic kingdom, but no crown to wear. There's also one of your trademark subject matters, the mundane sex life. 'She goes to bed/ Leg by leg/ Nothing said'.

CD: That's pretty true about a lot of relationships. After the nesting stage of a relationship you often go into the mundane.

At the end of this song she ends up staggering out to the pub and getting blind drunk.

CD: And why not? I feel for her. This character's in a tight space and says 'two can play at that game'.

It's quite a liberating moment in the lyric.

CD: I was hoping to attract a more sophisticated woman in my life. I hoped if we played this live they might come charging down the front shouting, 'Chris, you are the man. Come back and sleep with me and we will have a very intelligent relationship.' But it never happened. I was living in a deluded world, which I have done all my life.

'IS THAT LOVE?'

CD: This was written around the time I got married. I remember being in the bathroom and seeing Cindy's wedding ring next to the soap, which inspired me to write the lyric. I don't think it was particularly about our marriage, but it started off a sequence of ideas in my head.

I'm not strapped to the song emotionally but it was a great live number and sums up being on the road and having fun. It's a comfortable pair of jeans as a song.

GT: Like many of the songs on *Argybargy* this was originally mid-tempo, so we sped it up and it made more sense like that, coupled with my playful revisiting of the '1812 Overture' in the chorus, which made me laugh.

You like to amuse yourself when writing songs, don't you? Do you like putting in-jokes in your music that only you would understand?

GT: It wasn't like that and never has been, but when I write I do want to make myself happy. I've never wanted my music to be a joke and I take what I do incredibly seriously, but if I can put something in a song that will make me laugh then I'll do it.

The only time that mine and Chris's music ever became corrupted was after *East Side Story*, when we got the 'New Lennon and McCartney' tag. We went through a period of slightly pretentious writing, but fortunately we quickly drifted back down to earth.

CD: This was another song where Glenn's arrangement kept the listener's attention. Each piece of the story has a different section, and it has a Beatles-esque arrangement vocally when my voice comes in to complement his.

GT: I was influenced quite consciously by The Beatles here.

CD: That single high note on piano is also reminiscent of The Temptations and then there's an act of genius by Glenn when the tune goes from minor to major in the last verse. I always used to get it wrong onstage and Glenn would get very cross with me.

The semi a capella ending works well live, like an open invitation to the audience to sing the last line.

CD: It's like when you sit in church and don't know all the words to a hymn but you can sing the last line really loud because that's the one bit you know.

GT: That ending was Elvis's idea and he played the piano part accompanying it.

CD: We recorded the video with the artist Barney Bubbles and danced with mops turned upside down. Barney used blurred photography and swapped all the colours around. It was ahead of its time, like being in The Factory in New York with Andy Warhol. Oddly, the song became the only Number One of our career, in Israel.

'F-Hole'

CD: The lyric sums up characters who would have lived in Greenwich in the '60s, in Thames Street, which is right on the river. When I was at school, Thames Street was a road you didn't walk down for fear of being beaten up. I'm really proud of the turns of phrase in the lyric and the way the lines rhyme. It's a lyric I wish I could write today because it has such descriptive imagery.

It's quite a patronising lyric in parts. 'The youngish damsel figure/ With her tongue tied to a trigger' conjures up images of a foul-mouthed fishwife. Then the description of her trying to be classy: 'Sipped her snow balls poshly like a judge/ But left her lipstick traces on her mug.'

CD: When I was a boy my mum used to drag me to mothers' meetings, where I'd be mollycoddled by women like that who would leave lipstick all over me. They would think they were royalty, whereas they were absolute scum, but it didn't matter because without that characteristic they'd be very depressed. They gave themselves the authority to be like the Queen in local pubs, but I could understand why they did so.

What about the title?

CD: It should have been 'Fuck Hole' really, but we thought it was best left to the listener's imagination.

This is arguably the most unusual track on the album musically, with a very complex string arrangement.

GT: That was arranged by Del Newman.

How did you come by him?

GT: Del came to do strings on the stuff we recorded for RCA that never came out. We'd also got Del in on *Argbargy* for 'I Think I'm Go Go' and 'What The Butler Saw', which Miles specifically excluded from the album.

Why did he exclude it?

GT: Because he said it sounded like Barry Manilow, which just goes to show how much he listened. Anyway, Elvis has always liked Del, so we brought him in. It's fair to say that Elvis liked the more odd musical side of what we were doing and was happy to take things further. I was pleased about that but I suspect Chris was happy going down to the pub on this one.

Gilson excels on this.

GT: Yes. It's such an odd song because it didn't have a straightforward beat, and I demoed it with a Moog triggered by a drum machine. I'd done this in a very crude fashion, which was rigid in its feel. Gilson gave the song a far more emotive quality when he played it in the studio.

There's a startling butt edit from 'F-Hole' into the next song, 'Labelled With Love'. It's a shock to the system, going directly from this 'far out' track that's off in all sorts of directions, into a slow country ballad.

GT: That was Elvis's idea. The string arrangement dovetails perfectly into the opening chord of 'Labelled With Love'. Within that context 'Labelled With Love' sounds fantastic, after that build-up, whereas on its own it lacks that context and is quite pedestrian.

CD: What's also interesting is that the old slag at the end of 'F-Hole' picks up her guitar and starts playing her favourite country songs and the chords go wrong. It's quite a surreal image, almost Fellini-esque and then it goes straight into 'Labelled With Love', a country song where she tells the story of her life. It reminds me of Jacques Brel in that you don't expect the story to end like that.

'LABELLED WITH LOVE'

This was one of your biggest hits.

GT: That was odd because we weren't even going to include 'Labelled With Love' on the album until Elvis heard it. I was playing him a cassette of demos and started fast forwarding when it got to 'Labelled With Love' but he said, 'Stop there. I want to hear that track.'

CD: When he heard it Elvis loved it, and within an hour we'd recorded it.

GT: And it became the only song on that album that was a hit.

CD: 'Labelled With Love' was an adult lyric in a way that the older generation could latch on to and understand. My mother absolutely loved it. The story is about the end of a relationship after the war. I'd been reading about American soldiers in Britain during the war who married English girls and whisked them off their feet to the States.

We were playing in San Luis Obispo, California, one night in a small cockroach-ridden theatre and a woman working backstage said to me, 'You're from Deptford, aren't you?' I could hear her English accent and asked where she was from and she said, 'I'm from Deptford too, but when the war came I married a soldier and I've never gone back.' That person could easily fit into this song.

Was this originally a country song?

GT: Yes. That was why I hadn't wanted it on the album originally, because it didn't sound like the kind of song Squeeze would play.

CD: Elvis was really into country music and introduced us to George Jones and Loretta Lynn. He gave us an education in American country, which I'd never listened to before. From that point onwards I started buying country cassettes at truck stores in America and listening to them.

GT: To be fair I had been listening to some Hank Williams before, but Elvis really broadened my knowledge of country music. It was one of those barriers you cross when you think something is square and horrible but then discover it has a heart beating inside. I discovered there were loads of great artists who I'd avoided listening to because I lumped all country music in together.

There's some fantastic storytelling in country music.

GT: People like Elvis, Nick Lowe and Kirsty McColl used a similar turn of phrase to that found in country music. Humour was used to devastating effect in country songs.

Can you give me an example?

GT: A song by George Jones that I'd heard around this time contained the line, 'I put a slim gold band on the right left hand this time.' Absolutely fantastic.

'Someone Else's Bell'

CD: Another song of domestic bliss. Not a strong part of the album for me.

GT: Chris was writing a lot about infidelity at that time and I suppose we were all having tastes of that. Once again it's the little details in the song about how the relationship is crumbling. There's a line that says everything you need to know about the subject: 'Our eyes don't seem to contact/ Never much to say/ Except perhaps excuse me/ Or pass me the ashtray.'

Yes, it sums up the complete breakdown of communication.

GT: And the fact that you stop bothering. It's pure genius and even now it makes my hair stand on end.

CD: There's a lot of references on this album to the period of a relationship that takes place after the nesting stage. It's a transitional stage when you find out if the relationship will last forever or not. I must have been observing it around me. Even though I'd just got married, it's fair to say that I was never at home because the minute a record was finished we were out on the road.

I didn't have an opportunity to observe the real meaning of marriage in a way that my parents might have done. One of the reasons I got married was because it was expected of you in those days. Obviously I was in love at that time, but there was no time to explore that relationship. Cindy and I had two children together and they're great kids. I regret the fact that I didn't spend as much time with them as I wanted to when they were growing up, but I had a career to cultivate and without cultivating the career the family wouldn't have existed.

'MUMBO JUMBO'

'Mumbo Jumbo' has quite a strange time signature?

CD: And a barrelful of chords.

GT: I'd like to call our next compilation album *A Fistful Of Chords*, which would sum our music up well.

This is the only song of any note that I ever wrote on tour. I wrote it on a piano in a hotel function room. Almost every song musically on this album I can point to a set of influences that were working on me. The chorus is very much like Buddy Holly's 'Peggy Sue'.

CD: It reminds me of classical music insofar as it's tightly arranged and the melody moves all over the place in very dramatic fashion. That banging sound in the background was me giving an AC30 amplifier a good kicking with the reverb set to full whenever the downbeat came.

What can you tell me about the song lyrically?

CD: This character and the character in 'Vanity Fair' are pretty much the same girl. It's interesting that *East Side Story* is almost a thematic record. I didn't know this at the time because it was written so quickly, but I guess one story bled into another.

There was a girl from Chesterfield who used to come and see us who was always really made up, like a character in Coronation Street. It fascinated me that a young woman would spend so much time on her looks. I really like plain women with freckles and no make-up, so when I was confronted with women totally made up it scared me off. It was like meeting a Red Indian in the middle of the desert.

I thought that her make-up was like war paint, as if she was thinking 'I want to attract a man, so I'm going to cover myself in paint, smell like a rare exotic flower, and hope for the best.' I thought this was fascinating. The nearest I got to grooming myself was pouring a bottle of Brut over me and wiping something under my armpits.

There are a lot of references to farm animals in this song. There's a 'barn', 'cattle', 'hens', a 'pen'.

CD: I was playing with puns. Elvis was brilliant at puns and he was a huge influence on me. His album *Get Happy* was full of lines that could mean two things.

GT: That mad turn of phrase and association was a side of Chris's writing which became less dominant as time went on, and I regret its passing. Sometimes he picked out words in such an odd way. In this song Chris wrote, 'Kissing curls and boyish girls/ For all the pearls in all the world, wouldn't have me.' All that crammed together sounds great and conjures up vast images, yet it's not quite literal. It has a dream-like quality.

'VANITY FAIR'

GT: Del Newman was heavily involved in the arrangement of the strings. I wrote a piano part for this but when it came to playing with the orchestra I bottled out, to my eternal shame. The verses are quite simple but the introduction and the middle section contain lots of extra sounds. It's very tuneful, but densely packed musically. The fact that the rest of the song is simple made it easier to do that because those extra little bits never sounded intrusive.

CD: This has an absolutely stunning melody and beautiful arrangement. It's one we never really did live which was, in retrospect, a lost opportunity.

At the risk of sounding melodramatic, this is a very mature song. One that's almost beyond your years at this time.

GT: Yes it is.

John Cale would have hated it.

GT: He would have done.

CD: John Cale would not even have touched it with your barge pole.

This was very popular among your fan base, wasn't it?

GT: Yes. It's strange the ones that fans pick up on. There's another called 'Maidstone', which no one liked apart from me and ended up as a B-side. More people used to request that than nearly anything else.

CD: Another thing about 'Vanity Fair' was that we were recording this when we heard that John Lennon had been murdered. As soon as we got the news, there was a deadly silence followed by us leaving for the pub. The alcohol ban went straight out of the window because we couldn't possibly work in those circumstances. No one could understand why anyone would possibly want to kill John Lennon. We got all our mates like Nick Lowe to come down and got completely rat-arsed, then went back in the studio and started playing Lennon songs.

'Messed Around'

CD: This was always a good one for hoping to attract the opposite sex onstage with lower body movements. I don't even attempt that these days.

It's a good old rock 'n' roll song, and one that Jools would surely have loved playing.

GT: Yeah. There was definitely a feeling of 'See what you're missing out on, Jools. Look at all the fun you could be having.' Paul did a great job on it and we recorded it virtually live in the studio.

CD: It actually sounds like Jools playing on it. It's a breathtaking solo by Paul. Piano playing does not get any better than that. When we recorded this I felt as though I'd finally arrived, that I was in a proper band with real men. Glenn's guitar sounds very Scotty Moore, with a distant amplifier. It's reminiscent of one of Glenn's earlier solos from when we were younger and a great way to end an album.

GT: The song showed what a great band we had at that time, one of Squeeze's strongest line-ups. *East Side Story* was definitely the end of our first peak. It was downhill afterwards.

CD: We were reaching a pinnacle, which was hard to match on the next album. It felt like we were coming round the last bend in a 10,000-metre race. We were exhausted and it was becoming apparent that there was less and less time to write, and more and more time spent going on the road. It started to suffocate us.

***

1981 HAD been a momentous year for Squeeze, in which they had recorded the best album of their career to date and worked alongside the inspirational figures of Elvis Costello and Jake Riviera. According to Chris, 'Moving to Riviera Global was like moving to a larger gang. Squeeze used to call ourselves "The Blob", five people moving around together, chained invisibly at the hip. When we joined Riviera Global we were part of a bigger blob with Elvis and his band, Nick Lowe and Dave Edmunds. It was a great community of hearts and minds and a very exciting time. I also became a father that year.'

But life in Riviera's gang was about to go sour. Having stated his desire to work without a contract, Riviera arranged a meeting with the band some months after the completion of *East Side Story* and presented them with a document hundreds of pages long, which he demanded they sign. After much soul-searching the band informed Riviera they wished him to continue as their manager, but that they would not sign his contract. Riviera's response left no room for negotiation. 'He told us to "fuck off",' says Chris.

Out of the two songwriters, it was Glenn who was most adamant against adding their signatures to the deal. 'I was incensed. Chris also felt very let down but he wanted to go with it anyway because he didn't want to leave Jake. I find it interesting that Chris thought of John Wood as a father figure for me because I always thought Jake was a father figure to Chris.'

Chris admits to having 'an enormous soft spot for Jake', whom he describes as 'a very imaginative old-school manager'. Glenn's view is rather less charitable, describing Riviera as 'very destructive and dangerous'. He cites an extraordinary incident in the US when record company boss Jerry Moss came backstage in San Francisco to congratulate Squeeze on their performance supporting Elvis.

Glenn claims that when a beaming Moss told the band how much he liked *East Side Story*, Riviera grabbed the mogul by the nose and dragged him round the room shouting, 'You liked the album did you? Side two, track two, what's it called?' Squeeze's response was to freeze on the spot. 'To my eternal shame we did nothing,' says Glenn. 'It was a moment that was so shocking that we just stood there. I'm pretty sure that this incident led to that album doing nothing in the States. Jake was shooting a hole in our sides. It sounds like a terrible conspiracy theory but I cannot think of any reason unless you were fucking insane why you would do that.'

Despite the disappointing failure of 'Tempted' to get past Number 35 in the British charts, blamed in part by Glenn on Riviera antagonising A&M, the band did have unexpected success in the shape of 'Labelled With Love'. Climbing to fourth place, the song was Squeeze's third-highest UK chart entry of all time. The band had mixed feelings about its success. Glenn in particular felt embarrassed that at the age of 24 one of his songs was being championed on Radio Two, which was then a middle-of-the-road station. 'We'd released all these fantastic singles that had done nothing and it felt strange when this became regarded as our flagship piece. It sent out a strange signal about what we were.'

A joke by the band that backfired unwittingly helped the country ballad's success. 1981 had heralded the tacky series Stars On 45 – unspeakably awful medleys of hits by bands like The Beatles, Abba and Stevie Wonder – and Squeeze thought it would be funny to cobble together an assortment of their own hits on the B-side, which they crudely named 'Squabs On Forty Fab'. 'It was a brutal shoehorning of all our hits to that point into one tempo which absolutely murdered the songs,' says Glenn. 'We did it for a laugh but it got almost equal airplay to "Labelled With Love". It was such an own goal because people didn't know we were joking.'

6 *Sweets From A Stranger*

FOLLOWING THE artistic triumph of their fourth LP, Squeeze's next album, released within 12 months, was a classic case of 'After The Lord Mayor's Show'. The band was exhausted after five years on a never-ending cycle of recording and touring, and desperately needed to recharge their batteries. Yet with Squeeze making further inroads into the lucrative American marketplace and songwriters Difford and Tilbrook receiving overdue critical acclaim for their craft, a sabbatical was never an option.

The result was the band's artistic nadir, *Sweets From A Stranger*, an album sorely lacking in direction and ambition, its flat, uninspired sound unrecognisable from the peaks scaled on *East Side Story*. Listening back to the songs more than two decades on, Glenn and Chris squirm at the bizarre musical experimentation and mundane lyrics, and believe that this merely illustrates the inevitability of Squeeze's break-up the following winter.

1981 had been a monumental year for Squeeze, but it ended on a low note with the disappointing decision by Paul Carrack to quit the band. To lose one keyboard player in a year was unfortunate; to lose two in less than two years was disastrous. And although replacement Don Snow was a more than able musical replacement on the ivories, the band's chemistry had been badly damaged.

'It was very upsetting to the band when Paul left,' agrees Glenn. 'As football pundits say, no disrespect to Don Snow, but the chemistry within the band and our relationships changed dramatically.'

Carrack's departure was understandable, because the dynamic duo who were so dominant during Squeeze's 25-year history were always likely to leave his vocal and songwriting talents on the shelf. Citing his desire to forge a solo career, Carrack left 'The Blob' with their good wishes and, just like his predecessor, would make a fleeting return to the warm bosom of the Squeeze gang a decade later.

Legendary producer Gus Dudgeon, widely credited with helping to make Elton John a worldwide star, was originally called to work on *Sweets From A Stranger* and helped the band cut a version of 'Black Coffee In Bed'. Inexplicably, the band changed their minds about working with Dudgeon and replaced him with Phil McDonald, formerly The Beatles' engineer.

With Glenn in his most domineering phase, McDonald found himself browbeaten in the studio and unable to steer Squeeze away from the dangers of over-experimentation. As Glenn himself admits, 'Phil was a really nice chap and we got on very well with him, but he didn't have the strength to rein us in. I was particularly headstrong on this record and it resulted in some of it sounding awful. The spirit around the band at the time was a bit fractious and it must have been a difficult record for Phil to make.'

Work began in the spring of 1982 in Ramport Studios, owned by The Who, in London's Battersea. The band found conditions there ideal, despite its reputation as being haunted. 'We did have experiences in there of it actually turning very cold without explanation, and there was a feeling there that wasn't very nice,' explains Glenn. Working in such ghostly surroundings was perhaps apt because by the time recording had been completed, Squeeze resembled dead men walking.

***

'Out Of Touch'

This is probably the weakest track on the album, isn't it?

GT: I thought it was great at the time but that's a view I no longer share. We'd recorded a great version of 'Out Of Touch' earlier with Paul Carrack.

CD: Paul's version stands head and shoulders above this one. This is really naff. There's no personality to it whatsoever and to follow *East Side Story* with this was shooting ourselves in the foot. It's a ridiculous sounding song.

Were you aware of this at the time?

CD: I was definitely aware of it, but I just went along with it.

It has a very kitsch 1980s sound.

GT: I was really excited by it. We'd done lots of stuff with Moogs and drum machines already, but on this album our experimentation became laboured rather than joyful. I thought it was forward-looking when we recorded it, but now it sounds very much of its time and not in a good way.

Is Gilson playing synth drums?

CD: Yeah. Those synthetic drums sound horrendous. Listening to it now I just wince.

GT: Gilson was starting to get upset that we were moving away from the traditional.

CD: The only good about this song, and the album generally, is Glenn's singing. It's stunning.

'I Can't Hold On'

This is a much better sounding song. It doesn't sound dated like 'Out Of Touch'.

CD: 'I Can't Hold On' could have existed on *East Side Story*. Lyrically it's an extension of some of the characters on that album. We used to do this live and it was a good crowd song to get everyone moving, in the same way as 'In Quintessence' or 'Someone Else's Bell' did. But it's not a great moment for me lyrically because it doesn't say anything. I was beginning to lose the plot here.

GT: Don Snow's piano playing on this is brilliant. He's a fantastic keyboard player. I like the changes in the song, and the differences between the harder verses and the slight left turn taken in the chorus.

CD: Dear old Don. He was a great keyboard player and was hugely upset that he joined the band just when it was about to end. He put in a lot of work with the album and touring the album, and I felt for him. He was a nice lad, a bit of an all-rounder, who could play the saxophone and drums as well. He was an amusing character to have in the band, especially with his experience in The Sinceros and other New Wave bands.

'POINTS OF VIEW'

GT: This is a great band performance marred by a slightly poncey vocal performance by me.

Why do you think it's poncey?

GT: I was at a stage when my voice started changing. I started getting more control over my voice but in getting that control I started adding unnecessary inflections, like Whitney Houston at the end of 'I Will Always Love You'. One of the greatest dangers for singers if they have control over their own voice is that it becomes an athletic tool which deadens emotion. Another thing to mention is that there's a lot of alcohol in these songs.

They're alcohol-soaked, aren't they?

GT: It reflected the way we were and I can think of no finer thing in songwriting than reflecting the way that you are as honestly as possible. This was before Chris had begun to see the other side of the coin, the potential damage caused by drinking. At this stage large-scale drinking was normal behaviour in the band.

CD: This is fantastic. If Hall And Oates had done this, it would have been massive. Glenn's vocal is just supreme. When I hear him sing like this I just want to hug him and say what a great bloke he is. How we get from that to 'Stranger Than The Stranger On The Shore' infuriates me.

'Stranger Than The Stranger On The Shore'

CD: I have to apologise to Glenn for not punching him when he played the ochorena on this.

I was going to ask what that sound was. It's like listening to a snake charmer.

CD: Glenn bought this in a health food shop and he was determined to use this on the album at whatever cost because he'd paid for it.

GT: It's something I still proudly own. I do make a point that if I ever buy an instrument of using it at least once on a record, which justifies my buying it.

CD: When Glenn started playing it in the studio I left the building. I said, 'Okay. If you think this is good I'm getting out of here because this is crap.' He said, 'Well The Troggs had one on an early song.' I said, 'I'm sorry, Glenn. I can't take it. It's disgusting.' We fell out hugely over that bloody thing. Whenever I came in the room it would always be there, somewhere visual just to piss me off. I used to think that when he went out of the room I would take it and lob it in the Thames.

GT: That's very funny. I have to say I have no recollection of leaving it lying around like that.

The lyric makes a reference to your ongoing unhappiness with your management. 'The contract's been signed with a stroke of my blood/ I'm drowned by the name that sinks in the mud.' It suggests that you felt you had been exploited.

CD: Well, we had been. There was another song called 'The Axe Has Now Fallen', based on the fact that Miles's middle name was Axe. It was all about our relationship with him and how we felt totally had-over by him.

GT: We were also pissed off because we'd been through exactly the same situation with Jake as we had been with Miles, if not slightly worse. It's not a very nice feeling when you realise you've been fucked over.

'ONTO THE DANCE FLOOR'

What do you think of this?

GT: I like this one more. It's slightly self-conscious and has a definite 1980s sound, but I remember this for having a strong band performance in the studio. All the instrumentation was live. It's another example of a tune that could make you feel slightly queasy in a Bowie-esque way.

Was it your intention to make it unsettling?

GT: Yes. There's a fine line between quirky and self-consciously quirky. 'Onto The Dance Floor' is naturally quirky in a way that 'Stranger Than The Stranger On The Shore' was not, so it works for me.

CD: This does nothing for me at all, yet we go from the bizarreness of this to the absolute serenity and beauty of 'When The Hangover Strikes'. This is pure genius and Tilbrook at his utmost brilliant best.

'WHEN THE HANGOVER STRIKES'

GT: This is the first track that I'm proud of on this album. Del Newman's string arrangement, and Chris's lovely attention to slow-moving detail in his lyric, are terrific. Obviously, this was a subject we both could identify with at that time. Musically, the playing is understated in a way that is very untypical of us at this time. All of us, particularly me, would never play one note when we could play eight instead, so to be that restrained was remarkable.

Considering the vast amount of experimentation on this album, what made you write a 1940s croon?

GT: I'd started listening to the albums Frank Sinatra made for Capitol in the '50s, which he recorded primarily with producer Nelson Riddle. The instrumentation on those albums was fantastic and contained a certain mood and direction to them that had nothing to do with the record that had come before. Elvis Costello is the only person I can think of who does that these days. Sinatra would also explore themes within albums, and not be afraid to make some of those themes dark. I wasn't thinking this consciously when I wrote 'Hangover'. It's just that when I listen to any sort of music some of it trickles out in one way or other.

CD: Lyrically this was the finest song on the album for me. All the imagery is so correct and goes beautifully with the music. We always hoped that Sinatra would record it. I think a cassette went off to his manager.

GT: That's right. It was considered for his next album but Sinatra decided that he didn't want to sing a song with negative connotations about drinking. It was a great shame.

This was rather an odd choice for a Squeeze single.

GT: I was convinced it would be a smash hit, which just goes to show what Mr 'Finger On The Pulse' Tilbrook knew. I thought, 'The kids'll love this. They'll go crazy for it.' But it was about blokes getting hangovers, which was totally unsexy.

CD: The fact that the record company would endorse it is amazing. It wouldn't happen now.

'Black Coffee In Bed'

CD: This lyric was inspired by my picking up my notebook one day and seeing a coffee stain on it, which inspired the first line. It was a very vivid image for me and inspired this song of loss and regret.

I like the change of pace and mood at the start of the refrain which begins, 'Now she's gone and I'm back on the beat.'

CD: I didn't get to grips with the emotion of the song until recently when I sang it myself with my own outfit. I don't sing it like Glenn does but you can't help but feel that change in the lyric and melody when singing it.

How Glenn manages to switch from that to a really intriguing different guitar solo over a completely different piece of music is extraordinary. He did the same thing on 'Another Nail In My Heart'.

GT: The backing vocals by Elvis and Paul Young were the icing on the cake.

It's funny that Elvis sang on 'Black Coffee In Bed' because lyrically it's similar to his track 'Good Year For The Roses'. In particular, his line 'The lip-print on a half-filled cup of coffee/ That you poured and didn't drink' could have been written by you.

CD: That's interesting. I'd listened to a lot of country music at this time and lyrically it was attractive to be writing to that kind of metre. The fact that Glenn put a soul melody to it shows the unique quality of our writing. I brought it in as a country lyric, and he put a Hall And Oates arrangement on it. We always thought we recorded it too slow, though.

GT: It's far too ponderous. It could never be a fast song, but it certainly had the opportunity to be slightly perkier. My vocal is mannered and not very good at all, and I can't stand to listen to it now. It was influenced by what Paul Carrack had brought to the table but without Paul's voice it didn't sound right. We recorded a great demo with Gus Dudgeon but we really fucked it up on the record, which was entirely down to me. This is one of the few Squeeze songs I'd happily re-record because I think I could do a better version.

CD: We ended up playing this in every tempo you can imagine. It's like 'Take Me I'm Yours' in that you can bend it in different directions.

GT: We made a lovely kitsch video for this. It was the start of the storytelling video time in the early '80s, so we recorded a video featuring a story that made no sense, featuring us looking moody and as artful as possible.

CD: That video explains everything you need to know about this album. We're caked in make-up, rather like the women I wrote about in the last album, and look totally out of place and not credible at all. We seem totally lost. The director was the guy who made Michael Jackson's 'Billie Jean' video. We might as well have got ourselves perms, worn green and red leather jackets, and learnt to dance.

'I've Returned'

The beginning of the song is delivered almost like a war cry.

GT: Yes. It's slightly grandiose-sounding, which is not my cup of tea really. On the whole it's not a bad version. It's a bit like Bruce Springsteen's 'Born To Run'. And yet another song about drinking. Only Chris could write a line like 'You've thrown my jigsaw all over the floor/ We're at the deepest deep.' That line is so un-rock 'n' roll, which contrasts perfectly with the music. At the point where the music is dramatic, it appears that the lyric is about to convey something really important, but it says, 'You've thrown my jigsaw all over the floor.' It still makes me laugh now.

CD: 'I've Returned' could have been on *East Side Story*. It's a lyric that reflects our early writing, so I suppose we were beginning to repeat ourselves. We were cocooned in a web of touring and it was suffocating our skills. We didn't have any time to observe.

It's a very upbeat song. I imagine this would have gone down well live.

CD: We used to do this as the first number in the set, to replace 'In Quintessence'. When we made a new album we would filter out old songs and replace them with ones that were similar in tempo, in a way that appeared seamless.

'Tongue Like A Knife'

CD: This is one of our songs that leans in the theatrical direction. It's about two characters in a volatile relationship, like Elizabeth Taylor and Richard Burton, the kind of people who live with oil paintings above their fireplaces. It's like looking in the window of someone else's house and observing what goes on inside.

The man in the story appears to be a working-class guy who is trying to impress the woman, but is a bit of an oaf, spilling his drink on the floor.

CD: Yes. She's in a country house and he's a bit of an idiot, fumbling with his whisky. As a young man I was infatuated by rich young women who had a better education than me. I loved hanging out with them and trying to understand what it was that they had and I didn't. I hoped that by hanging out with them some of their education might fall off on to me.

GT: This is one of a set of songs where Chris visited his interest in the upper classes and his fascination with their lifestyles. David Enthoven, who was our manager at this time, came from an independently wealthy family and we met some incredible people around that time. For instance, going to the Guinness family castle was mind-boggling. We saw a different section of life that was welcoming, interesting, and funny. We got the impression that all this could be ours if we wanted it to be. Musically, it contained another great arrangement by Del , who really fleshed out the song.

At the end it sounds like 'These are a few of my favourite things' from *The Sound Of Music.*

GT: Chris was playing that in the studio and Del picked up on it in the arrangement. It was a lovely touch.

'HIS HOUSE HER HOME'

Chris, you're singing much higher than usual here.

CD: Yes. This is my Peter And Gordon number.

Can you explain that?

CD: Peter And Gordon were two guys from the '60s who sang in ridiculous camp voices. They wore roll-neck jumpers and black-rimmed glasses, and looked very sophisticated. This was me trying to be sophisticated, but just sounding camp.

How come you ended up singing a song as high as this?

CD: Glenn would always ask which songs I wanted to sing and I would usually make an excuse and procrastinate. When we got into rehearsals Glenn would sing everything brilliantly, so I'd slip into the shadows and hope he'd forget. Towards the end of recording he'd say, 'You still haven't decided,' and force me into a decision. 'His House Her Home' was the crust end of the loaf. It sounds like it was in the wrong key to me, so maybe he was teaching me a lesson.

GT: I worked very hard on trying to get Chris to sing up there, but I was aware that he felt I'd played some cruel joke on him by getting him to do it. He could definitely sing that high, but the fact he thought he couldn't was enough to render him unconfident and that slightly shows in his vocal performance.

You have a very distinct voice, Chris, but you don't seem to have much confidence in it when you talk about it.

CD: I'm confident now, but it took me 27 years.

Can you explain what the lyric is about?

CD: It's obviously about adultery and contains the characters from 'Tongue Like A Knife'.

So the husband is watching from a picture on the wall, like a lord of the manor?

CD: Exactly. It reminds me of a scene in the Hammer House films, with a picture on the mantelpiece that has eyes which move. It's about being in a relationship where there are young children and the father isn't around.

GT: It's another side to the coin of Chris's many songs about break-ups and their ramifications. It's about the impact this has on kids, with a stranger moving into their home.

'THE VERY FIRST DANCE'

CD: This is atrocious. We put our trademark octave vocal on this, because that's what we were known for, but there's no passion in it.

GT: Musically it was influenced by The Beach Boys, so I went for this odd vocal arrangement, which if I'm not mistaken, Chris went down the pub for. I like the experimentation of the song, but I can't say it's entirely successful. It sounds a little ponderous to me. I'd probably go to the pub now if this was being played.

I know that synth drums were very much in vogue, but when you've got a drummer like Gilson, why did you need them? They make everything sound so wooden.

CD: I agree. There was something called a Simmons kit, which had come out. It was basically bits of plastic wired up to a basic computer that triggered drum parts. Gilson had one and we used it a lot on this album, but I hated it. It was like those funny toys of Glenn's that he used to get out. I used to think, 'Why are we bothering? We can plug in a guitar and sound brilliant and here we are experimenting with stuff which takes up loads of time and is rubbish.'

You mentioned your sounding camp on 'His House Her Home', but I'd say you sound far more camp on the backing vocals here.

CD: On which bit?

Where you're saying "The very first dances" over and over again.

CD: That isn't me, fortunately. It's Don Snow, but it's terrible. It's our Spandau Ballet moment.

'The Elephant Ride'

GT: This is one of my favourite songs. It's beautiful and very much influenced by The Beach Boys in its arrangement, if not the tune. I'd been listening to *Pet Sounds* an awful lot at the time and this was one of the songs where rather than oppose the mood of the lyric, I tried to reflect it.

CD: This comes from a set of songs with 'elephant' in the title. It was a story I came up with about a skinhead who had fallen in love with an Indian girl in Charlton. They couldn't hang out with each other because their parents wouldn't go along with the cross-pollination of their relationship. I thought it would make a good musical, because it was a racial story.

Similar to Romeo And Juliet.

CD: Yes, and I liked the fact that it was about a skinhead, a soft skinhead, if you like. I wanted to work on this idea more but there wasn't enough time, so only two of the songs came out, this one and 'Elephant Girl'.

***

MORE THAN two decades on, the two halves of Squeeze's songwriting partnership wince when questioned about *Sweets From A Stranger*. Both Glenn and Chris regret being rushed into the studio by a record company eager to capitalise on the band's growing popularity in the States. This decision would have catastrophic consequences, adding to and exacerbating existing tensions, and leading to the band being ripped asunder by the end of the year.

Not surprisingly, the album "stiffed" in the UK, with first single 'Black Coffee In Bed' unable to make the Top 50 and the follow-up 'When The Hangover Strikes' failing to register in the charts at all. By contrast, the LP was a success on the other side of the Atlantic, carried along by the momentum of *East Side Story*, but also no doubt helped by Chris's unconscious decision to move away from the Squeeze tradition of writing about London. For once, Americans were not left scratching their heads at lyrics mentioning the Arndale Centre, beanos in Southend, and 'bits of old skirt'. But for their British audience, Squeeze's new songs had little passion and sounded dull and uninspired.

Although lyrically inferior to *East Side Story*, Glenn is critical of his own role in the lacklustre *Sweets From A Stranger*. 'I think some of the songs were good and blame myself particularly for not having my finger on the pulse. If we'd gone with a producer who could make a professional record and had whipped us into shape, it could have been a different sounding album, but I didn't see that at the time.'

Desperate to regain Squeeze's lost momentum, A&M asked them to come up with a new single, the first seven-inch the band had released outside of an album since *Packet Of Three* five years earlier. Glenn had already worked out arrangements for two new songs, 'Action Speaks Faster' and 'Annie Get Your Gun' and asked the band to choose between them.

The latter was a unanimous choice and the band were instructed by their label to go to the studio with Alan Tarney, who had produced Cliff Richard's recent string of hits. Glenn played the demo version of 'Annie' to Tarney, who went off to ruminate on what he had heard. When the band were called back into the studio a few days later, they were stunned to find that Tarney had recorded the entire backing track himself and merely wanted Glenn and Chris to sing over the top.

Tarney had taken the original ideas from the demo, processed them though his Fairlight sampler, and added the guitars himself. Glenn recalls, 'It was like we were in The Monkees. Alan did a very good job, but it was devastating for us because we could all play so well, although I didn't mind as much as the others because I was singing the lead vocal.' Gilson, in particular, was outraged, and insisted on overdubbing some drum parts.

Despite receiving heavy radio play, 'Annie Get Your Gun', with its catchy title stolen from a musical of the same name, became the latest in a long line of failed Squeeze singles, stalling at Number 43. The song's main legacy was its subsequent popularity as a live number, becoming a cornerstone of the band's live set.

Yet another lengthy tour to promote *Sweets From A Stranger* was already underway and the atmosphere within the Squeeze camp was at its lowest ebb. Glenn and Chris were bickering and Gilson's behaviour becoming increasingly erratic. Always a heavy drinker, Gilson was now suffering from alcoholism, and was becoming increasingly aggressive. Unnerved by his semi-psychotic conduct, the band's management hired a security guard on the road specifically to look after the errant drummer.

'Gilson was going through a terrible time, which unfortunately made it hard work for all of us,' claims Glenn. 'Having a security guard just made Gilson want to get into trouble even more. He'd try all sorts of tricks to evade him and be running about all over the place trying to cause fights and generally not being very nice. It spread a horrible air over the band.'

Chris has similar recollections of this period and describes Gilson's personality in 1982 as 'a mixture of Keith Moon and Wolf Man. He was a firecracker always five minutes from going off, which made life interesting.' Yet instead of firing Gilson, the pair's respect for their drummer precluded any such decision. 'For all his problems Gilson was still the most inventive drummer we ever had and one of the warmest people you could meet,' says Chris. 'The disease he had, alcoholism, was not his fault and you could argue that without his strong personality Squeeze would never have been the band that it was.'

Both Glenn and Chris were becoming increasingly unhappy with life within 'The Blob' and on a train journey across Germany while promoting the album, decided that the band's time was up. 'I was having sleepless nights and thinking "This has got to stop",' recalls Chris. 'On the train I said to Glenn, "I couldn't sleep last night, thinking about the band. Something has to change." He said he agreed and that we should call it a day. As much as my belly turned inside out thinking about it, it was absolutely the only thing we could have done.'

Although acknowledging that taking a sabbatical might have been a better option, Glenn agrees that the band's disintegration at this point was inevitable. 'With the gift of hindsight what we should have done is rest, but at that point there was no way of telling which way things would go. Also, the fun had gone out of it, which was the only time in my career that's ever happened.'

The duo, who had already decided to continue their songwriting partnership outside of the group, called a band meeting in typical Squeeze style in a Putney pub. When their decision to liquidate the band was announced the atmosphere became increasingly unpleasant. According to Chris, Gilson was 'devastated', John Bentley 'beside himself with rage' and Don Snow 'didn't know what had hit him'.

With the decision to split the band now made, neither Glenn nor Chris were able to enjoy any sense of relief, having made the extraordinary decision to embark on a three-month farewell tour. 'It was like being on death row,' laughs Glenn.

The tour culminated in an appearance at the Sunsplash Festival in Jamaica in November 1982, with Squeeze putting in a dreadful last performance, and going out with a whimper rather than a bang. 'It was the most bizarre gig,' remembers Chris. 'I got as smashed as I possibly could before going onstage. When I look at the video I can see I was playing all the wrong chords and had gone completely Keith Richard, dancing around like a headless chicken, and bumping into amplifiers. Glenn looks really miserable and Gilson is playing too fast.'

The final parting of the ways was a strangely subdued experience, as Glenn recalls. 'We sat in the van, drove back to our hotel, walked into the same lift and all got out on different floors, said "see you later", and that was it.'

Afraid of being talked out of his decision to quit, Chris instructed David Enthoven to book him on the first flight to London the following day. Having continued drinking large quantities of rum after the show, Chris fell asleep in a rowing boat on a lake and only just made it to the airport in time. When he embarked on the plane mightily hung-over Chris discovered that he was on board a charter flight full of rowdy Grateful Dead fans leaving the festival. It was not an enjoyable trip home. Glenn and Don bizarrely stayed on for a holiday in Jamaica with the keyboard player's girlfriend, while a disconsolate Gilson and John made their way back to Blighty.

The release of a singles compilation album to mark the band's break-up at the end of 1982 brought matters to a neat conclusion. The album, entitled *45's And Under*, was the brainchild of David Enthoven and became Squeeze's largest selling LP of all time. In addition to swelling the band members' individual pension funds, the album also succinctly pieced together Squeeze's career for the record-buying public and helped listeners to comprehend the sheer volume of strong material the group had produced. Ironically this would help the band to pick up from where they had left off when they made the surprise decision to re-form three years later.

Before that realisation could occur, Glenn and Chris would discover just how tricky life would become without the safety blanket of Squeeze around their shoulders.

7 *Difford And Tilbrook*

FREE FROM the shackles of non-stop touring and recording, Glenn and Chris took some time out in London and begun to rediscover their appreciation for the simple things in life. By early 1983 the novelty of walking to the local newsagents every morning was wearing off, and the offer to collaborate on a musical seemed the perfect way to recover the pair's passion for music.

John Turner, the in-house writer at The Albany Theatre, Deptford, approached them with a script based around the songs from *East Side Story*, and Glenn and Chris immediately jumped at the chance to work in a completely new arena. Having auditioned local musicians to play in the pit, the duo took part in three months of daily rehearsals at The Albany, working alongside a director and choreographer. Glenn, in particular, learned the value of teamwork.

He says, 'I worked a lot on the arrangements for the musical and had to tailor songs to what the musicians were capable of performing. On *Sweets From A Stranger* I'd got my own way too much whereas on this I had to learn about taking other people's opinions into consideration properly. It was a great learning curve.'

Entitled *Labelled With Love*, the show ran for three months, and Glenn and Chris were virtually ever-present in the audience. Although enjoying the opportunity to spend six months living in London – the longest consecutive period they had enjoyed at home in seven years – they turned down offers to take the show to the West End, believing the show was too parochial to achieve success north of the river.

A by-product of the musical's success was Glenn's tempestuous first marriage. Pam Baker was a wardrobe designer at The Albany, a brassy, confident woman who enthralled Glenn but whose forceful personality and frequent demands would in time help to widen the gulf between her husband and his writing partner. At a party marking the end of the musical, Chris had a premonition that his relationship with Glenn would change irrevocably the moment he witnessed the blooming of his friend's relationship with Pam.

'I looked on to the dance floor and watched Glenn dancing with Pam and thought I was never going to see him again. I left the building and drove down to the country feeling jealous because Glenn and I were so close and I knew that our relationship had changed that night. My instinct was absolutely correct. I did see Glenn again but I'd kind of lost him because I was completely blocked out by their relationship.'

Interestingly, Glenn experienced similar feelings when Chris had married Cindy and started a family three years earlier. 'I'm ashamed of it now, but when Chris started settling down, getting married and having children, I thought he was nuts and probably didn't make any secret of it. I thought we should be concentrating on our career and resented him for it. I never told him, but I would be surprised if he didn't know.'

In order to flesh out *Labelled With Love*, Glenn and Chris had written a new song called 'The Amazoon', containing one of Chris's increasingly rare lyrics about London life. Going under the moniker The Long Honeymoon the pair released the track as a single, produced by Laurie Latham, who had secured his reputation working with Ian Dury And The Blockheads and Paul Young. With a lack of publicity and minimal public interest in the duo's output, 'The Amazoon' failed to chart, but is looked back upon with fondness by one half of the songwriting duo. 'It's a brilliant lyric from Chris about how the pubs were changing from old-fashioned boozers to places where you got umbrellas stuffed in your drinks,' says Glenn. His partner is less enthusiastic, describing the song as 'one that gathers dust at the bottom of the pile.'

A cover version of 'The Amazoon' was planned by hip hop legend Grandmaster Flash, and Glenn and Chris flew to the Sugar Hill Studios in New York to re-record the song. Unfortunately, Grandmaster Flash's band broke up before the recording ever saw the light of day.

Having got a taste for life in the studio again, thoughts turned to recording the debut *Difford And Tilbrook* album. A handful of songs had been left over from the *Sweets From A Stranger* demos, notably 'The Apple Tree' and 'Action Speaks Faster', while others were hastily written shortly before recording commenced with celebrated producer Tony Visconti.

It was at this time that Chris's fears of being undermined by Glenn's new wife began to be realised. 'Pam called me to ask if I'd written any lyrics for this album and whether she could read them before Glenn. I found it very difficult to handle, that after all these years writing together there was suddenly a third party who I'd have to filter the lyrics through. I checked it with Glenn and he said he wanted her to be involved. I had to accept it, but it was difficult.'

A band was quickly cobbled together from musicians recommended within the business and some who had successfully passed auditions. The ambitious line-up contained two drummers, Larry Tolfree and Andy Duncan, alternating between drums and percussion, while Keith Wilkinson was appointed on bass, and Guy Fletcher on keyboards.

The latter, who went on to join Mark Knopfler's Dire Straits, left the fledgling band almost as soon as the recordings were finished. His unfortunate replacement lasted a matter of weeks before being dispatched mercilessly. The musician, whose name cannot be recalled by either Glenn or Chris, had been working on the cabaret circuit as a lounge player. 'He didn't make the transition and we swept him up and plopped him down again' says Glenn. 'He was heartbroken.'

Difford and Tilbrook's eponymously titled album was a mixed bag, containing inspired pop tunes and laughable grandiosity in equal measure. The best track on the album was 'Love's Crashing Waves', released as a single in June 1984. Musically, Glenn was influenced by the Philadelphia sound of Gamble And Huff and The OJs. His counter melody and opposing of bass lines with chords was also reminiscent of Beach Boy Brian Wilson.

Lyrically, Chris admits that 'Love's Crashing Waves' was based on his songwriting partner, confessing that 'the only way I felt I could communicate with Glenn was to write lyrics and try to post a message to him.' The song, which reached Number 57 in the UK charts, dealt specifically with Chris's concern over Glenn's relationship with Pam. "The line 'Malicious gossip will never profit when hearsay is its foundation' was a reference to the gossip within the band that constantly surrounded Glenn and Pam's relationship. People were speculating things, that she wouldn't last, or that she'd kill him with drugs.'

Much of the speculation surrounded the couple's developing heroin habit and Glenn's colleagues' fears that he might become addicted to the Class A drug. 'I know that it wasn't a good thing to have done, but I enjoyed heroin at the time,' Glenn explains. 'It took me to a place where television became endlessly fascinating.

'People blamed Pam because she had taken heroin in the past but, in fact, I was the instigator and eager to find out what it was like. We launched ourselves into it in a casual way, but then it became less casual. We never injected heroin but it did get to a point where I thought "We've got to stop this now", so we did.'

Chris also refuses to blame Pam, but says he was appalled at Glenn's alleged glamourising of his secret habit. 'I was very sad when he admitted it to me and also worried because he was very proud of it and thought it was a great thing to be involved in. Although I enjoyed my drugs and alcohol, that extra step into smoking heroin was never an option for me and thank God for that because I don't think I would have been here. As an addict I would have enjoyed it so much that smoking it wouldn't have been enough. I was furious with Glenn for doing it because I thought he was going to get harmed and I'd lose him.'

Fuelled by six years of artistic and financial success, it was perhaps inevitable that two men who so enjoyed inebriation would dabble with hard drugs. Although Glenn's selection of heroin as his drug of choice was potentially more damaging, Chris was himself heavily using another Class A substance, cocaine. 'I'd just discovered coke at this time and it was more enjoyable than anything. I was escaping to my den to write and some of the songs on *Difford And Tilbrook* are very descriptive of how I felt at the time.'

Perhaps Chris's best song of his cocaine period was 'On My Mind Tonight', one of the few highlights of this album. 'I wrote every line of this in one sitting. It was exactly what I was seeing. I was sitting in my study in my house in the country, in a bungalow. It was summer and I'd taken some cocaine and was watching the moths at the window. The line about being "confined to solitary" is indicative of my feeling of being lonely, yet living in a family. As a writer you need to create space for yourself to be able to work and because I had a family everyone else suffered as a result. There are different ways of doing it, but in those days I did it badly, sneaking off and taking cocaine while everyone was asleep and watching the sun come up in the morning. But I wrote a couple of good songs on it.'

Much of the lyric was based around an American fan of the band for whom Chris had an unrequited passion. Their paths had first crossed at a Squeeze gig in Boston some years earlier when the girl had dressed up in an Indian squaw outfit. Chris remembers. 'I looked at her in the audience and wondered why she was dressed like that. When I sang "Cool For Cats" she went bananas and I realised she was dressed up especially for that song. I went off stage and my mind was fixated on her, but I was devastated because I thought I'd never see her again.'

When the band made the short journey from the venue to their tour bus, the girl introduced herself as Linda, and she and Chris became pen friends for many years. At this stage a happily married man, Chris made no attempt to take the relationship further but fantasised about her frequently over the years.

It was only during Squeeze's US tour of 1993 that Chris finally broached the subject of a fully-fledged relationship. 'I went out to lunch with her and told her I'd made a decision that I couldn't keep up the charade anymore. I said "It's great being a pen friend but I know that somewhere in both our hearts we'd like there to be more of a relationship so I'm afraid we have to say goodnight." She replied, "That's interesting because I'm getting married next week." I hadn't expected that, but I'm glad it happened because it gave me the exit sign. We never stayed in touch after that.'

'A Man For All Seasons' was another minor highlight of the album, although Chris denies Glenn's claims that 'this was one where Chris was having a pop at me'. Certainly the opening line, 'Now the woman wears the trousers' could well have described Chris's feelings towards Glenn and Pam's marriage.

Chris retorts, 'I don't think the lyric is anything other than two characters whose roles have changed. At that time the world was becoming a feminine place and Britain had a woman prime minister, Margaret Thatcher, so it felt like we were being controlled by our mother again. The band was being run by our mum and my marriage was being run by my mum. I guess that was the tip of the iceberg lyrically.'

Pressed on the direct inspiration that Glenn's marriage had on his lyric, Chris admits, 'The characters could be Glenn and Pam, I guess, if you wanted them to be. It was the first time in our relationship where a woman was wearing the trousers, so it was fair enough for me to say that, although it was subconscious.'

Indicative of Chris and Glenn's fractious relationship was the magnificent, moody video for 'Love's Crashing Waves'. Filmed at Brighton Beach, a force-five gale arrived unannounced during recording; the enormous waves smashing brutally against the sea wall perfectly demonstrated the turbulence of the duo's partnership.

The video shoot also brought Chris and Pam into open conflict, over the question of Chris's outfit. As a talented clothes designer, Pam was determined to give Glenn and Chris a makeover but the latter's calculated insouciance heightened tension within the warring triangle. 'Pam styled Glenn's clothing for the video and wanted to design mine too. I got my friend Scott Crolla to design my clothes and made the point of going completely in the opposite direction to what Pam wanted. It was like this when we did the tour. She would say "Chris, you've got to try and get something that matches Glenn," but I said I didn't want to do that. So Glenn would come on wearing a 16th-century frock coat and I'd come mincing on, Max Miller-style, in a three-piece suit made out of floral curtains.

'I'm sure Glenn wasn't impressed either but I wasn't doing it out of spite. I thought if we were going to start getting into clothes we might as well have some fun and be the opposite of each other, which is what we are.'

Twenty years on, Glenn still fails to see the funny side of Chris's refusal to play ball with Pam's ideas. 'He did it in a way that was very hurtful to me. Because Pam had been designing my clothes, and she was my wife, I wanted to give her credit on the record, so in the sleeve notes I wrote "Glenn's Tilbrook's clothes by Pam Baker." Chris responded by putting "Difford's togs by Scott Crolla." He was definitely having a pop at me and I didn't think it was very nice.

'I loved Pam's clothes, but I'm eternally scruffy and never have the application to be able to make things look good on me. If I wear smart clothes I end up looking like someone who is trying to look smart rather than looking naturally stylish. I don't think that was Pam's fault. She encouraged me to try something new, but the others just sniggered at me. Perhaps they were right.'

Further evidence of the paranoia and mistrust felt between Chris and Glenn at this time concerned the former's lyric to 'You Can't Hurt The

Girl'. Glenn believed that the song was an obvious reference to his previous girlfriend with whom he had broken up shortly before meeting Pam. 'The only thing I can think of about this song is Glenn chastising me because he thought I'd written it about his previous girlfriend,' moans Chris. 'He thought I had snuck it into the selection just to wind him and Pam up and said something in the studio about it, but I told him this wasn't the case.'

Glenn was certainly made aware, both during the Difford And Tilbrook period and upon the reformation of Squeeze, that Pam was disliked by his colleagues. He understandably sought to defend his wife's integrity. 'Pam was unfortunately almost universally unpopular with people, whereas my previous girlfriend, who I'd been with for years, was well-liked. I felt very protective of Pam because of that and also because of the wedge that had come between me and Chris.

'I didn't feel I got a lot of support from Chris and any attempts I made at friendship with him were rebuffed. This made me feel quite insecure so Pam was there to prop up my security and I needed that.'

Glenn's decision to bring Pam on the tour bus created more disharmony. 'The band became a bit like Spinal Tap in that I brought Pam out on the road with us, which must have been hard for everyone else. In my own defence, I didn't feel that I had any support from within the band, but unfortunately my way of approaching things just made it worse for everyone else. I think that my experimentation with drugs didn't help.'

Chris claims that for the remainder of Glenn's marriage, Pam cast a shadow over their writing partnership. He says, 'Even when we got Squeeze back together Pam behaved as if she was more important than the rest of us. We might be standing onstage in front of 20,000 people but she thought she was more important and I couldn't handle that. We'd never had a female character in our gang with that strong a belief about life and about what it was to be a woman. I understood where she came from and respected her views. It's just the way she employed her views that upset me.'

Despite his evident discomfiture at the woman who had 'taken over our gang', Chris acknowledges his part in stoking up the disharmony within the ranks. 'I was as much to blame in that I was a difficult person to be with. Glenn and I didn't talk to each other for about 18 months. It was a bizarre carry-on. We would be in the same pub together and not say a word to each other.'

Side two of the *Difford And Tilbrook* album continued the record's extraordinary schizophrenia. Alongside the experimental but catchy 'Hope Fell Down' were the mundane 'Tears For Attention' and the utterly embarrassing 'Wagon Train', an attempt to relive the cowboys-and-Indians vibe of the first verse of 'Cool For Cats'. The album ended on a high note with the anti-nuclear anthem, 'The Apple Tree', originally intended for *Sweets From A Stranger*.

Chris's lyric was inspired by his grandparents' house in Charlton, which contained a Second World War fallout shelter in the garden. The shelter, which still contained 1940s helmets and was semi-maintained, had an apple tree that had grown through the roof. 'I thought it was an amazing image,' explains Chris. 'The tree had grown through what was an object of bleak and desolate fear. It made me think about how delicate things were in the world at the time. The Cold War was at its height and as a father I was worrying about it.'

Glenn and Chris were surprised when the song, which lyrically was a veritable mouthful, was covered by Elaine Paige. Actress and comedienne Emma Thompson also recorded a version for her television show in the late 1980s.

As their first album as a duo, *Difford And Tilbrook* had been an ill-conceived project, poorly executed. The quality of Chris's lyrics had nosedived in direct proportion to the amount of narcotics he was consuming, while Glenn's obsession with 1980s gadgetry deprived many of the songs of their soul. In an attempt to put clear blue water between Difford And Tilbrook and Squeeze, the duo had seemingly forgotten what had made them such an extraordinarily talented team.

In addition, working in the studio with Tony Visconti had proved less than inspirational. Chris's curt recollection was of 'working with a producer who I don't think was in the room at the time. We obviously looked up to him because of his reputation but his heart wasn't in it at all.'

Glenn is less critical of Visconti's role, and believes it's unfair to say that he wasn't interested in the record. Yet when A&M heard the recordings, they ordered them to be remixed by an outside party. On Glenn and Chris's request, Eric Thorngren was brought over from New York to take over.

Thorngren had worked briefly with the band at Sugar Hill, and his association with Glenn and Chris would continue for many years to come. Despite bringing some much-needed life back to the songs, Thorngren found it impossible to paper over all the cracks.

Surprisingly, this album retains a high degree of popularity within the loyal Squeeze fan base and is regarded by many followers as 'the lost album'. Yet the over-riding feeling outside the band was that the pair were badly missing their former colleagues, Gilson in particular.

Because of the violent seasickness caused by five years riding the storms on board the good ship Squeeze, Chris and Glenn had felt it necessary to rearrange the deckchairs and rename their vessel. Yet, to those on the band's periphery, it was clear that dismissing their fellow officers had failed to steer Chris and Glenn out of choppy waters, and that they needed to get the old crew back on board quickly to prevent the ship from sinking.

Although the dangerous rocks ahead were apparent to many, Glenn and Chris could not yet see them and were fully prepared to battle against the tide on the Difford And Tilbrook liner. Fortunately for them, a lifeboat was soon to pass, hauling them aboard and saving them from artistic oblivion.

8 *Cosi Fan Tutti Frutti*

DESPITE THE evident commercial failure of *Difford And Tilbrook*, both men claim they were happy for the project to continue and had no intention of reforming Squeeze. The pair had no immediate plans for further recordings or live performances as a duo, but the death of the mother of one of Glenn's close friends in early 1985 inspired the singer to put on a show, to raise money for the hospice where she had spent her final months.

Having arranged the show at the Saxon Tavern in Catford, Glenn went along to see Jools and Gilson perform together at a venue in the capital. At this stage, a Squeeze reunion was still far from his mind. But Glenn was impressed with what he saw, particularly that Gilson's spark, so badly missing towards the end of Squeeze's initial career, had returned. When he spoke to the pair backstage he realised that Gilson had got his life back together and had quit drinking, having spent a year working as a south London minicab driver.

The thought suddenly struck Glenn that Squeeze should get back together for one night and play at his charity gig in Catford. He was surprised to find both men enthusiastic. Gilson was a man reborn, teetotal and slim, while Jools had struggled to establish his solo musical career – although his parallel vocation in TV had taken off in impressive fashion. A quick call to John Bentley also found the bass man happy to forgive and forget and resume his duties in the band.

When Squeeze took to the stage in January 1985 the small pub was packed to the rafters. The atmosphere both on- and off-stage was electric. 'We sounded really fresh and the most surprising thing of all was that it was great fun,' says Glenn. 'I hadn't been expecting to feel like that at all, and I realised that this was what it would have been like had we been given a break a couple of years earlier.'

Chris had slight reservations about the gig 'because I was not sure whether Gilson was going to kill us, but the minute we got to play it was electrifying. I remember it so well. It felt like the first day at school. When we rehearsed we were shuffling around not looking at each other, but as soon as we hit the first part of the first song it felt magic.'

Afterward, the band were unanimous in their belief that the show should not be a one-off and that with a less exhausting schedule, Squeeze could reach great heights again.

At around this time Glenn and Chris's legal action against Miles Copeland had ground to a halt, with both sides claiming an honourable draw, but with the songwriters no closer to regaining the missing 50 per cent of their publishing dues. Jools had retained Copeland as his own manager and suggested strongly that the band hire the American's services again.

Although still bitter at what they saw as his underhanded dealings, Copeland charmed the pair – 'bedazzling us all over again', according to Glenn – and the three men shook hands and agreed to let bygones be bygones. Both Chris and Glenn wisely realised that Copeland, whose empire had gone from strength to strength in his five years away from the band, could open a lot of doors for them on either side of the Atlantic.

Squeeze being Squeeze, the band's reformation wasn't as simple as expected. Despite his recall for the band's one-off charity gig, John Bentley found himself out in the cold, to be replaced by Keith Wilkinson. 'John was a very unfortunate casualty,' admits Glenn. 'I'm now of the opinion that we undervalued his playing with Squeeze and didn't realise what he'd contributed. Having said that, Keith had been fantastic on *Difford And Tilbrook*. He was a great bass player, who sounded a little bit different, which is what we wanted.'

The band decamped to Brussels – the first time they had recorded abroad – in order to work with Laurie Latham. The producer had temporarily moved to Belgium for tax purposes after the phenomenal success he had enjoyed with Paul Young's album *No Parlez* 18 months earlier.

Squeeze enjoyed their time in Brussels, behaving in as juvenile a fashion as possible within the liberating space of their newly-reformed gang. One morning, towards the end of the recordings, Glenn and Jools indulged in a mock sword fight with makeshift weaponry picked up in the studio. As the playground antics unfolded, Glenn managed to severely injure one of the keyboard player's middle fingers. The result was that Jools was sent to hospital where his digit was put in a splint. With studio time running low, one of Jools's younger brothers, Chris, then aged 19, was flown to Brussels to add the overdubs. Little did he know, Chris would eventually become a full-time member of Squeeze.

Although an enjoyable record to make, the resulting album, *Cosi Fan Tutti Frutti*, was a disappointing hotch-potch of songs, reflecting the folly of rushing the band back into the studio before they were ready.

***

'Big Beng'

CD: 'Big Beng' is a sort of Indian/Pakistani drug reference. This album is laced with cocaine and alcohol in large measures and contained some fairly dark lyrical content. I managed to create some of that darkness for myself in my hotel room in Brussels.

This sounds to me like a David Bowie song and shows off Keith Wilkinson's bass playing off to a T. To start the album with this was telling people we meant business. It was a pity we never sang this live because it was a killer song.

It has a very distinct 1980s sound, though. I think it sounds rather dated.

CD: Laurie Latham's production is a bit like that. If you hear a Paul Young album of the same period it wears the same footballer's haircut of the time. That is not to criticise Laurie's production because it was very skilled, but this album sits in its own time and space. When he works on Jools Holland records they don't sound like that at all. At that time everyone was using lots of effects on bass and had new synthesisers and foot pedals. Consequently they are on every track.

'By Your Side'

GT: This song was about ten years old. Sometimes you write songs and it isn't the right time to record them, particularly in the early days. Once we'd got over that initial rush of writing and surge of adrenalin, we'd slowed down a bit, and because we had such a massive catalogue of songs that we hadn't touched, from time to time we'd dip into the books and pull one out.

CD: I really liked this version of 'By Your Side', although the bass playing sounds very much of the time. I never enjoyed Squeeze when we erred on the side of reggae. I've always hated white people playing reggae. I listen and think, 'No, you have it totally arse about face. The bass drum and the snare and the bass do not go there.' So when we used to do reggae I used to wince.

Having been brought up on ska music and reggae as a skinhead I thought I had a bit of a qualification on this and felt uneasy about playing that style of music. There were very few bands around who could do it properly without sounding dull.

What about UB40?

CD: UB40 made a living by doing the whole thing properly. They have actually got Jamaicans in the band and that is where their roots are, whereas Squeeze's roots are in Greenwich. Having said that, 'By Your Side' works like this, and I like the original version too, which is more like James Taylor.

When you played this live it was quite stripped down.

GT: Yes, we recorded a version like that on a live album. The album version had a massive sound, but very good bass playing from Keith, which I think made the song as a whole.

'KING GEORGE STREET'

CD: Lyrically I'm very proud of this. I was born in King George Street and the song is very much about that road and the characters who lived there. I lived in a bungalow that was built during the war and in our street there were three pubs and a telephone box. There were Protestants and Catholics living there and everyone hated each other. This song is about one family from the street.

What I wasn't vouching for was how many chords Glenn would write for it. When he turned up in rehearsals with the chord sheets for everyone to learn, he left the room and we all looked at each other and asked, 'What is he on?' At the time we thought Glenn was losing the plot but when I listen back to it I think it's brilliant. When I play this to people I'm working with now they say, 'Slow down. The chords have changed.'

GT: I seem to remember there being a fair bit of animosity towards it from the band because of the fistful of chords. That many chords were alright if you've written the song and are into it but if you're not it can be a real pain in the arse to get around.

CD: When it became a single I took a copy over to my mum and dad and they loved it. They'd moved from King George Street by this time but were really pleased that I'd written about something which they could really associate with.

CD: This was the first song of Chris's for a while where I could see exactly the same story unfold in my mind. It's great when a lyric takes you on that journey, and we'd been missing that for some time.

'I LEARNT HOW TO PRAY'

The big production sound really works on this.

CD: Yes, but that tambourine is really annoying.

Was that Glenn playing?

CD: No. It was probably a machine.

GT: 'I Learnt How To Pray' is the sound of two men trying too hard, me and Chris. It is a polished vocal performance and sounds perky but I think the song is absolute pants. I don't believe it for a second.

What do you mean by that?

GT: I just don't think there's any soul in it. I think it's only on the album because we needed a certain number of songs and so we came up with this. At this time we got self-conscious in our writing and I don't think I was trying hard enough.

CD: What the song does touch upon is the situation of a man having a female as a best friend and he crosses that borderline of friendship and sleeps with her. I was trying to convey that when this happens, a friendship can disappear in an instant.

I know from relationships I have with female friends that at the height of conversation we could easily be kissing and getting in a relationship, but it would ruin our friendship, so I don't ever cross that line. It's an intriguing subject.

Years later I felt very deeply about a woman I knew well and wrote a song called 'In Another Lifetime' because it was the only way I could ever imagine a relationship with her.

'LAST TIME FOREVER'

CD: The tune for this had been written early in our career but I rewrote the lyric, inspired by a story I'd read in a newspaper. A body had come to the surface in a lake and the police had tried for weeks to discover who it was and who had murdered them. They eventually discovered that the bed linen covering the body had a dry cleaning ticket on it, fastened by a safety pin and perfectly preserved.

The police tracked it down to an airline pilot who had murdered his wife about five years earlier and buried her in the lake by weighing her body down with bricks. He'd told his friends and family that she'd left him because he was always away from home, which sounded feasible.

We recorded a video at Camber Sands and re-enacted this woman's last picnic on the beach with her husband. At that video Pam turned up with lots of clothes for us to wear and although we were all aghast, I wore this satin blue dress coat with tails that she brought.

The song got a lot of radio play and we played it live for a while. It's got a sample from the film *The Shining* at the beginning.

Which bit?

CD: Where a voice says, 'A momentary loss of muscular co-ordination.'

Did you have to get permission to use it?

CD: No, we just nicked it. Jack Nicholson was a Squeeze fan anyway, so it was alright.

How did you know he was a fan?

CD: We went to a nightclub in Los Angeles and he was there. I remember shaking hands with him and he said, 'You guys are fantastic.' Later that night I played cards at that club, which I'd never done before in my life. I was really pissed and sat down at a craps table and won continuously for an hour and a half. Suddenly everyone was my best mate. It was like some bad Mexican film. I thought I was going to get taken outside and cleaned out. I don't know how I got home, nor do I know what happened to the money.

'NO PLACE LIKE HOME'

CD: This is a really powerful song, where the lyrics and music embrace each other strongly, and one that was always great fun to do live. Jools really excelled himself, as he did on 'Last Time Forever'. We'd reached a stage where Jools was playing parts that sounded like they were parts of the song rather than just Jools just playing rock 'n' roll piano. On *Cosi Fan Tutti Frutti* and *Frank* his piano playing was jaw-droppingly good and frankly I haven't heard him play better since.

It's another song of domestic bliss, with a dramatic, visual lyric. It's a bit like a scene from *EastEnders*.

I like the image of the man holding the waste paper basket over his privates while he's being attacked. It's unusual to have a song about domestic violence by a woman on a man.

CD: Yes, but that was about something I was experiencing.

So it's an autobiographical lyric?

CD: No, it's not about my relationship but I knew of people who had been in similar domestic situations. Women only get upset like that when they have good reason, because the communication with their partner is really bad, which is usually down to the man. I've had women be violent against me and they've had every right to because I've wound them up.

GT: It's a great lyric and Laurie's production was fantastic and really brought the song out, especially when you bear in mind that when I had written the music, it was very straightforward and sounded more like Stealer's Wheel. Laurie moved it on several notches and gave it more of a sense of drama, and I copied Robert Fripp for my guitar line, a continuous droning sound.

CD: The sound is quite brittle, which sums up the lyric. It surges forward in all the right places, like the soundtrack to a movie. With something on the screen this song could be really powerful and, if I ever get another musical off the ground, this would probably be one of the songs I would use. Lyrically the song says so much, and even though people say that musicals should be based around your hits, I'd stick my neck out to include this one.

'Heartbreaking World'

This is a Difford and Holland track. Do you like it?

GT: No, I don't. I was quite upset at this time by Chris writing with Jools because they had both got very close and I was jealous of that. I also thought that the lyric was absolute bollocks. I still do, actually. What's it about?

CD: Jools had actually written some of this lyric himself, so we met halfway, but it doesn't mean very much to me now. It was written at around the time of Live Aid and was a bit self-conscious.

Glenn often used to ask me to write songs about what was going on in the world but I wasn't any good at it. I'm not Paul Weller or Elvis Costello, who can do that brilliantly. I'm good at what I do and when I work outside in a different arena I'm not so good. It would be like me trying to write a song about the ozone layer. People would say, 'Come on Chris, get a grip,' whereas Joni Mitchell could do that very well.

The song refers to a football fan dying watching his team. This would have been written around the time of the Heysel Stadium disaster and the Bradford City fire.

CD: That's right. We were actually living in Brussels when the Heysel disaster happened.

The only affection I have for the song is that Marti Pellow nicked a whole verse out of the song, used it in a Wet Wet Wet song called 'Angel Eyes' and I made some money out of it.

To be fair to them they called my lawyer and owned up and I said if you give me a songwriting credit, I'll be as happy as Larry. So I got a royalty split and we've been friends ever since.

For my money the song is let down by the drum machine, my pet hate.

GT: I like drum machines. I think there's definitely a place for them. Even though I don't like the lyric, it's probably one of the nicest sounding songs on the record. It has a good arrangement.

'HITS OF THE YEAR'

The lyric concerns the story of a plane hijack.

CD: Yes, but it means very little to me. It's another 'Wagon Train', a cabaret song best kept for some future existence.

There's a lot of playing with mood in the song. There's an air of calm, and then mystery, fear and finally absolute terror, signified by your grating guitar solo. It works quite cleverly.

GT: I suppose so, but I can't see past the point of not liking the song. It's one of those songs where there was a different lyric originally and where I preferred the demo. It had a different feel, part of my ongoing battle to include anything dancey. If I wrote anything vaguely dancey the band would take it away from that and do something else. In this case the song lost whatever it had in its translation.

CD: We had to make a video for this and we were talked into doing it with a film director in LA. We flew in, feeling rather the worse for wear when we arrived, recorded the video, and then came straight back. After all that, it's the worst video you can imagine, recorded in front of a blue screen. When we'd left, the director put all these goings-on behind. It was meant to be MTV-like, so we had to conform to what they wanted, but it cost about $100,000. A total waste of money.

'BREAK MY HEART'

GT: We'd written this song for Kiki Dee originally and then it ended up in *Labelled With Love*, the musical. It was a very pretty song, but almost the same comments I made about 'Hits Of The Year' apply to it. It was ugly, not because of Chris's vocal, but because of the way we recorded it. We made a pretty tune less pretty.

CD: I always loved this song. The melody was terrific, and really worked with the lyric. When Glenn said I needed to sing a song on the album I told him I really wanted to sing 'Break My Heart', which wasn't on our original list.

Unfortunately, I had a real problem with my confidence and it shows. Laurie and Glenn were very patient with me, trying to get me to sing in tune, but I wasn't in a great personal space, so every time they told me to sing it again my insecurity was getting worse and worse. I was a complete wreck by the time I'd finished and it sounds pretty bad, but when you're singing with somebody like Glenn it's a tall order trying to keep up.

Did you feel intimidated by how good Glenn's voice was?

CD: Not intimidated. I just knew I didn't sound good then. I wanted to be the Bernie Taupin of the band and just write lyrics and stay at home. If at the end of this album Glenn had said, 'We don't want to take you on the road. We'll find another guitar player, so stay at home and write the lyrics,' I would have said, 'That's fantastic.'

That's remarkable, especially when you said what a buzz you got when you first got back with the band.

CD: Yes, but I didn't have the skill to make that feeling from the first gig at Catford last throughout the year. I should have thought to myself, 'What a great energy that was. How can I make it last?' Although I enjoyed the places we played at around this time, like The Pier in New York and the Nassau Colosseum, I didn't feel I was up to scratch compared with other members of the band. I didn't see myself as the full shilling, which is sad.

'I WON'T EVER GO DRINKING AGAIN'

GT: I still play this song live but I play it the way I wrote it, which was as a country song. It was entirely Laurie's idea to take it to another area, but it was an interesting take on the song. I think the lyric is very funny in places: 'When daylight appears/ It's the third time around/ And I swear I won't drink ever again with that crowd.'

CD: This is one of my better drinking songs, one that was written in bed in a hotel room in Brussels. All the lines in this song sum up the way I felt. I used to go down to the Saint Bar in Brussels or sit in my room drinking or taking coke on my own. It's a fun drinking song.

The music has an off-kilter, almost disorienting sound.

CD: Keith had a lot to do with the influences on many of the rhythms on this album. He took on a strong role as a member of the band. He didn't come in and slip gently between the sheets. He jumped straight in the bed.

Gilson played drums well on this album, considering the technology that was around that we worked with. He was in sober spirits and he adjusted really well.

GT: Rhythmically, Gilson's contribution to this song is great, but it also shows up how his contribution had been weakened by our usage of new technology. This made it a weaker record from the word go, which was a shame.

***

SQUEEZE WERE back in business, but the recording and touring pressures that had brought the band to its knees three years earlier were again taking hold.

Cosi Fan Tutti Frutti was similar to both *Sweets From A Stranger* and *Difford And Tilbrook* in its level of inconsistency and, a few memorable moments aside, had failed to move the band significantly forward. Each of the band's first four albums had shown a steady improvement, but since the glorious *East Side Story*, now four years old, the band were artistically treading water.

Both Glenn and Chris look back with some regret at not being allowed more time to write stronger material and think it was unwise to have created song arrangements ad hoc in the studio. In the same way that *Squeeze* was a rehearsal for the second album of the band's first period, their comeback album *Cosi Fan Tutti Frutti* is regarded by both songwriters as merely the warm-up for the far stronger *Babylon And On*.

The album, despite its undoubted high points, such as the magnificent 'I Won't Ever Go Drinking Again' and 'King George Street', which may never otherwise have been written, also sounds dated. According to Glenn, this is less of a criticism of the band and fabled producer Latham, and more to do with the prevailing musical attitude of the time, dominated by 1980s technology.

'I've consistently dissed Laurie over this album, which I'm sorry about,' explains Glenn. '*Cosi* is the album that sounds most of its time, but I have to say that Chris and I weren't up to full steam in our writing. There's some great songs on the album but there are some very weak ones as well. What frustrated me was that we barely played a single note together in the studio and everything was recorded to click track and guide keyboards.

'It was very much the fashion of the time to make records in that way, but it didn't convey any of the power of the band. When we rehearsed the songs immediately afterwards they sounded ten times better than the record because we could really play. If we'd used that album as a set of demos and gone into a studio again to cut them it would have been a significantly better record.'

9 *Babylon And On*

FOR THE follow-up album of the band's second coming, morale in the Squeeze camp by and large remained positive. Despite the continued impetuosity of the Difford-Tilbrook axis, the spiritual rebirth of a sober Gilson and the return of Jools as court jester kept much of the tension between the two warring partners at bay. In addition, Squeeze had employed another two musicians who were both easygoing and content to play second fiddle to the band's stars.

Keith Wilkinson was now an integral part of the line-up, his input to the last album much appreciated by his colleagues, while Andy Metcalfe had played with the band since the *Cosi Fan Tutti Frutti* tour. That album had been so heavy with emulators and synths that a second keyboard player had been required and Metcalfe, best known for his work with Robyn Hitchcock, had got the job, and stayed in the band after they came off the road.

The title of the album *Babylon And On* itself indicates the positive mood of the camp. A clever play on words chosen by Chris, which referred to the band members' tendencies to 'babble on and on' for hours on tour.

After rushing the recording of their previous LP, Squeeze wanted to take their time on this occasion. As a result, the album was the most expensive the band ever made. Much of late 1986 and early 1987 was spent working in a total of six studios, including the ultra-modern Air in London and the Hit Factory in New York.

At one stage, the band were forced onto a hastily organised month-long tour, having gone way over budget. This decision was a blessing in disguise, because the time spent playing the new material to live audiences revolutionised many of the songs and helped make the album Squeeze's finest record in six years.

Crucial to the album's success was the production team of Eric Thorngren and Glenn. A man of great energy, Thorngren was instrumental in keeping the songs sounding as simple as possible, in contrast to Squeeze's previous record. Also, he acted as a perfect counterfoil to Glenn, who continuously desired musical experimentation.

Originally, Thorngren's role was as sole producer of the album. But having made what he considered an equal contribution to the record's sound, Glenn requested a co-production credit for his work. Thorngren obliged, but the request resulted in a minor disagreement between Glenn and his colleagues.

Glenn stands by his proposal, by pointing out the extent of his extracurricular role on previous Squeeze albums. 'I know I upset some people in the band by pushing for a production credit, but in my defence I didn't get enough credit for the work I put into earlier records. When John Wood co-produced records with us, I was always at the forefront and everyone was happy to let me do that. It was not as though people were fighting to have their say. On *Babylon And On* they were happy for me to put all that work in again but not happy when I wanted a credit. It wasn't a financial thing, I just wanted professional credit for the work I'd put in. So I thought "Fuck you, I'll pursue it anyway."

'I put my foot down in a way that I now regard as ungracious and subsequently got less respect in the band. I think Chris resented me for it and also felt increasingly alienated by my relationship with Pam, which was entering its final stages. In fact, this whole period was probably the lowest point of mine and Chris's relationship. We were never close at any point but we were getting further apart rather than closer. Fortunately, it started to get better after this record.'

Chris, not surprisingly, has a different take on events and claims it would have been 'more tactful' for Glenn to have brought up the subject at the beginning of recordings. 'If you start an album and you say on the first day, "I want to be the co-producer", everyone knows that's the case from the beginning. But if you get to the end of an album and someone puts their hand in the air and wants to be co-producer because they've done more work than everybody else, that's a different thing altogether.'

What both men agreed upon was the desperate need for the album to be a success. In addition to the recordings' vast expense, which had eaten away their advance payments from A&M, the band were living increasingly opulent lifestyles. Glenn, in particular, was troubled by their predicament. 'Our living requirements were beginning to intrude on what we did. Financially our advances had to be increased so that we could maintain the lifestyles we'd become used to. I felt at the time that this was like putting the cart before the horse, that it was dangerous to live off those advances rather than the money we were earning. But we carried on doing it for a while.'

Fortunately, *Babylon And On* would become Squeeze's highest selling studio album, almost going gold in the States, and providing a brace of hit singles. The family silver was safe for another year.

***

'Hourglass'

CD: This was the first time we wrote together in the same room, which was Glenn's idea. I'd always thought of writing as a bit like masturbation: something you do on your own, not in the same room as another bloke. However, I went to Glenn's house and within an hour we'd written 'Hourglass'. Lyrically it doesn't mean much but we had some fun writing it. Glenn counteracted some lyrical ideas and I added some musical ideas, then he demoed it and made some changes, and finally the band got hold of it and changed it some more.

GT: I came up with the idea of the chorus, which are nonsense words really, but I loved the idea of a rapid delivery, which is what that chorus required. When I got the lyric I thought it was curiously negative about our chances, given where we were as a band at that time, and it was also ironic considering it went on to be a chart hit both here and in America. Maybe Chris was disappointed with the album before and was thinking that we had peaked.

It was one of those songs that was much more dance-orientated when I wrote it than how it ended up. Unlike some of the other things that Squeeze flattened out, we delivered a good band performance together in the studio.

Eric added some good effects and created a break that hadn't been there, which gave it a slightly more contemporary edge, although it still had that Squeeze sound, so it was a good combination. At one stage there's one really long note that Chris thought sounded ugly, but that made me want to keep it even more.

You're credited on this with horns.

GT: They were synthesised horns. In those days we'd never spend 300 quid on a horn section for a day when we could spend several thousand pounds on a synth and overdubbing it over the course of a week.

You had a video directed by Ade Edmondson.

GT: Yes. Jools knew Ade and he was fantastic to work with, and overflowing with ideas. To be fair, Jools came out with some of the ideas, because he was becoming very visually literate, which is something I've never been.

CD: The reason this song exists in my mind is purely for the video, which won an MTV award. Jools co-directed it, without a credit, and it was a feast of clever photography and great costumes. It's like surreal art.

'Footprints'

GT: Again this sounds like Chris was in quite a bad space. Take the lines 'I spent too much money/ I looked far too glad/ Now I have so little of what I once had.' To be honest, I didn't share those sentiments at all. It wasn't how I felt about where we were.

Was it a personal lyric, Chris?

CD: It might have been. My divorce had kicked in and I was starting to lose money. I stayed in a hotel at the Tower of London for about three months and didn't look at the bill, which was ridiculous, so that explains the lines Glenn has quoted. I lost my house and my cars, and I'd moved into a small flat, so my life was changing. Part of the lyric refers to a couple of good friends of mine who had sobered up. I thought that their giving up drink was interesting, although I didn't want to stop yet. It's a regretful song in that way.

GT: Gilson's playing is great. He really thought about his parts and the song and helped it motor along. This was also the first song for a long while where I used a harmony between guitar and bass, like we'd done on 'Another Nail' and 'Piccadilly'. It really worked well on 'Footprints' and a lot of credit for that has to go to Keith.

'TOUGH LOVE'

GT: This was the first alcohol song to be written from the perspective of being aware of the damage it can cause, as opposed to just having a headache. When we originally wrote this, Chris had written a lyric that wasn't particularly good, so he was asked to write another one. I'm glad he did, because this is so powerful. It's right up there with some of our best songs.

It was inspired by Gilson, wasn't it?

CD: Gilson told me a story he'd overheard somewhere about a terrible relationship between two people. I found it upsetting that a relationship could be quite so grim, and it also felt a little like my relationship, so I wrote 'Tough Love'.

How did the song relate to your relationship? The violence?

CD: If you're asking me if I've hit any of the women I've been with, I can say honestly that I have. I'm very sorry about that. I've also been hit in return, and it hurts. I take responsibility for my actions, but when you're under the influence of vodka and cocaine all hell can break loose.

Did you feel that your alcohol and cocaine use was getting out of control?

CD: I was more aware of it because a few of my friends had sobered up and I was curious, but there was still a few more years of drinking left in me and I wanted to enjoy them.

Glenn and I used to play this in our acoustic set and it was more powerful like that.

The music is written against the grain of the lyric, isn't it?

GT: You have to remember that I'd written it to a different lyric. It was a tune I liked and had the original lyric stayed the same it would have been an average song, but the replacement lyric Chris came up with was stunning.

There's some lovely accordion playing on this by T-Bone Wolk, from the Hall And Oates band, who we brought in. He gave the song a bit of a swing. Gilson's role was also crucial. It's unusual the way he plays what is essentially a waltz-time song. The beat he has on the hi-hat combined with a waltz time in between the snare and kick drum is really clever. The reason it works isn't because it's clever, but because it fits perfectly with the song.

'THE PRISONER'

GT: This is one of Chris's songs in the tradition of 'Woman's World', but it marks his growth as a lyricist in that it's infinitely more subtle as a lyric.

CD: It's an observation of everyday relationships, with the masculine *Sun* reader, who has an 'IQ of 21'. The woman is kept prisoner at home.

There's some wonderful imagery, such as the line 'Baked like a cake but without the file.'

CD: I like that as well. I enjoyed playing with words and was inspired in the early days by the way Elvis Costello did it. He doesn't do this so much now, but there's a real art to playing on words.

At the end you create a happy ending. She's broken out of jail and run for her life. You seem to like positive resolutions at the end of your lyrics.

CD: I think resolution is good. It's quite a dark lyric and Glenn put a bombastic rhythm track around it, which was immense fun to play live. It was like being in The Who, with all these chords going off and a fantastic drum rhythm in the background that sounded like an animal coming towards you.

GT: Eric and I had to fiddle about with this song to get it right. It was a good performance by the band but it was brought alive by the fact that Eric muted out half of what we played, which gave it some dynamic, and made it more exciting.

I was aware that the parts of both Gilson and Jools were very important to the song. The biggest change between Squeeze Mark One and Squeeze Mark Two was that I'd learnt more about how to give people space on records. I'd taken on board the idea of songs being tailored to fit the people playing them rather than musicians moulding into the space I'd created for the songs.

This is one of the reasons why I feel like our second album back together was like our first album should have been and was far more representative of how we sounded.

'853-5937'

The title is your old phone number, isn't it?

GT: That's right, and it's a song of which I'm heartily ashamed. All I've got to say about this song is that it was one of Squeeze's only hits in the States, which tells me so much about how not to value hit records. This is my answer-phone jingle, which regrettably I decided to turn into a song. Chris very obligingly came up with the lyric, but I hold myself solely responsible for this utter waste of time.

CD: The record company wanted this included in the set because it was getting a lot of airplay, but Glenn refused point blank.

I'm pretty disgusted with it myself. It's a nonsensical lyric, married to the tune in no-man's land. How we managed to create such a monster and see it become a hit single amazes me.

One thing of interest was the fact that people across America were phoning that number and causing mayhem.

GT: Yes, it was one of the last songs that was allowed to have a telephone number in the title. We made the front page of *USA Today* because so many irate people were getting calls. That was the only good thing about the song.

'In Today's Room'

This is quite funky.

GT: Yes, it is funky. I have a soft spot for this song. It was me pretending to be Prince. It was always hard to get Squeeze to do dancey things like this, but for some reason they went for it this time around. Musically it sounds quite off-the-wall and Jools's playing is terrific. The lyric is not a literal lyric, which I like. It contains a lot of imagery as opposed to a story, which was unusual for Chris.

CD: I was inspired by listening to Prince as well, and wanted to write something that would be in his neighbourhood. The lyric is a collection of lines rather than a complete story.

Musically, it had so many permutations that it got beaten around in the studio hundreds of times and ended up being a mish-mash of several ideas.

'Trust Me To Open My Mouth'

The follow-up single to 'Hourglass', this reached the mighty heights of Number 72.

GT: Barnstorming. It's quite an ordinary song really, although I liked it more at the time. I was influenced by Michael Jackson, probably for the first and last time in my career.

The song is about adultery. Was it about you, Chris?

CD: I don't think so. The fact I was going through a divorce meant I may have been writing about me but through a third person. I can't recall.

GT: I came up with a lyric for this, that Chris very tactfully suggested we didn't use, and one that makes me wince now. I saw myself as a sort of guitar gunslinger and singing 'I oughta stick to playing catgut.' The thought of it is really painful but it didn't get on the record, thank goodness.

It has some nice Hammond by Jools.

GT: Jools's part was great. I've noticed that I'm enthusing about the fact that it was like a band again. This was a band record; it's not about moods and atmospheres, it's about people playing, but with some contemporary production. It sounds of its time but it doesn't sound dated in the way that the last album did.

CD: We did another tremendous video, directed again by Ade Edmondson, in which we had a huge mouth that we all played inside. Musically it's a stonker to play onstage because it has a lot of guts.

'STRIKING MATCHES'

GT: By this stage Chris could not bear to work with me and recorded his lead vocal when I wasn't around. I was happy for him to do that because the result was a great vocal performance by him, which had been missing for a while. Whatever it took to get him there was fine by me. Also, Monique's parts in it are fantastic, so I take no credit for the way the song turned out.

You mentioned Monique Dyan. Who was she?

GT: Eric's girlfriend, and later his wife. She's got a great voice and we used her on the next album, *Frank*, as well.

CD: The duet between myself and Monique works a treat and it was good to have a track like that on the album. It's a fun song and although lyrically it's not about anything particular, just two characters, I think it's okay to have that kind of story line in songs, a flippant message. I don't think everything has to be that deep, unless you're Bob Dylan.

I really like the line 'there's some of her in the teeth in your comb'.

CD: Yes, it's another bathroom song. This has a similar domestic clarity to 'Is That Love?', which along with this song and 'Tempted' could easily be in a musical of their own.

'CIGARETTE OF A SINGLE MAN'

This is my favourite song on the album.

CD: Funnily enough, it was also the favourite of our A&R man at the time, Chris Briggs, but Glenn didn't like it. I thought it had a spring in its tail. It was quite a romantic storyline, really.

It apparently came from your watching a man looking lonely in a pub.

CD: That would have been in the Rose and Crown at the bottom of Crooms Hill, which was full of images like that. It's a gay pub now.

'Who Are You?'

This is another mood song.

GT: Yes it is. I can't recall much in the way of specifics, except it reminds me that we are getting further into the album and still coming across a lot of songs which are good and that we worked hard on.

CD: I don't remember anything about this.

***Babylon And On* is a far more polished album than *Cosi Fan Tutti Frutti*.**

GT: It is, and it shows how we had taken our foot off the accelerator on *Difford And Tilbrook* and *Cosi*. I think we'd learnt from that and discovered how to apply ourselves properly. We worked hard on the record and while not every track is a gem, there is a really good standard. We got ourselves back on track with this album and the band was in very strong shape.

'The Waiting Game'

CD: I've always liked 'The Waiting Game' and remember vividly the moment I wrote this. I was sitting downstairs in my house and could hear the stomping of feet dancing on the wooden floor upstairs. 'I wasn't in the mood for laughing/ So I sat silently in my chair.'

There used to be endless parties in that house and during most of them I would sit in the garden or downstairs and not participate. So 'The Waiting Game' means a lot to me because that's exactly how I was at that time.

The storyline about waiting for a girl to turn up is nothing to do with what happened, though. It was just an extension of the idea. I witnessed that feeling of the first verse and then extended it into a story.

It was an achievement to record it live in the studio with an orchestra, with Del Newman conducting. I felt a bit unsure of what was happening, trying to play along with an orchestra. To be honest, I was well out of my depth with my guitar, but I went along with the vibe of it. The whole record was like that really. It was a lot of me just getting through it, really.

GT: Recording 'The Waiting Game' was absolutely fabulous, the only time in my life I've ever played live with a 60-piece orchestra. To have all that coming through your headphones and singing along was a real pleasure. For me it marked a real growth in confidence because when we had used an orchestra previously on 'Vanity Fair' I'd backed away from the chance of being involved. This time I embraced it and it was lovely.

Del (Newman) did the arrangement. I always liked working with strings. It gave a bigger picture, which that song was crying out for, because actually it's a bit weak. It's a nice enough tune but it's one of the few lyrics I don't think a lot of on this record.

'Some Americans'

GT: I was amazed at our insensitivity on this song, sneering at Americans. It was like going round someone's house and picking holes in their décor and a bit cheeky seeing as though we'd been touring America regularly. I liked the sentiment of criticising Ronald Reagan but at the same time I was scared by what the knock-on effects might be. Nevertheless I said nothing and went along with it and I was quite pleased with the tune I wrote.

CD: It's a terrible song. Thank God we never played it live.

Particularly in the States.

CD: Maybe we should have played it in the States to get a reaction. More seriously, this shows the level of our songwriting prowess at that time. We'd got diverted into getting this drum machine and that rhythm box to sound fantastic together, and the craft of writing songs had gone to the side. It was more about technology, and sculpting a pattern.

One story from these recordings sums up the album perfectly. One of the very first computers that could sequence keyboard and drum sounds had come out. I was still in touch with Andy Duncan, who had one of these machines, which was called a Green Gate. I somehow convinced Glenn and Eric that Andy should come in with his box of tricks and that the whole album would change and it would sound amazing.

They bowed to my greater judgment, stupidly, and Andy came over with his Green Gate machine, plonked it on the table, plugged it in, and eight hours later – a whole day's studio time – it still wasn't working. I kept saying it would be fine.

The next day Andy brought it in and it was starting to make piss and fart noises. I was waiting for it to break into life and be the saviour, but it still didn't work, so we sent him packing with his machine.

Then a huge bill came in for a couple of grand for his work and it was instantly decided that I should pay it myself because I'd completely wasted a whole day's work for the band. At this point I thought, 'This isn't right. Why should I be made to suffer when everybody went along with it?'

Fortunately, I didn't have to put my hand in my pocket in the end to pay for this bloody machine. It was a good lesson and from that day on I just kept clear. I thought, 'I don't know what I am doing. I'm miles out of my depth. Leave Glenn to it because he knows what he is doing.' From that day on I just stuck to making the tea.

***

THE SUCCESS of *Babylon And On* had justified the faith Miles Copeland and A&M had in the band. Its high sales added to Squeeze's self-confidence, which at last seemed to be recovering from the battering the much-derided *Sweets From A Stranger* had given it five years earlier.

It is apparent, however, that Glenn and Chris see the record very differently from one other 17 years down the line. Glenn rightly feels proud of the musical step-up that the album signified, and lauds the co-production team's success in utilising an abundance of new technology without sacrificing the traditional Squeeze sound.

Chris acknowledges the quality of the record's sound and points out that the two hit singles and impressive album sales justified its vast expenditure. What prevents him from being fond of the record is what he regards as its lacklustre lyrics.

'I'm not attached to this album lyrically. The album as a whole is more of a summing up of a vibe rather than of any lyrical depth. There's nothing apart from "Tough Love" that I would hold my hat on, from a lyrical point of view. I think it's scraping the barrel in some respects, but maybe there's a lesson in that. If you just let go and don't try too hard then you can let success in. Maybe I was trying to be too clever sometimes.'

In an effort to consolidate Squeeze's growing profile in the US, the band were booked as the support act for David Bowie on his Glass Spider tour. They also headlined at Madison Square Garden for the second time, an indication of the high regard in which the band were held stateside. Touring with Bowie was a great success and the support act often went down better than the main attraction, who at the time was stubbornly refusing to play any of his greatest hits. According to Chris, there were so many people at a show in New Jersey who had turned up solely to see Squeeze, that many thousands had left the auditorium before the Laughing Gnome himself appeared onstage.

Despite being on tour with him for a number of weeks, the members of Squeeze never got to meet Bowie, who would be whisked to the stage in a limousine minutes before he was due to perform. Similarly, the singer would make a rapid exit as soon as the lights went down after his last encore.

By a coincidence, Chris had been a member of Bowie's road crew back in 1972 on the star's *Ziggy Stardust* UK tour. 'I met David while I was a roadie for him, although I use the word roadie loosely. A friend of mine, Willie, was his tour manager, and I tagged along and helped paint things for the set and fetched wood from the yard. I was more of a gofer. David was wonderful to be around, like someone from Mars.'

During the course of the album's writing, recording, and subsequent touring, Glenn and Chris's private lives changed significantly. The latter's marriage to Cindy was in ruins and had, in fact, already come close to being dissolved shortly after *Cosi Fan Tutti Frutti*'s release. At one stage an emotional Cindy threatened to use her husband's lyrics of infidelity and cruelty from the 1985 album in a divorce court. Chris's response might explain why he occasionally suffered physical violence at the hands of his spouse. 'I said I'd be honoured if she used my lyrics in court.'

The recording of *Babylon And On* beckoned Chris's inevitable divorce, but making the 'Hourglass' video would usher in happier times for the troubled soul. Chris chatted up a make-up girl called Heidi on set, and the pair started dating seriously, eventually marrying and having two children. 'This whole period was a time of great turmoil,' Chris explains. 'I was suffering from the trauma of losing sight of my children, while on the other hand I was madly in love and blissfully unaware of life.'

By this time, Glenn's marriage to Pam was close to disintegration and Chris, frustrated at being on the road with a woman he regarded as an implacable foe, spilled out his anger one memorable day. The setting for this spectacular row between Glenn and Chris was Salt Lake City, where Squeeze were filming the video for 'Footprints'. The argument was ferocious and intense, and left a cloud over the entire recording.

Chris now confesses to 'deeply regretting' his role in the bust-up. 'We had the most awful argument during the making of this video and didn't talk to each other for months afterwards. There were times that I'm sure Glenn wanted to punch me because I must have been so insular and unavailable to him, which is sad when you've got such a good working relationship, to mess it up in such an idiotic way.

'The fact was I just didn't like Pam and had no way of challenging her. We'd been on tour and Glenn thought I'd said something to her about his behaviour, via a third person, and I swear to this day I hadn't. I felt I'd become a whipping post for the fragility of their relationship and it brought this division down the middle of our relationship and within the band.

'Onstage you could almost see a brick wall appearing between me and Glenn and it was horrible. One day in LA, one of our management team, John Lay, dragged us into a room and said "you guys have got to talk." We proceeded to speak aggressively about why we were upset with each other and then carried on not talking to each other afterwards. From the outside the band were growing, we were doing great gigs, and were working hard, but the apple was beginning to get a bit soggy on the inside.'

10 *Frank*

IN BETWEEN the release of *Babylon And On* and the recording of *Frank* came Squeeze's now-customary change of personnel: Andy Metcalfe left for new pastures, and was replaced by Matt Irving. Jools's increasing commitments to projects outside of the band had already necessitated a second keyboard player, but his lengthening absences were becoming a serious problem for the band, especially for head boy Glenn.

Christened 'Alan Whicker' by the band because of his constant jet-setting, Jools's television commitments meant that for lengthy periods Squeeze could not play gigs on Thursdays or Fridays. It also meant that Jools would fly-in physically and mentally drained for weekend shows. One instance, Chris recalls, shows how Jools's juggling act was beginning to take its toll.

'I went across to Jools one day onstage and he had his head in one of his hands. I pulled his arm away for a laugh and found he really was asleep, but somehow managing to play with the other hand. It was really annoying, especially to Glenn. We had to have a second keyboard player but we all knew that having Jools in the band gave us an extra profile.'

Jools's obligations outside of Squeeze meant that he was absent for much of the recording of *Frank*. This was exemplified by the photographs of each member of the band, which were included inside the sleeve. Every band member had a strip of passport booth photographs included, with the exception of Jools; his booth was empty, save for an orange curtain. Accompanying the photographs was the terse comment: 'Jools was on holiday,' although Glenn insists this remark was meant to be tongue in cheek.

Despite his part-time role in the band, Jools's impact on *Frank* was enormous, and Chris and Glenn rightly regard the record as the boogie-woogie man's finest hour in Squeeze. It would also be Jools's last album with the band.

Worried by the exorbitant costs of recording *Babylon* and his realisation that financial hardship might be imminent without a drastic reduction in budget, Glenn suggested that the band use a cheaper studio to make *Frank*. His colleagues wearily acceded, perhaps not fully understanding that they could no longer afford to pour as much money into records as the likes of U2 and Dire Straits. Chris explains, 'Glenn took us by the scruff of the neck and said, "We're not making any money? What can we do to change it?" I really didn't give a shit. I was having a great time and didn't think it was necessary to do things on the cheap.'

Having enjoyed the best facilities that money could buy in studios like Air and the Hit Factory, the band set up camp in the rather more basic surroundings of The Chocolate Factory in New Cross, south London. Chris was particularly unhappy at their fall from grace.

'The environment was not very creative for anybody,' he moans. 'The sound there was awful and nobody looked forward to going to work in the morning. It was depressing, with hessian brown and orange walls. Gilson absolutely hated it and Eric Thorngren could not believe what we had to put up with. For example, there were ants coming out of the desk. One of Glenn's mates was making sandwiches for us as well. We were really cutting corners.'

Glenn's recollection is that the band had simply wasted too much money over recent years and, however tough it might be, they must cut their coat according to their cloth. He also believed, with some justification, that the band had been using too many unnecessary effects, and that they were talented enough musicians to make a more simple record. 'A conscious decision was made not to use many effects on the record. It was going to be dry and very much recorded live and we pretty much stuck to that plan.'

The resulting album was an artistic triumph. Chris was back on form with a batch of clever lyrics, Glenn showed his continuing development as a musical arranger, and the band sounded hungry and accomplished in equal measure.

Before the first song, a 15 second out-take from the studio recordings is aired entitled 'Frank', which was the name of Gilson's dog. This extract illustrates how the band indeed recorded songs live in the studio, with one musician asking who is going to count the band in. Jools replies 'Fatty,' referring to Gilson and, after a few seconds of hushed silence, the once porky but newly slim drummer Gilson replies, 'I'm not fat.' A laughing Jools agrees to 'take that back', and the intro to 'If It's Love' kicks in.

***

'If It's Love'

It's a very joyful song and those backing singers give it a gospel vibe.

GT: It's funny because when this was originally written it was rather less optimistic. It was originally called 'If I'm Dead', and had a very dark lyric. An A&R person tactfully suggested that we might care to make it less depressing after he heard the demo.

CD: 'If I'm Dead' was, as you might imagine, a dark and dismal song and when it was pointed out that it wasn't very catchy to sing about being dead I changed it.

GT: When Chris re-wrote the lyric it became a perky song, but it's one of those tracks that if you pull it apart too much you find there's not much there. It's not a song of substance, but I'm fond of it nevertheless. I like the optimism of it.

CD: What springs to mind most about this is not the lyric but the video. We made it with a director called Bob O'Connor, who gave us a little room each in which we made our own little documentary. Each time the camera came to us we had to have done something different in the room. It was a very inventive idea. Gilson decorated his room, for instance. I sat and smoked a pipe.

'PEYTON PLACE'

GT: This is one of our more complex songs, and was never an easy one to play. We worked very hard at it and it's one of the tributes to Squeeze at this point that it sounds quite effortless.

Peyton Place is actually in Greeenwich and this lyric returns to the tradition of Chris singing about something local, which I think is always a good idea. It's one of the best songs of the second Squeeze period.

CD: There is something really powerful about this lyric. Glenn was pulling his hair out because I was using television titles for the songs and this was another title from a '60s TV show.

GT: The piano solo is something that Jools worked really hard at. I remember looking at him through the glass when he was doing it and he looked like a man possessed because he was so into it. He was able to lend a jazzy lightness of touch to what isn't an easy selection of chords to solo over, so it needed a great deal of thought. It was fantastic to see how much Jools had grown as a keyboard player over the years.

CD: The piano solo is beyond belief, one of the most fantastic I've ever heard Jools play. It was the first time I could remember him taking some homework away and working out in advance what he was going to play. There was a tendency for Jools to swan in and out of whatever it was that we were doing, but on this particular track and some of the others on *Frank* he really nailed it.

'ROSE I SAID'

CD: I would say 'Rose I Said' was one of the strongest lyrics I had written for a while. It's as strong as 'King George Street'. I wrote a whole load of lyrics at this point that were long stories. It must have been awful for Glenn to try to put them into a three-minute song. He had to be very inventive melodically here. On tour I was always amazed that Glenn could remember every word. It was the same with 'Melody Motel'. I wouldn't have been able to remember all those words in a million years.

This lyric has some very strong imagery. The 'mouth full of sandwich went all over the place' and 'I picked with my tongue at the bread stuck in my teeth.'

CD: Yes, I think I did a pretty good job on this song. We had great fun recording it.

What can you tell me about it musically, Glenn?

GT: Every now and then I try and write a song that's really straightforward and this is one of those. This falls into the same category as 'If It's Love' in that I like the song and the performance of it, which is very spirited, but it doesn't distinguish itself in any way.

'Slaughtered, Gutted and Heartbroken'

Your vocal sounds just like Badly Drawn Boy, Chris?

CD: I think you mean that he sounds like me.

GT: This really shows off Chris's vocal renaissance at this time. It's a fabulous delivery and the song is a great vehicle for this Squeeze line-up. Everybody shines on it. Jools's playing and Gilson's swing approach are particularly good. It's an arrangement we all worked at. And what a fabulous title for a song.

CD: The song is very much about me, I think, and when I sing this I feel very attached to it. Other songs, like 'Striking Matches' and 'Cool For Cats', were about things that are pretty removed from me. 'Slaughtered' is actually a song that means something to me and I can enlarge upon it. When I play this in my own set it feels totally my song.

Your delivery conjures up an image of you leaning on the mic unshaven, bow tie undone, clutching a bottle of whisky and smoking a fag.

CD: That's a good image. Glenn gave a lot of his time for me to get in the right key and making me feeling comfortable with it. Glenn's guitar playing is sublime.

GT: I originally wrote it as a horrific reggae song, which thank goodness we changed. This version harked back to the types of music we played a lot when we first got together, which was r 'n' b and blues. We never recorded a lot of that stuff but we used to play it in the early days. It had that throwback element to the song, but there's a real lightness of touch about it.

'(This Could Be) The Last Time'

CD: This is an album filler.

Not a song you are particularly proud of then?

CD: Absolutely not. It sounds like somebody else, not Squeeze. It's the Ringo Starr song of the album.

GT: The only thing I'd add is that Keith's idea for the backing vocals during the chorus was good. It was a song I was really enthusiastic about at the time, but I can't really see why now. The lyric's okay, but the tune is neither one thing nor the other.

I thought I was Roy Orbison when I was writing it, but quite plainly I wasn't. I had that operatic thing he used to do in mind, the way the changes happened in the chorus, with very dramatic stops. But in the cold light of day I realised that it wasn't Roy Orbison, but Glenn Tilbrook on a bad day.

'SHE DOESN'T HAVE TO SHAVE'

CD: This was how to win the girls over. I can remember playing this and when Glenn sang the first couple of lines you would instantly feel the connection with the first three rows of girls. I'd think, 'Yes, the bait has worked. I am a gentleman. Come to my dressing room after the show and we will talk about periods.' This song could in fact be termed a 'period piece'.

This song was written about 200 yards down the road from where I lived in 1981. It was a time-of-the-month song and no one had ever written one of those, I don't think. I thought this was a song that needed to be written.

GT: I have mixed feelings about this one. On one hand I love what it's tackling, the idea of writing a song about periods in a straightforward way and intertwined with a relationship. It's slightly heavy-handed in its approach, though, and sometimes sounds patronising.

'Cry as much as you like/ I'll do the dishes.'

GT: Exactly. 'There you go, love. Sit down and have a biscuit.' I think Chris meant well but it didn't quite come off for me.

CD: Maybe there was still a part of that patronising bastard lurking in there.

Although the girls in the front three rows didn't think so.

CD: No. My charm had worked.

GT: The vocals at the end are my favourite point of the song, where it says 'There's a point where you reach,' which is one of the few lyrical contributions I ever made. I felt the song needed something extra to bind it all together. What's curious about this song is that a lot of people still like it and I get fans shouting out for it at gigs, so it struck a chord with some people.

The band's first publicity shot, Bridgend, Wales, 1975 (from left to right: Jools, Harry, Paul Gunn, Glenn, and Chris. (Lawrence Impey)

Glenn, Chris and Jools rehearsing at Greenwich Swimming Baths in 1975. (Lawrence Impey)

Sign here please: Glenn writes an autograph, flanked by Chris and John Bentley before a show at the Fulcrum Centre, Slough, June 1981. (Sue Nicholls)

Give us a kiss: Don Snow puckers up as Chris looks on and Glenn's eyes go to the floor. Sheffield, December 1981. (Sue Nicholls)

Chris looking moody in London, March 1981, with John Bentley behind. (Sue Nicholls)

Harry Kakoulli, circa 1977: A good head of hair and popular with the girls, but a 'fumbler' on the bass. (David Bailey)

Gilson Lavis: 'A big hairy bear' swapped the building site for the stage. (David Bailey)

Jools looking for a light, while standing at Squeeze's favourite venue – the bar. (David Bailey)

Glenn and Chris do their best Status Quo impression at the Top Rank, Reading, November 1981.
(Sue Nicholls)

Glenn swaps the guitar for the keyboards at the Top Rank, Reading, November 1981.
(Sue Nicholls)

'This summer there won't be a cloud in the sky.' Filming a video on Brighton's West Pier, 1995. (Mitzi Bagpuss)

Chris and Keith strum away, circa 1995. (Mitzi Bagpuss)

Keith Wilkinson: One of many who found their songwriting ambitions thwarted by the Difford/Tilbrook duopoly. (Mitzi Bagpuss)

Glenn cracks a smile before yet another soundcheck. (Mitzi Bagpuss)

The smile says it all. Glenn enjoys performing more than anything else. (Mitzi Bagpuss)

Glenn playing another highly original guitar solo. (Mitzi Bagpuss)

'It's cool to be a cat, it's cool for cats.' Chris sings, circa 1981. (David Bailey)

Glenn celebrates his birthday in August 2004 with wife Suzanne and the author. (Simon Hanson)

Chris takes a request from the audience, circa 1994.
(Kirsten Marzec)

'LOVE CIRCLES'

Do you regard this as one of your finest moments as a singer, Chris?

CD: I don't know if I'd say that, but I'm very proud of this song because I think it's a very powerful lyric.

It contains all sorts of details about the mundane parts of a relationship. For instance, there is the 'matching dressing gown' nesting stage and later the 'phone goes back on the hook' when there's no passion left.

GT: This is Chris at the top of his game. It's a brilliant, funny lyric and, as you say, has that Chris speciality of taking little details and making them speak volumes. That is such a great talent.

So which stage of your relationship with Heidi were you when you wrote this?

CD: I was definitely at the matching dressing gown stage, poncing around on hotel balconies, eating croissants and drinking finely ground coffee.

I felt it was important in the lyric to witness all the different stages of a relationship and how they seem to come in circles. This was released as a single and had a budgerigar on the sleeve. Danny Baker used to play it all the time on his radio station. It was his favourite song of the year.

GT: My inclination musically was to do nothing that detracted from the vocal. It's a very simple song, although we did an unusual amount of harmonies, more than you usually get on a Squeeze record. Perhaps the only thing I don't like about it is my stupid guitar solo.

Why is it stupid?

GT: It's another of these wilfully atonal things that happens immediately after Keith's bass solo. A 46-year-old Glenn would give the 32-year-old Glenn a slap around the chops and say, 'Why don't you just play a nice solo, you git?'

The song's sentiment concerns the difficulties people face in making relationships last. Being in the music business must have made holding down relationships particularly difficult for you guys.

GT: Yes, it was very hard to hold down a relationship and also hard for those you're in a relationship with to fully get their head around where you are. I have rarely been what you would call famous, but nevertheless I've been on the peripherals of it for a long time and no matter what stage you are at people will recognise you and come up and chat as if they know you. If you're with a girlfriend and they have no experience of that beforehand, it takes a long while for them to get used to it.

'MELODY MOTEL'

CD: This was influenced by the Luven Brothers, who were the forerunners of the Everly Brothers. They wrote very clever songs about the horrible things that went on in small-town America. One of their songs was called 'Knoxville Girl', which is about a girl who gets drowned in the river. I wanted to tell a story that was like that, an American story rather than an English story.

I dreamt up 'Melody Motel', which was a place where there was open prostitution, where men could drive up, get a key to a room, and when they got in the room there would be a girl in there. In this story one of the girls is murdered.

GT: I love this song and I think we successfully made it sound like a genuine country record, as opposed to a pastiche. Chris's lyric was really seedy and lurid and reminds me of an American tabloid story.

Gilson's approach on drums was very unusual. The temptation for a drummer would be to play this like a swing number whereas Gilson actually played it quite rigid with the rest of the band swinging around him. This gave it a whole new feel.

I was pretending to be Elvis Presley's guitarist, Scotty Moore. I had in mind the riff that he would play as Elvis left the stage.

CD: The melody Glenn put together is awesome and Jools's piano playing is just fantastic.

GT: Jools was playing a Bo Diddley part on the piano, which slotted together well with Matt, who was playing accordion. There's a brilliant solo from Jools. Although I moaned about him not being in the studio very often, when he was there he really did the business. By far and away this is my favourite album with Jools in the band.

'Can Of Worms'

'Can Of Worms' concerns the effect of marriage break-ups on children and the role of stepfathers.

GT: I identified with the lyric instinctively because I remember after my parents had split up my mum introduced me to a bloke she was seeing and I was viewing him like a prospective dad. It was a very strange process.

Chris writes here about how kids pick up on things and how perceptive and adaptable they are, which is something I remember from my own childhood. You can take an incredible amount on board and deal with it in a matter-of-fact way.

CD: The lyric is not based on me, but this kind of situation was all around. It's part of modern day relationships where people shack up with someone who's already got kids. It must be a difficult bridge for a man to cross if they're not his kids, I guess. I wrote a similar song called 'Tightrope' on my last album.

At the time of writing 'Can Of Worms' I had recently had to tell my children that I'd left their mum and that I was with a new person whom I really loved. I wanted them to be involved with Heidi but I found it hard to mould the two camps together. When kids are that young and you split up it's really devastating for them. My soul drops when I think about it because I remember how heartbroken I felt whenever my dad went out to the shops, and he'd only be gone an hour.

GT: Musically I almost like this song. There are just a couple of bits which if I had my time all over again, I would change. Again, I was being deliberately awkward musically and I wish I'd have played it straighter.

'DR JAZZ'

This was the only Squeeze song to be written entirely by Jools, both words and music.

GT: I believe he'd had the song for a while. It's head and shoulders above anything else Jools had written with Squeeze and exposes a lot of warmth in his piano playing, which was often missing elsewhere.

CD: I admired the fact that he had gone to New Orleans to write this song because that is where his heart lies musically.

The kind of song Jools brought to the table added an extra string to Squeeze's bow.

GT: You're right. This is better than say, 'Messed Around' on *East Side Story*, which I liked, but was a pastiche. 'Dr Jazz' is not a pastiche. It sounds like the product of its influences, but with our personality in it, as opposed to our playing to a set formula.

It was a lovely delivery by the band because we were all into the vibe of the song and it's a tribute to us that we were able to deliver it as well as we did.

'IS IT TOO LATE'

GT: I don't like this, for the same reason that I do like 'Dr Jazz'. I tend not to like pastiches. It's an easy thing to slot into an album and in my defence it was fun to do, but the lasting impression is of a quick hit with no after taste.

CD: This reminds me of 'Messed Around', another rockabilly song. The lyric says very little and the song does just enough to get on to an album.

***

SQUEEZE HAD every reason to feel optimistic after producing an album artistically superior to the commercially successful *Babylon And On*. As Glenn has pointed out, Squeeze were actually sounding like a band again rather than a disparate collection of individuals, with each band member bringing his own style to the songs' arrangements.

The music press was also back on side, finally convinced of the wisdom of the band's reformation four years earlier. A typical plaudit came from *Q Magazine*, which awarded *Frank* four stars in October 1989: 'For all its unassuming matiness, as typified by the tortoise adorning the sleeve, the glamorously titled *Frank* is Squeeze's most winning work since *East Side Story* eight years ago.'

Despite its positive press, the album sank without trace and is now almost impossible to buy without resorting to either eBay or American second-hand internet sites. Chris himself has been unable to track the record down, having lost his original copies during various house moves. 'This album is a lost chestnut, really,' he sighs. 'Considering it came off the back of a big record it kind of disappeared.'

The fall from grace was painful for the band, although they must have been thankful not to have accumulated a small fortune in studio fees this time around. Glenn remembers his horror when told by A&M's radio plugger that the single 'If It's Love' stood no chance of being playlisted. 'This was even before the record was released and I thought "Fucking hell, this is a guy who's working for us telling us that. Things must be bad."

'Yet again we were suffering from falling between two stools, whatever stools they were. At the time Genesis, Mike And The Mechanics and Status Quo were getting on radio, so we never got any attention. After this point, every minor hit we had came completely out of the blue. In fact, if you look at our career, "Cool For Cats" and "Up The Junction" were the only consecutive hits we ever had.'

Within months of the album's release Jools decided to call time on his life in Squeeze, although this second departure was far easier for his bandmates to handle. 'I never gave it much thought,' admits Chris. 'He'd been and gone before and by this time Glenn and I had started to do acoustic tours on our own. We were getting closer together on the songwriting and performing side and I was beginning to feel that the future for Squeeze would be just the two of us, really.'

Glenn was equally relaxed about Jools's departure, having seen five keyboard players depart from the line-up in under a decade. The singer was also reaching the conclusion that he and Chris were becoming the major focal point of the band. 'I saw a quote recently from Joe Strummer saying, "As soon as you change one member of a band, it's not the same", but I don't agree. I know that some people think there was a classic line-up of Squeeze but I think we had several of them. People can feel fondest of one group rather than another but we produced some fantastic stuff with all of them. The only person besides me and Chris who was vital was Gilson.'

Jools's final contribution was the lauded live recording 'Round And About', which was released on both LP and video in 1990. Shortly afterwards the band were knocked sideways by the news that they were being dropped by A&M after recording nine studio albums with the label. 'I was distraught,' admits Chris. 'It was like your parents had died suddenly or kicked you out of their home. I really felt we'd hit rock bottom and was on the phone to Glenn saying, "What the hell are we going to do now?"'

The decision to axe Squeeze after 12 years was in large part due to the sale of A&M to Seagram. When the new label's accountants went though the books to do a little spring cleaning of their inherited acts, they discovered *Frank*'s poor sales, and Squeeze were immediately cut loose. This devastating body blow was softened within 48 hours when Warner Brothers stepped in with the offer of a new deal, but Glenn now realises that there was to be no coming back from Squeeze's commercial decline.

"*Frank* was a crushing disappointment because we were hoping to build on the first two albums we'd released after getting back together. From this point whenever we released an album there was the same cycle of hope followed by disappointment. It was incredibly frustrating because from *Babylon* onwards we experienced an upward curve of our records getting better and better, while our sales were going in the opposite direction."

Any hopes within the Squeeze camp of a long and profitable partnership with the American giants would vanish in little over a year. The failure of their next LP, *Play,* to shift sufficient units, resulted in the band being dropped by Warner, only to return almost immediately to the bosom of A&M. For Squeeze, such a comic turn of events was fast becoming the norm.

11 *Play*

WITH THEIR move to another label complete, Squeeze might have been forgiven for thinking that they had arrested their commercial decline. Yet an ill-advised tour to America supporting rock dinosaurs Fleetwood Mac would bring home to the band just how far they had fallen from grace.

Their management, now consisting of Miles Copeland and John Lay, felt a high-profile support tour would get the band heard by a different audience and regain American interest. In fact, at the vast majority of shows, most people refused to take their seats until Fleetwood Mac came onstage.

From headlining at Madison Square Garden three years earlier, Squeeze were now playing to empty stadiums. Any illusion of a glorious stateside return had been smashed.

'That tour was a total waste of time and possibly the most distressing thing we ever did,' moans Glenn. 'It was soul-destroying.'

When the band weren't playing in deserted aerodromes they resorted to hustling smaller gigs to make ends meet, after Fleetwood Mac began cancelling tour dates at random. 'We were mucked around by them,' says Chris. 'At any moment one of them would say they were ill and they would cancel gigs. They could afford to do that, but we couldn't. We were stuck in the middle of nowhere with all our gear in their truck, which was a very unhealthy place to be. In the end we got all our gear off the bus so that we could play some gigs on our own.'

Although their personal relationship remained highly combustible, Glenn and Chris knew that the coming year was crucial to turning around their sharp commercial decline, and both vowed to knuckle down to work. It was clear that the ending of Glenn's first marriage in 1988, and subsequent relationship with second wife Jane, had eased much of the tension with Chris, who was going through a similar period of wedded bliss. The autumn of 1990 saw Heidi announcing that Chris would be a father again the following June, although it would become clear over the resulting 12 months that her husband's happiness was at best surface deep.

Glenn himself became a father for the first time in October 1990 when wife Jane gave birth to Ted, who was followed 18 months later by the pair's second son, Louis.

Initially enthusiastic about the new act on their roster, Warner Brothers gave Squeeze their pick of two producers, Nile Rodgers, who had just worked on the B52s' *Cosmic Thing* album, or Tony Berg, who had recently worked with Michael Penn and Wendy & Lisa. Embracing Berg's left-field approach to production, the band chose him, but for a variety of reasons the recording process descended into a prolonged nightmare.

The initial recordings took place in late 1990 at Peter Gabriel's studio in Box, Wiltshire, with Steve Nieve of The Attractions filling in on keyboards. However, Warner Brothers were insistent that the album be completed under their noses in Los Angeles.

In January 1991 the four permanent Squeeze members moved into a house in Beverly Hills and, unaware of Chris's growing sense of personal desolation, Glenn believed that this might help to rekindle the pair's friendship. Nothing could have been further from the truth.

Desperately missing his expectant wife and away from the comforts of home, Chris was descending further into the depths of alcoholism and felt an urge to regain his own space. 'I felt resentful the whole time I was there. The studio was in Tony's garage at his house, so he was able to be around his kids the whole time, which I found really hard. I'd been cut off from my kids and also Heidi was pregnant, so I felt very angry and frustrated.'

Chris spent much of his time in LA listening fretfully to a short wave radio in Berg's pool room next to the studio, as the first Gulf War unfolded. 'I kept a diary every day, all about the bombing that I heard on the radio. It was a very strange time.' Within a week Chris was on the verge of mental collapse and had moved out of the band's rented home to his own apartment 30 miles down the road, in an attempt to shield his almost uncontrollable drink and drug bouts from view.

Two horrific incidents illustrate Chris's diabolical state of mind. 'Once, I left the studio about three in the morning having clearly drunk too much. People were saying I shouldn't get in the car, but I ignored them and proceeded to drive the wrong way down the freeway. I woke up at about two the next afternoon with no recollection of how I'd got home. Gradually it all came back to me and I realised that I'd nearly been killed. God knows how I survived.

'Another time I got lost in a Mexican part of town and could hardly see out of the windscreen. People were harassing me in other cars because I was driving so erratically.'

Eventually, Chris could bear no more and took what was arguably the best course of action for himself: returning home. Having been kept in the dark over Chris's spiralling mental state, Glenn was perhaps understandably far from happy at being abandoned. When the other band members also began beating a hasty retreat to Britain, Glenn realised that he had been lumbered yet again.

He recalls with some chagrin, 'Once again I was in the position where everyone else had buggered off, which was hard for me. I enjoyed making the album but I didn't enjoy being out there by myself. Robbie Robertson from The Band came into the studio to work on his record and said, "Where's the rest of the band?" I said, "They're back in England." He said, "That's happened to me too."' To cap it all, after spending six weeks virtually alone with Berg, Glenn found himself denied the co-production credit he felt his work deserved.

Although the finished recordings were among the most polished Squeeze ever produced, the relationship between Glenn and Berg was far from smooth. Glenn recalls lengthy sessions where the producer had his ear glued to the telephone, leaving him to soldier on alone in the studio. On other days, Glenn would arrive at work to find that Berg had added his own guitar parts to tracks without even acknowledging the fact.

'It was a funny way to go about things. Tony is a lovely player and came up with things that I could never do. I don't know whether he thought I was so sensitive that I couldn't possibly stomach someone else playing the guitar, but that wasn't the case.'

Chris's recollections of his brief time in the studio were of Glenn and Berg at loggerheads, and he believes the pair were too similar in personality and outlook to make the partnership work. 'They were probably too alike and their relationship suffered as a result. They were both great guitar players and both had an ear for production and melody, so they were always battling.

'Glenn would virtually lock himself in the studio to do his solos. When I was leaving for England, Tony came outside to speak to me. He was upset and told me that he needed to talk to me about Glenn. He said he was finding it difficult to communicate with him and I said, "Well, join the queue."'

Glenn counters this assertion by pointing out that Berg made similar comments about his partner and claims the producer had a manipulative streak. 'Tony was a really creative guy and great to work with, but I think that there was a little bit of dividing going on, which I think came from him. Tony was prone to saying some things to one person and other things to another. There was quite a lot of politics going on between Tony and Warner and us on that record.'

Chris believes that both Glenn and Berg were deeply passionate about the record but that their inability to communicate their ideas to one other led to a clash. He added, 'I don't mean this to be critical because making a record is a really tense time. Emotions and tempers are very close to the surface. On every record we made there was tension.'

In spite of this underlying tension, *Play* would become one of both Glenn and Chris's favourite Squeeze albums.

***

'Satisfied'

GT: I have to give credit to Tony for his production on this. I always thought that 'Satisfied' was a mood song, capturing post-coital loveliness, when you're in the throes of immediate, fantastic love. It was a simple song for me to write because it slotted into place and in the studio we added a veneer of sophistication not there originally.

CD: We did have a problem with the chorus. I remember Tony saying, 'When we get to the chorus why does the chord have to go down instead of up? The chorus never lifts.' We fought to keep it as it was and succeeded. It is very Squeeze. We didn't want it to be too successful, after all.

GT: I never understood why this was released as a single because two other songs on *Play* are of the very best we've ever written, 'Letting Go' and 'The Truth'. I don't think that 'Satisfied' is in the same class.

CD: We did a great video that got close to describing the wonderful bliss of the lyric. We filmed it in the desert and it started to rain. A chap who lived in a shack there said it hadn't rained there since 1934 and that we'd brought it with us.

'CRYING IN MY SLEEP'

'Crying In My Sleep' is a jaunty little number.

GT: Jaunty is a good word for it. We went round the houses with 'Crying In My Sleep' because of my ongoing battle to get something vaguely influenced by dance music into Squeeze.

There are lots of session musicians playing.

CD: Yes. There was a horn section who were brilliant. They could really play. This is more of a production than a song really. As a song there's not a lot there.

Were you in the studio when this was recorded?

CD: I was in my usual place, sitting on the couch at the back.

GT: Tony didn't really understand what I was aiming for with this song, so it ended up being a horrible bastard son of our ideas. He was pulling it one way, I was pulling it another, and it ended up somewhere slightly uncomfortably in the middle.

I would have liked it to have been straightforward, dancier and somewhat tougher. The melodic content and the song was there, but once you have the melody and lyric, you can do any number of things to a song.

Sometimes the best thing you can do is to toughen up a song rather than make it sweeter, because I do enough of that in the tune already. It doesn't need any more. The brass parts were really well played but slightly naff and it sounds more like a TV theme tune than a song.

'LETTING GO'

CD: This is one of the most brilliant songs which Glenn and I have ever written. I can't listen to it without choking up. Glenn's music is so stirring. It was a very difficult song to play live because the chord sequences are very intricate, but on the odd occasion when I got it right I was almost crying because it was so emotive. It's such a sad relationship, like a really sad Picasso painting.

GT: We got this one absolutely right. It's a very melancholy lyric, and I'm sure most people have experienced that stage in a relationship where it's not quite over because you can't quite summon up the courage to end it. Half the song is about the avoidance of acknowledging that the relationship is over, and I think the way Chris tackled the subject was great.

I was trying to be Prince melodically when I wrote this, and of course it sounds nothing like that, but to me it captures the mood of the lyric. It's not one where I've gone for the opposite effect. Steve Nieve's playing on this is great and Gilson's playing is brilliant. I'm also quite pleased with my backing vocals on this. I was being Abba. There you go. Abba and Prince in one song.

Gilson's playing brushes, isn't he?

GT: Yes, he swaps between brushes and sticks but it's wonderful, restrained, intelligent playing. Steve's keyboards are pivotal to the song. He's one of those players who will do three entirely different takes and won't remember what he's done on the last one, but each will be brilliant in its approach. He's so naturally gifted, so I built my guitar around what he played.

CD: The beauty of the song is definitely in the keyboard playing. I'd always wanted to work with Steve because we'd been friends for many years, and when he came in to the studio it was a dream come true. He played that really fantastic baroque-type harpsichord. As I said, this is truly one of the high points of our songwriting career.

'THE DAY I GET HOME'

CD: This was a fun song to make. You can hear my short wave radio at the start.

The lyric is about the joys of returning home after being on the road.

CD: That feeling of coming home after being on tour is very special when the simple things about English life come straight back to you. As soon as you fly into British air space you notice that everything is green and then you see a red London bus and the jet black taxis, and it all seems an extension of your persona. Then you get a cab across south London where you live, put your bags down, and you can smell the cheese on toast from the grill.

I thought Glenn was very inventive on this particular song. In spite of the negatives, the one thing about working with Tony Berg was that Glenn really rose to his game musically and became crafted in everything he did.

GT: When I wrote the music it was like The Pogues, very raucous and fast, and I wanted to do it with the accordion and fiddle. It was a jaunty, two-step number, but the version we recorded was prompted by Tony, and brought out qualities in the song that I hadn't seen.

There's an air of melancholy about the song that passed me by at first. I just thought it was a straightforward knuckle-headed 'it's been great being on tour, it'll be fantastic getting home'. But actually there's another element to it, which I hadn't spotted, that touring can take its toll. Overall the mood of *Play* is quite melancholic. It's not an 'up' album and this song could have been very 'up' but because it was dark, it added a whole different dimension.

Had you begun to find touring a chore by this stage?

CD: Yes. For me touring had become a little bit of a dead weight. By this time I had moved out into the country, to Kent. Basically I wanted to put up a fence and stay within its boundary. I had to do that in order to discover that I then had to tear the fence down and explore another part of my life. For me it was an essential part of my life's journey.

'THE TRUTH'

What can you tell me about the lyric?

CD: Glenn always said I never lived in reality for very long. I was always very economical with the truth because my imagination took me to another world. This helped me to be creative but it could also create a distance between myself and Glenn or whoever I was with.

'The Truth' is a kind of apology in a way. It's saying, 'Yes, I did lie. I did cheat. I was a complete arsehole.' I'm not making excuses, but maybe there was a reason for me to be dishonest, because I couldn't handle the truth. Going off into my imagination meant there was a fine line between my songwriting and reality. It's only now that I'm beginning to realise this and I find it difficult to even think about. It's OK to have your head in the clouds but you must have your feet on the ground, whereas my head was in the clouds but my feet were up there as well. 'The Truth' was a message from me to Glenn and others, apologising but saying 'this is how I am'.

GT: This was a very bold song for Chris to write. Part of Chris's talent as a lyricist it is that he can be fanciful in his storytelling and there are borderlines where you're never quite sure where fiction begins and truth ends. For Chris to put that in a song was incredibly powerful and I'm sure everyone can identify with it to a certain extent. There are always issues in people's lives where they make the decision about whether the truth is told or not. This is one of Chris's very best lyrics.

Did you have problems with Chris and his battle with the truth?

GT: I've never found Chris to be straightforward. Certainly in the past he had some problems stating his opinion about things and would rather just say whatever people wanted to hear. In certain circumstances that's fine, but ultimately it's unsatisfying because one doesn't know where one stands when dealing with someone like that. I know Chris was having a lot of problems at this time and I'd never hold it against him but that side of him is difficult to deal with.

The music has a country feel to it.

GT: It has, although we went all round the houses with this one. When it was first written it was more like a raucous, heavy rock song, which didn't sound right. It was a bit like 'Jet' by Wings. We went through a number of permutations but now I can't imagine it sounding any other way than it did on the record.

'HOUSE OF LOVE'

This is quite an odd arrangement. It jumps all over the place.

GT: It does jump about a lot, but I really like it. Bob Clearmountain's mixing was absolutely fantastic. It's one of those songs that's deliberately awkward and not exactly easy listening but neither is it unfriendly. It's just difficult.

This is probably the most produced song on the album.

GT: That's really in the mix. We gave Bob the song and we said, 'Go as mad as you like' and he did, adding the phasing and those weird delays. He's got such good ears.

CD: This is a terrible song. I got the feeling from Glenn that this was going on the album whether I liked it or not. Every time I told him I didn't think it was good enough he would put 100 per cent into making it work because he was angry at my going back to England. When this went on the record I was very disheartened, but what could I say?

'Cupid's Toy'

CD: This is about a young lad who goes into a club and thinks he is Jack The Lad, but the twist of the story is that he can't pull it off. There's nothing awe-inspiring, musically or lyrically. It became a production number, like 'Satisfied', and so much had been spent on its production that it had to be on the record.

GT: It's an observational song and musically I think it sounds very polished. I was slightly shooting myself in the foot with the middle eight, which doesn't measure up to the song, but it's catchy and we worked hard on getting the mood right. There are a lot of overdubs but they are all very sparse. They add colour, but you're not really aware of them when you listen.

'Gone To The Dogs'

CD: This was a song we were asked to write for a sitcom about dog racing. We went to the dogs at Walthamstow, had some dinner, observed what went on, and took it all in. It didn't make the TV but it did make the album.

This is in the old Squeeze tradition of London songs.

CD: 'Gone To The Dogs' and 'Sunday Street' were the two English songs on the album and they stick out a bit.

GT: It's always interesting in your writing career to occasionally refer back to a period of your past, either musically or lyrically. You'll never have the same take on things but it provides a reference point and this song very much refers to the start of Squeeze. I like the lyric much more than I like the tune, which is very inspired by Sly Stone and 'If You Want Me To Stay'. I wish it had been slightly less so.

'Walk A Straight Line'

This is quite a pared-down song.

GT: I'd written it much more poppy than it turned out. Again, Tony Berg was quite instrumental in bringing out the song instrumentally. Bruce Hornsby played the accordion wonderfully. I like the sparseness of it. I'm not good at being sparse so it was nice to have some help from Tony.

The story deals with the life of an alcoholic. Was this autobiographical?

CD: It opens with the lines 'I need some help/ Help to decide/ Whether it's our love/ That steps out of time.' That was me saying that I needed some help, although I camouflaged it by writing this story about two people getting married. He is an alcoholic who can't walk down the aisle straight because he's so drunk all the time.

Around this time I had been to a treatment centre and had an interview. I filled in a form and was told I should come in, but I said I couldn't at that moment, because I had to go on tour and record an album. He took me into a room full of people having treatment and I thought, 'My God, they're all nutters, I'm definitely not coming back here.' I went to my car and drove away as quickly as I could. I just wasn't ready for it.

A lot of people investigate treatment, have a prod and say it's not for me just yet, but eventually they go back. This is a really important song for me because I was owning up to the fact that I needed help.

Describe your average day as an alcoholic.

CD: It was very organised. I'd get up about 11 or 12 o'clock in the morning, go to the studio or start whatever I was working on. It would feel like I was wearing a Norman helmet all day because of the hangover. By the early evening I'd think, 'I quite fancy a drink, I've got a bit of a thirst on.' Then from about six until three in the morning I would be hard at it. Once you've drunk so much it doesn't take a lot to get you back in the groove. You're topping up the whole time because your blood is just cooking. If you have one glass you're back on form again. Suddenly you're Jack The Lad and you're off and running. It would be accompanied by 20 fags and finished off with a bag of bat food, as we used to call it.

The thing about being an addict is that you can be quite controlled with it and say that between the hours of say six and twelve I'm going to drink, and the rest of the day I'm not. You think that no harm will come to you but over a period of years it really takes its toll.

'Sunday Street'

CD: This is another reminder about what is great about London. I'm not particularly fond of it. It's just a description of a Sunday in London. It was our first single from the album and got a lot of airplay. It was another of Danny Baker's favourites but got absolutely nowhere, although that was like water off a duck's back to us by then.

GT: This is another jaunty Squeeze song and Warner Brothers leapt on it as being most like the old Squeeze. It was possibly the most 'air guitar' solo I ever played and very unlike me. I've never done one like that before or since. The song has an air of optimism about it and it's one of those ones that, in spite of being very descriptive, conjures up exactly the same pictures in my head whenever I hear it. We had two of the guys from Spinal Tap on this record, Christopher Guest and Michael McKean.

Did you get your amp up to 11?

GT: Certainly did on that solo, mate.

'Wicked And Cruel'

GT: The backing track was recorded as a completely different song. Warners objected to the subject matter because it was a graphic description of giving birth. I thought it was a really great song but they would absolutely not have it because it offended their sensibilities. There was a culture clash between the way in which Chris was writing and the way Warners saw things, so it had to go.

CD: Glenn has a far better memory than I have. I really don't remember that.

GT: 'Wicked And Cruel' was an older lyric I hadn't done anything with and by this point Chris was back in London. I picked this out of a song book and shoe-horned it in to fit the music. Chris had no idea what I'd done.

Did you say, 'It serves you right for going home'?

GT: There was an element of that. I was very pleased with how this song turned out. I had a terrible cold when I did the vocal, so it sounds very rough and actually benefits from that. I like the lyric because it has a lovely line in petty vindictiveness which appeals to me.

'When I die I'll return as a housefly/ And land upon her wall.'

GT: Yes. She hates spiders so much, that they get sprayed down the bathroom plug hole. It makes me laugh.

Gilson is prominent on this.

GT: Yes, and Keith's bass playing is really good. I seem to remember Gilson and Keith and Chris were all there at some point, but mostly at the beginning. Keith had to re-do his bass part. It's much more rocky than Squeeze would normally play. The drum part does not exactly go along with that flow, possibly because Gilson was playing another song when he recorded his track.

CD: Everything was spot-on in the production. There was no margin for error like there had been on *Frank*. The record had to be Yves St Laurent. We played this a couple of times live and it had a lot of balls to it.

'THERE IS A VOICE'

There's a butt edit from 'Wicked And Cruel' into what is probably the darkest song on a very bleak album.

GT: I saw this as Chris's despair leaking out. It was the first song I wrote for the record. I couldn't quite understand what Chris was going through at that time.

CD: This lyric is indicative of exactly how I was at the end of this record. 'There is a voice within us all/ That says destruct/ Go to the wall.' It sums up beautifully the way I felt. Glenn and I had quite an intense battle over this lyric. He kept saying to me, 'What do you mean, "Each day is a night"? Explain yourself.' I would say that they were just the same to me, that day is night and night is day. I tried to explain to him what I meant but he didn't get it and kept asking me to change it. Yet every time he sang those words, it sounded right.

GT: In some ways I had as much of a clue about what was going on in Chris's life as anyone who had bought the album. We didn't talk about it much. I'd just get signals from what he was writing.

Like 'The Truth', because it was a personal lyric and not a story song, it was more powerful. Everyone can recognise an echo of that sentiment within themselves. However strong or weak, that impulse to break things up and destroy them is there.

CD: Musically, I think Glenn's tune is genius. I'm very grateful that he picked up this lyric and made the song what it was because it's magical. When I look at the lyric it's basically saying that I've got to get off my arse, look into my soul, and get a grip. A year later I had.

In the interviews we've done for this book we've travelled from an 18-year-old boy in 1973 to someone who between 1990 and 1993 had reached a brick wall. The great thing about songwriting and being in a band is that you get an opportunity to share this with other people. That's why I don't mind talking about it.

A lot of people I know in the industry won't talk about this stuff but I think it's really important to share your darkness and shed light on other people's darkness. The only way I got well was to listen to other people. I remember seeing Elton John on TV one morning talking to David Frost and I cried my eyes out in my hotel room. I thought, 'Elton has got this exactly right. Why the fuck can't I stand up and realise the same thing?'

***

GLENN CAME back to England to be rejoined by his bandmates in Real World Studios, where they added various overdubs and mixed the album with Bob Clearmountain. The end result was the smoothest, most accomplished sound the band had ever produced.

'Four songs make the album for me,' says Chris. '"Letting Go", "The Truth", "Walk A Straight Line", and maybe "Wicked And Cruel". They are the songs that are important to me but the production of the album is really strong. Audibly, it's a beautiful record to listen to, so that even though I don't particularly like 'Crying In My Sleep' or 'Cupid's Toy', when I listen to them they sound good. The production was the be all and end all of the record and the musicianship was brilliant. But for me personally it was a really dark record because of what was going on in my life. I was semi-detached from the album and in fact Tony Berg played all the guitar I would have played.'

The mood of the album was certainly sombre, and saw Chris's fabled use of humour in his lyrics almost entirely disappear. Only the jaunty 'Sunday Street' hinted at the chirpy Squeeze sound of old, an element of the band's songwriting that would return only briefly on their final three records.

Play's underlying sense of gloom was mirrored by Squeeze's confusing relationship with Warner Brothers who, without any warning, decided to limit promotion of the record to a bare minimum. Glenn remembers the extraordinary turnaround from Squeeze being the label's darlings to virtual outcasts in the blink of an eye.

'We'd been A&R'd to perfection and spent a lot of time working on the two songs they wanted as singles, although I'd never have chosen to release "Satisfied" nor "Sunday Street". Lenny Waronker was the A&R man on the album and kept telling us it was brilliant. It felt like at last we were working with people who understood us. Then the day the record came out we were told that Warners weren't going to do anything with it.

'The people at Warners were very talented but they didn't express themselves in any way that we could understand. It was like dealing with a hall of mirrors.'

The following year, 1992, might well have heralded the end of Squeeze, with Gilson's second departure, and Chris's abandoning of the band, as he finally sought help for the alcoholism that was threatening his very existence.

The prelude to the drummer's departure was his recent separation from his wife and subsequent decision to start drinking again. Gilson's old demons quickly resurfaced and, according to Chris, his behaviour became 'increasingly difficult'.

At a stormy band meeting Gilson and Squeeze parted company, although both sides have differing recollections of the circumstances. In an interview with *Mojo* in January 1996 Gilson recalled, 'I was kicked out after an American tour. I'd just separated from my wife and was in a bit of a state. I'd been sober for seven years and I decided that having a drink would be a good idea. So on this tour I was a bit of a mess, and very depressed. When we got back there was a band meeting and I was told I wasn't needed any more...If anybody's to blame it was me for taking it too seriously, because it's all a game.'

Both Chris and Glenn deny this version of events. According to the former, the band tried to protect Gilson from the worst excesses of his own behaviour, but found caging the tiger an impossible task. 'We called a meeting and Gilson sat down in our manager's office and he just walked, rather than be pushed.'

Glenn is even more vociferous in his denial and recalls that Gilson was becoming increasingly frustrated at the band's lack of success, magnified by their axing by Warners after just one album. 'Gilson wasn't kicked out at all. I would never have kicked him out. He felt we were banging our heads against a brick wall and after we were dropped by Warners we were left in yet another void.

'Gilson also wanted a share of the songwriting and Chris and I were both against that because I don't believe we were ever U2, coming up with songs together. The band would play a full part in the way the songs sounded but Chris and I wrote them. I felt I could play a full part in an arrangement of "Fly Me To The Moon" but it still wouldn't make it my song. Gilson was also tired of touring, and in a band environment you can only be as happy as the person who is least happy. You can't but feel enmeshed in that. So he left.'

Within a few months Glenn found himself performing on a strenuous Squeeze tour of America as the only original member in the band. Unbeknown to the singer, his musical soulmate of 18 years had been on the verge of a nervous breakdown, fuelled by almost two decades of alcohol abuse.

'Chris was really struggling with his drinking, which I was blissfully unaware of. I hardly ever saw him socially, so I never realised how much he was drinking. He was very secretive and distant, so when he turned himself in I was completely flabbergasted.'

Chris's decision that he couldn't face a tour of the States was made in dramatic fashion. While the rest of the band were checking in at Heathrow Airport, Chris made a short phone call to the band's gob-smacked manager John Lay to say he wouldn't be coming with them.

'I woke up that morning with a terrible hangover and feeling very sick. I packed my bags, drove to London to say goodbye to the kids, and when I got to their house I got upset about going away again for six weeks. I knew exactly the sort of tour it would be, with everyone drinking heavily, and I suddenly realised that I couldn't go.

'I called a friend of mine who had been in treatment and said, "I really need help." Within 15 minutes he was round at the house, put me in the car and drove me to a treatment centre. I phoned John on the cell phone from the car and was in bits. The next thing Glenn phoned and said, "Come on. Get on the plane. It will be alright." At this point I couldn't really speak, so my friend picked up the phone and said to Glenn that I was ill and needed to be looked after. Glenn accepted it very reluctantly. The next thing I knew I woke up in the centre.'

A shell-shocked Glenn continued the tour, playing with Keith, new drummer Pete Thomas and Steve Nieve on keyboards. 'In this situation I just had to get on with it. We did the tour and I said we should split the tour money as though Chris had been with us. I'm not trying to say what a good bloke I am, but Chris was in a bad place and I wanted to help him out.' However, when Chris went through a second personal crisis seven years later and failed to make another US tour, Glenn's attitude had hardened, which widened the rift between the pair and hastened the break-up of their partnership.

In July 1992, Squeeze were offered a slot supporting Bryan Adams at Wembley Stadium and got a message to Chris asking if he would like to rejoin for the gig.

Still recovering in the clinic in Canterbury, Chris ruminated on what to do. 'It was going to the biggest gig we'd done in this country. I thought about it long and hard and spoke about it with my new friends at the centre, but I decided that it wasn't important for me to play Wembley. My goal was to get well.'

Glenn relished the occasion and claims that playing without Chris by his side helped give him 'full reign' of his personality, something which he believed had been suppressed by Chris's more sedate stage presence. 'I asked the entire Wembley audience if they'd like to get up and go mad or if they fancied a minute's quiet so we could lie down and have a sleep. They chose the minute's quiet, so we laid down onstage for a whole minute. It was a fantastic moment because it tested everyone's nerve.

'Mine and Chris's approach to being onstage was to be the least offensive to each other and so the more extreme bits of my personality would be ironed out. I remember taking a whole audience of 2,000 outside into the car park once and he absolutely hated it. He liked the division between us and the audience and felt very uncomfortable at being out of control, so I thought I'd better not do it again. We cancelled each other out in many ways but he cancelled me out more because there weren't things that Chris wanted to do that I found distasteful.'

By this stage the band looked doomed. Their fraught personality clashes had if anything deteriorated further over the recording of *Play*, they had lost Gilson's influential figure, and Chris appeared on the verge of giving up the music business. Yet 12 weeks of intensive therapy revitalised Chris; the combination of his renouncing booze and the rebuilding of his shattered psyche acted as a catharsis. Within a year Squeeze were back on top of their game and making what would arguably be the greatest record of their career.

12 *Some Fantastic Place*

WHEN HE stepped into the outside world again in the autumn of 1992 Chris was a man re-born, determined to produce a groundbreaking record with his long-standing partner. Towards the end of his intensive treatment programme Chris had begun writing lyrics, many of which would end up on Squeeze's tenth studio album. 'I'd hit rock bottom when I went into the treatment centre but that whole 12 week period provided the most amazing turnaround in my entire life. It was incredible, almost like going in with two left feet and coming out with both feet in the right place.'

Chris was touched by the support he received from his many friends in the music business, including a phone call from Elton John and a long letter from former Squeeze member Jools Holland. He was also grateful for the help offered by his old mucker Glenn. 'One very inspiring thing for me was that Glenn was really open to the change in my life. He really embraced the fact that something had happened to me and was very inquisitive. We talked for hours and hours about it, which I think brought us closer together.'

With their friendship renewed, Glenn and Chris began writing songs together in the same room, something they had done just once before, when they wrote their last major hit, 'Hourglass'. Despite this newly-found camaraderie, which led to some of the best songs Squeeze had written for years, Glenn believed that Chris still found sitting in a room for long periods with him a difficult proposition. 'It was really great to work with him, even though it was probably the last time we did so. I still felt that Chris looked slightly uncomfortable, like he had a carrot stuck up his arse which he couldn't wait to get out.'

Yet again Squeeze went into the studio with a new line-up, with Pete Thomas continuing as a replacement for Gilson, and Paul Carrack returning to the fold after a 12-year absence. Carrack had been approached by Chris to rejoin the group, although neither of his former songwriting colleagues were under any illusions that his would be anything but a fleeting return.

Thomas's drumming was in marked contrast to his predecessor. Chris describes his style as 'that of a song drummer', in contrast to the more inventive Gilson. Chris explains, 'What I found inspiring about working with Pete was that he'd only been in the band a couple of days when he called me up and said, "Can you fax me all the lyrics?" I thought, "What's going on here? A drummer asking about the songs." He said, "I want to know what you are trying to say," which I found really rewarding.'

Having been stung by the unhappy experience of recording in Los Angeles, Glenn suggested to Chris and Keith that the three invest in their own studio. This would drastically reduce the cost of producing their albums and also ensure that Glenn wouldn't be left high and dry if the others lost interest. 'I thought that if I ended up doing a lot of the work in the studio then it might as well be somewhere that was close to where I lived.'

His two colleagues were not keen on the idea, something which to this day Chris regrets. 'I wish I'd had the foresight to say, "Let's put in 20 grand each and build a really great place in Greenwich and let other people in the community use it." Funnily enough, I was thinking recently that if we ever got back together again that this would be something that would be really useful to do.'

Glenn bought his own studio in Blackheath, called 45RPM, which he still owns and uses to produce his solo albums, while Chris later built a studio in Rye. In early 1993 the band decamped to 45RPM with producer Pete Smith to start laying down tracks amid a far greater sense of harmony than was evident when making *Play*.

***

'Everything In The World'

This opening song has such an accomplished sound.

CD: Yes, it's a great start to the record. It's saying, 'We're back in business.'

GT: It's often hard to write songs that are up-tempo and sound chirpy without seeming clichéd, and we really captured what the band could do on this. It had a very optimistic sound, which was nice because we'd missed it for a while. Despite some of the themes I think *Some Fantastic Place* is an optimistic album.

CD: I can't say too much about the lyric. It's just a good song. The riff is very powerful and reminds me of The B52s. It has that kind of rhythm and American radio vibe about it. Whenever I hear this I think about the video which accompanies it, which was mad. There's cross-dressing going on and people wearing all sorts of outfits.

The other thing about this track is that I can hear myself playing guitar. I really participated both on guitar and vocally. On previous albums I was not so bold as to do that.

GT: Chris would be the first to say that he's not a natural musician in the sense of picking up the guitar and playing easily. He can play but that's not his primary function and if we were up against it in the studio the quickest thing was for me to play his guitar part. It wasn't me elbowing him out but a matter of expediency.

'Some Fantastic Place'

This song is a tribute to your first girlfriend Maxine, who died in 1992.

GT: That's right. She was my first proper girlfriend whom I loved very much, and she contracted leukaemia. Throughout her illness she was very positive in her outlook and never lost her sense of optimism. I can't imagine what it must be like to be in that situation, but she never let it get her down. Sadly, her illness eventually got the better of her and she died, which was devastating for both Chris and I. She was a really smart and funny person and a very influential person for Squeeze.

CD: Maxine was the one who bullied Glenn into phoning me, and when we fell out while we were living together, she was the one who got us talking to each other again. She was a mother hen to the two of us and I appreciated her friendship. I went to see her in Lewisham Hospital, when the doctors had told her she had only a few months to live. In fact, she lasted another couple of years and went through every sort of medicine she could find.

Before I went into the clinic for treatment I went to see her down in the country. She was a bit green and had lost a lot of colour in her face. She said to me, 'There are two things you should be doing. One is to stop drinking because it is ruining your life, and the other is that you should spread your wings and start writing with other people.' When she died what she'd said made total sense. It was only when I went into treatment that I did my first writing outside my relationship with Glenn.

GT: When Chris gave me this lyric it was obviously about Maxine, although typically he never actually told me this. I sat down at the piano and the music just came out. It's such a lovely song and I remember playing it to Jane when we'd just written it and she burst into tears.

What I've found out since is that even though it wasn't a hit, it's a powerful song for lots of people who follow Squeeze. It comes to mean a lot to anyone who's had someone close to them die. It's actually my favourite Squeeze song. Anything that's from the heart can't be beaten.

CD: It was a very spiritual moment when I was told of Maxine's death. I sat in the garden of the treatment centre crying my eyes out. The band was touring in America and I could only speak to them on the phone. I wanted to be with Glenn and to hug him.

I sat there and wrote this lyric from top to bottom without pen leaving paper. A friend of mine who was there with me, a famous drummer, came over to me and handed me a cup of tea. I remember the taste of it to this day because the last thing I wanted was a cup of tea. I wanted a proper drink. I wanted to get over the wall and run to the nearest pub to get arseholed.

The following week the centre let me out to go to the funeral. I did not stay for the wake because it would have been too alcoholic for me. So Heidi picked me up, took me to the church where I had a good cry. The only member of the band who was there was Jools, who played the piano. Glenn was still on tour.

What's interesting about the music is that the guitar solo is lifted from one of the first songs we ever wrote in about 1973. It took me a long time to see what Glenn had done, but it was very clever because it linked the past with the present.

GT: The feel of the song was taken from three sources: 'My Sweet Lord', 'Oh Happy Day', and 'The More I See You', by Chris Montez, which had a dreamy, almost ethereal quality. I wanted to use the same vibes and am very pleased that I managed to capture that feel.

'Third Rail'

CD: If I'm not reading too much into it, alcohol is the third rail, the energy keeping my relationship and my life together. I suppose the lyric is questioning that dependence.

Are you referring to your relationship with Glenn?

CD: It's only when I look back and reflect that I wonder whether it was about Glenn, but I don't think so. I think it was about a relationship which had lost its energy. There was a lot of that going on in my life.

With Heidi?

CD: With all my relationships. When you get sober a lot of reflecting takes place. It's like going in the garden and turning the earth over. All the worms come up when you start pulling up all the weeds. Every time you pull up a weed another comes straight back at you.

It sounds like it was not an easy time for you, despite coming out of darkness.

CD: I had a new lease on life and was truly grateful but what it did was unearth lots of things, on which I had to spend time reflecting. I looked inward at what I'd been doing and that rubbed off on some of what I was writing at that time. I'm still writing about it today because I had 23 years of solid drinking without a day off, so it is going to take a lot of weeding out. I'm only 11 years sober. It can take a lifetime to sort all this out.

What about the music, Glenn?

GT: When I started writing this album I'd first got into writing with Cubase, a computer program. It sounds like such a natural guitar song, but I wrote it all on keyboards, even the guitar line on keyboards. Pete Smith said, "Why don't you just do it on bloody guitar?," which of course was right. I learnt how to play it on guitar and it sounded great.

'Loving You Tonight'

CD: At this time I was living out in Rye and doing a lot of driving between there and Glenn's studio, and also from the treatment centre in Canterbury. I was spending a lot of time in the car and had lots of ideas coming to me while I was driving. I had a little Dictaphone in the car and one day I was driving along the A268 and all this lyric was written. It was exactly what I saw on the journey.

"I see the signpost/ The road slowly bends/ Nothing in my life makes sense."

CD: I can see that corner now. Every time I pass it I think about that song. Glenn came up with this super romantic vibe in his tune and of course when Paul started singing it, the song became wonderful.

GT: The song wasn't written for Paul originally and had quite a camp arrangement when I wrote it, which thankfully we got rid of. It springs from the lyric, which is very simple, and I can't help but reflect on Chris's situation. He was taking stock of all the simple things that were nice about his life. We gave it to Paul and again he made it sound ten times better than it would have done.

Did you think that Paul's reappearance in the band would be shortlived?

GT: Definitely. Our line-up was changing continuously by this stage. I would have feared that instability beforehand but I learnt to embrace it and to enjoy it. I used to think, 'This is going to be Squeeze for the next year, and if someone leaves let's embrace that as a positive as well.' It was liberating for me to learn to appreciate that because it relieved so much worry. If you're constantly worrying about how you're going to keep a band together it's unhealthy.

'IT'S OVER'

This is another lamenting lyric, dealing with the break-up of a relationship.

GT: Yes, but doesn't it sound jolly? It sounds almost joyous and I like that. It goes back to that earlier Squeeze thing of writing against the grain of the lyric, which adds a different element. It showed that it might not be such a bad thing that the relationship was over.

I think that *Some Fantastic Place* benefited from getting Chris Braide involved, who at that point was only about 18. I'd started working with him outside of Squeeze and he was such a great vocalist who could reach the high notes that I couldn't. He was so keen to be involved in the album, because he hadn't appeared on a record before, so he was involved on the backing vocals for 'Third Rail', 'It's Over' and 'Some Fantastic Place'.

CD: I used to love doing this one live. It was like a John Lennon song. The extraordinary thing about this record is Glenn's voice. On *Play*, *Some*

Fantastic Place and *Ridiculous*, Glenn's voice had reached a pinnacle. He sounded very mature and lived in and there was no mistaking that it was Glenn singing. It could not have been anyone else on the planet.

When he went to the microphone in the studio to sing 'It's Over', he took so much time correcting himself, and yet every take sounded brilliant. It was awe inspiring to hear him sing.

'Cold Shoulder'

GT: 'Cold Shoulder' represents the final stage of Chris's writing about drinking. It's a powerful lyric and it must have been hard for him to write about that dark place in himself. The closing line is an absolute classic, "Then I fell over/ Into a bush." Given the tone of the song, it's tremendous and shows Chris still retained his sense of humour through all the darkness.

CD: I've fallen over into a bush and it's not a very nice feeling, and have driven into a bush as well. That's not very nice either.

Do you remember writing this?

CD: This is another song which came to me while driving home. It was pouring with rain and the image came to me of this guy with his head stuck in the cat flap, which was brilliant. I actually stopped at St Mary's church in Rye and wrote the whole thing down. It's one of the best songs we've ever written.

When we recorded it I came up with this guitar riff on my beautiful blue paisley Telecaster.

GT: The tune was written as a jazzy thing with about eight million chords and Pete Smith got on my case very hard to simplify it. We stripped and stripped, like a sculptor with a block of wood, until it was simple. We kept the tune but all the chords went, which made the song more powerful.

CD: Glenn's vocal on this is stunning; it's really chilling. I must confess that when I started doing my own solo shows I had a go at 'Cold Shoulder' but it was so poor in comparison I thought, 'I'd better leave this to Glenn.'

'Talk To Him'

I would guess this lyric is about the two of you. 'How come I don't talk to him?/ I didn't talk to him.'

CD: I suppose it's about my stubbornness and failure to communicate with Glenn prior to making this record. The fact that I would, if I felt something, rather just hold it than share it with Glenn. Whereas now I wouldn't give that an ounce of room.

GT: I pictured 'Talk To Him' as being more of a childhood thing, a not very popular boy at school saying 'look at me now'. I had as much of a clue about the fact that it was about me as anyone listening.

CD: On this album, instead of being the old me who would sit at the back of the studio and sulk about things I tried my hardest to roll up my sleeves and get involved. If I heard something I didn't like, I stood up and said so and made a point of having my opinion heard. I found this terribly rewarding.

The creativity of Keith's bass playing is worth mentioning, as was the removal of my vocals from the mix. At first it was a duet which Glenn and I sang, like 'Take Me I'm Yours', with myself singing the bottom end and Glenn the top. When it was being mixed by Bob Clearmountain in Bath I went into town to get some things. When I came back my voice had been taken out of the mix.

I sensed other people had been in a conversation about it when I was out. Glenn was a little distant, which was odd. Bob turned to me and said, 'Chris, I have tried everything to keep your voice on this song but it clashes with the bass because you have such a low voice. It was either you or the bass and unfortunately the bass won.'

How did that make you feel?

CD: Hearing it from Bob meant I had to put my hands in the air and say, 'That's OK by me.' It might have been different if I'd heard it from someone else.

'Jolly Comes Home'

GT: We resurrected this song from 20 years beforehand. It was a very poppy tune and was originally called 'Love Is A Four Letter Story'. I kept bringing the tune up because I really liked it, and Chris rightly thought he could do something with it that was better. His second lyric completely transformed it.

CD: I remember we did this live when we toured this album and it went down extremely well. It is like 'Labelled With Love' where people would listen to the lyric and hear a bit of themselves in it. There's no greater feeling as a songwriter than being onstage and watching people reflect on what you've written. And when people come up to you afterwards and explain how it affects them, it's incredible.

Since my website has been up I've had hundreds of emails over the last year from people who have been affected by things that I have written lyrically and Glenn has written musically, which makes it all worthwhile. The fact that we don't tour anymore doesn't matter because our music lives on.

'Images Of Loving'

GT: I haven't got much to say about it, except that it sounds like The Monkees, in a good way. It's one of those songs which is neither particularly great nor important in its subject matter but I just like the sound of it.

CD: At the time I wasn't especially keen on this one, but if anything it reminds me of the time I was having a relationship with a girl called Mary. I used to live with her and after we broke up she got together with Jools.

During what period were you living with her?

CD: From about the period for 'Cool For Cats'. She was married to Harry Kakoulli and when they split up I moved in with her.

That must have been difficult for everybody.

CD: It was like *EastEnders*.

How did Harry take that?

CD: He'd already flown the nest by then with somebody else. But then I played away from home and she found out about it and wasn't happy to have me back, and Jools ended up moving in with her.

'True Colours (The Storm)'

Written and sung by Keith, this meant there were four lead vocalists on this album.

CD: Keith brought this song to the table, with about six other songs that he'd written. He wanted at least one of his songs on the album because he felt that he was a fully paid-up member of the band. Glenn was more open about it and Miles was pushing for it because he was going to publish Keith, which I felt was a bit underhand.

GT: I'd been faced with the situation before, where I've been working with someone and they've given me something which is not very good. This can put you in a horrible situation, but I never felt like that about Keith's songs.

Did he have another avenue for his songs?

GT: No, he didn't. He'd been part of the band for a long while by then and I didn't see what the problem was at all.

CD: But the main thing was that if you are going to have a song on the album it has got to be good.

So you don't like it?

CD: Not particularly. We had got the opportunity to use ten or twelve great Difford-Tilbrook songs on this album and I was a bit bemused as to why we were doing it, except to accommodate Keith.

I felt distanced from it in the same way I would have felt distanced from anything which Jools wanted to have on a Squeeze album. I still had that urge to be parental about the band and didn't want anyone else coming into the songwriting family. Looking back, it's a very selfish way of thinking.

GT: This was originally written for a ukulele and was really sweet. A&M came down very heavily on it. They didn't like it and said we'd have to put on something different if we wanted it on the record. The re-recorded version was good, but no better than the original. I don't think A&M gave Keith the same respect as they were giving Chris and I.

'Pinocchio'

GT: This is a song that is totally unlike any other Squeeze track. There is a weary sound to it, more adult to the way Squeeze normally sound and it worked really well.

CD: I was listening to REM at the time and wanted to write something which was a bit obscure. This was the closest I ever got. I could never write like Michael Stipe, who is brilliant. I really looked up to REM as a band.

They are really cohesive and logical and come across as a great family, which is something I always wanted from a band and still do. If ever I'm lucky enough to be in a band again I would strive for the family relationship.

That's funny, because out of you and Glenn you seem to be the one who needs more solitude.

CD: That's true, but to my mind having a family relationship is about being in touch with all the people that work around you. It's about knowing your road crew and everybody who goes on tour. I want people coming up to me and telling me what they think about the show, whether it could be better. I don't want people just to do a job and think, 'I put the lights up, therefore that's all I do.' You should want people confronting you. It's like being in a circus when you go on the road. The band are the main entertainers of the show, but everybody is really important and when I look at REM that's what I think they have.

***

AFTER THE crushing disappointment of being dropped by two record companies in little over a year, the recording of *Some Fantastic Place* marked a major triumph for Squeeze. Chris's sobering up had helped his creative juices flow again and he and Glenn had recorded an album of outstanding, consistent material that sounded as upbeat as *Play* had been maudlin.

'I always look back on this record and that particular year as being the pinnacle of my writing career,' says Chris. 'I had this black cloud over me that had gone and I was open to communication. I really enjoyed being around Glenn and this fantastic new band that we had.'

Glenn is also full of praise for the new line-up, regarded as one of the best in Squeeze's history, and claims that Gilson's regretful departure had paid dividends in the band's sound. 'I've paid tribute to Gilson throughout this book and shown him respect, but the fact was that he was so unhappy that it became hard for us to function properly as a band. If you have someone who is clearly not into what they're doing, for whatever reason, then it's hard to enthuse about what you're doing.'

He also believes that the decision by both A&M and Warner Brothers to drop the band had helped the band to write better material. 'It bucked us up in a way that carrying on making records and being a success wouldn't have done. We had to pay attention to what we were doing and not slack off, which was a great incentive.'

The flip side of this creative refuelling was that Squeeze's career was on a seemingly inexorable commercial slide. It had now been six years since they had last enjoyed a hit single, and album sales were continuing to dip. The album was a potent mix of pop sensibility, unbeatable lyrics and superb musical playing, and resulted in another batch of impressive reviews from the critics. But it still wasn't enough.

In October 1993's *Q Magazine*, the album was awarded a fulsome four stars and the astute observation: 'This is another fine Squeeze album with the usual complement of perfectly realised songs and bittersweet kitchen sinkery.' Yet sales did not live up to the quality of the record, while the singles 'Third Rail' and 'Some Fantastic Place' reached a disappointing 39 and 73 respectively.

Despite welcoming Squeeze back into their fold with open arms, A&M were guilty of over-caution and a lack of confidence in the band, perhaps believing that a group of musicians who were pushing 40 was no longer marketable.

One extraordinary moment revealed exactly how low Squeeze were on the A&M agenda. The label had hired a boat for the afternoon from Plymouth to sail up the River Dart while Squeeze played some of their newly released material. Spirits were high as the managing director of A&M went to the podium to congratulate the band.

Glenn recalls with horror what happened next. 'The MD got up on the stage and said, "I'm so pleased to have Squeeze back. They've produced a fabulous record and this time we're really going to do it for them." Maurice Oberstein, who used to be head of CBS, was standing there pissed. Suddenly he shouted out "Well, what's your advertising budget for it then?" and everyone went quiet. It was like he'd shouted out "I wanna fuck my granny." There was this horrible silence. He'd punctured the whole launch, but rightfully so because A&M's spend on the album was minimal.'

By now Squeeze were becoming used to the fickle nature of the music business and starting to realise that their days as a major-league pop act were over. However, the renewed optimism in their ability to write top-notch songs, regardless of sales, allied to their being retained by A&M for a second album, gave them plenty of optimism for the future.

13 *Ridiculous*

SQUEEZE'S CREATIVE renaissance was by now in full bloom. Each of the band's previous four albums had shown a marked improvement on its predecessor, and *Some Fantastic Place*, despite a lack of proper marketing, had made a healthy financial profit. This was due in large part to the decision to use 45RPM Studios, and the band decided to hire Glenn's base again for lengthy periods on their follow-up album. With a batch of 14 songs written, Squeeze initially went into Chipping Norton Studios in Oxfordshire with co-producer Pete Smith to lay down the backing tracks.

Chris and Glenn had regained much of their original sense of companionship since the former's lengthy spell in rehab. But during the writing of *Ridiculous* tensions rose again, this time over the lyricist's decision to work with musicians outside the band.

Chris had begun attending songwriting weekends and during one of these creative getaways, had come up with the lyric for a song called 'Electric Trains'. When Glenn saw the lyric, one that Chris himself admits was one of the finest he had ever written, he was keen to start work on the song. Discovering that Chris had already given the lyric to another songwriter, Francis Dunnery, on one of these extracurricular weekends, Glenn hit the roof.

'I was really annoyed with Chris because he had given away a lyric which was so clearly a gem and an obvious song for Squeeze to record. I said, "What the fuck are you doing giving lyrics like that away?" My view is that if you're in a band like Squeeze you shouldn't give away some of your best stuff to other people.'

Chris was torn between his loyalty to Glenn and the fact that Francis had by this stage already written a tune to the lyric. He claims never to have intended to give the lyric away, but that Francis had stumbled across it and was so enthusiastic that he offered him first refusal. 'Francis saw this lyric on my laptop and asked if he could put a tune to it. He came up with something almost instantly and I really liked what he'd done. When Glenn found out, he was furious. It was as if I'd slept with someone on the side.'

'It put me in a very difficult position but I went back to Francis and said, "Glenn wants me to give him the lyric." Being the wonderful person Francis is, he agreed to give it back.'

'Electric Trains' became the opening song on *Ridiculous* and a minor chart hit, landing four places outside of the UK Top 40. Eight years later Chris resurrected the original version written with Francis and included it on his debut solo album, under the title 'Playing With Electric Trains'. 'Both tunes were brilliant, so I didn't lose out,' says Chris. 'I got two great tunes for one great lyric. It was all a bit girlie for a while between Glenn and I over this. It was like we were both saying "I'll slap you with a rose."'

Glenn believes that 1994 saw Chris beginning to divert the focus of his lyrical output away from Squeeze. 'Chris had the feeling that Squeeze wasn't going anywhere and started to concentrate his energies elsewhere, which I found hurtful. He was writing with lots of other people and, like with most things, never told me about any of them. I would find out by the by.'

Chris argues that his decision to work outside of Squeeze was merely to explore other avenues of songwriting, rather than moving away from Glenn permanently. 'I started to realise that it was possible for me to write lyrics for other people and that people wanted me to write with them. It gave me a sense of independence, which was very liberating, so I worked with people in places like Nashville and LA.

'It was not until some time afterwards that I realised Glenn was upset by it. In my defence as a lyricist, if people called to say they really liked my writing and wanted me to send them a lyric, I wasn't going to say, "No, because it will piss Glenn off."' Chris also makes the point that by the nature of their differing songwriting roles, he was penning a greater number of lyrics than Glenn was creating tunes, and wanted the opportunity to find more outlets for his work.

Glenn now accepts that his attitude was 'unfair in some ways' and that his partner had every right to want an outlet for more of his lyrics. But he stands firm in his belief that Chris's primary loyalty should have been to Squeeze and that he should have had the foresight not to give away lyrics that Glenn might want to work with. 'If Chris was going to give away his best lyrics how could Squeeze be expected to have any kind of success? I'm very protective of anything that I work with and was always fiercely loyal to Chris. I felt that at that point Chris didn't care what my feelings were.'

The now obligatory personnel changes for this album saw Pete Thomas leaving, because of his renewed commitments with Elvis Costello, to be replaced by Kevin Wilkinson (no relation of Keith). Paul Carrack also departed for the second time to concentrate on his solo career, although his position was left unfilled. Glenn filled in on keyboards on many of the songs, while Don Snow, now going by the name of John Savannah, returned for a guest appearance on 'Walk Away'.

The band's management had also changed yet again. Squeeze finally cut their ties with Miles Copeland and John Lay, and new man Paul Toogood was at the helm. Although Toogood would soon depart from the scene, Chris paid tribute to his desire during this period to make Squeeze a success. 'Paul's heart was in making Squeeze a big band again and helping us to play better venues. He was passionate about it and would drink beer with Glenn until the early hours of the morning, and then come and have tea with me in the afternoon at the Savoy. He could wear those two hats and somehow make the two of us communicate. He was a real gentleman, but he made some mistakes by spending too much money on tours. The band also has to take some responsibility for that, though, just like we have to take responsibility for our contract with Miles. I don't blame Paul.'

Taking the age-old route of moving a band into the country to live and work together, Squeeze and Pete Smith decamped to Chipping Norton. The studio was about to close down, so the band paid a minimal rent, and found life outside of London inspiring.

Smith was a personable figure, someone whom all the band members felt comfortable working with, and who knew how to fuse Chris and Glenn's talents harmoniously in the studio. With Chris still feeling the benefits of his personal renaissance, and the fallout from the writing of 'Electric Trains' put to one side, the band embarked on making what would be another impressive record. It was an album that would see Squeeze make their last foray into the pop mainstream and achieve the final commercial success of the band's career.

***

'ELECTRIC TRAINS'

This has a poppy arrangement, considering the wistful nature of the lyric.

GT: Yes. I have to pay tribute to Keith, who arranged the backing vocals that were a great counterpoint to the tune. Chris has this knack of being able to draw daft people together, like Julie Andrews and Jerry Garcia, and make it sound both funny and poignant. It was another song that mentions masturbation, so we were keeping the old flame burning for the Wanker's Charter.

This was a song we'd done the backing track for already, for another song, so when Chris eventually gave the lyric to me, I worked on it to make it fit.

What can you tell me about the lyric?

CD: It reminds me of being at 98 Coombe Avenue, where I lived with my parents. I had an electric train set under my bed and listened to The Grateful Dead and to 'The Sound Of Music', which was the first song I knew all the words to.

I can picture everything in my lyric vividly and when my brother listens to it he cries because he recognises the things in it as well. It's a very personal lyric, which is often the most difficult to write.

The story goes through the whole of your childhood until your early adulthood.

CD: Yes, it mentions counting my pubic hairs, which I can remember doing. I'm sure a lot of boys can connect with that pride at your first sign of manhood. It goes through the passionate relationships of my teenage years.

And it talks about the start of Squeeze. 'I played guitar and formed a band, I puked up all night long/ As people came to sit and stare as I raced through my songs.'

CD: That's right. It brings us right up to Catford Girls School where we did one of our first shows.

'Heaven Knows'

This is a song where the vocal was split between the two of you.

CD: It would have been funny if we'd had me and Glenn singing to each other, like a romantic duet. 'Heaven Knows' and 'Long Face' were virtually the same song, just played differently.

We sat in the studio at Olympic at the end of the recordings and we hadn't completed those two songs. We were rewriting them at the same time as they were being mixed. When there were gaps that needed filling with lyrics on either song, Mark Stent, the engineer, played the song over and over again in the studio and I sat with my laptop and wrote. Both 'Heaven Knows' and 'Long Face' were written and sung almost instantaneously.

On this album, as with *Some Fantastic Place*, I was increasingly involved in the recording: singing more, and playing guitar, and I really enjoyed it.

'Heaven Knows' was your biggest UK hit since 'Hourglass'.

GT: This concerned me a great deal. It reminded me of the success we'd had with '853-5937' in America and made me think long and hard about the music business. This song was A&R'd to death, because the record company liked it, so they made sure it got into the charts. It disturbed me that we would record a song that I didn't think anything of at all and find that it charted.

CD: The song was also used as the soundtrack to a film called *Hackers*, about kids breaking into the US defence system on the internet.

'GROUCH OF THE DAY'

CD: I felt like John Lennon on this one, with my legs astride and bouncing up and down on the pivot of my spine like he did. I love this song because it's so happy.

It's an autobiographical lyric. Heidi would say, 'Stop being such a grouch and get on with it.' It's a lyric about how blokes moan.

GT: Musically it shows that I'm relaxing. It's very obviously influenced by The Beatles and I was happy to just go along with that. It's a fun song without any importance attached to it. It's clearly a song about Chris because he could certainly be quite grouchy, and it made me laugh that he would acknowledge that in a lyric.

'WALK AWAY'

Don Snow, or John Savannah, I should say, came back for this track. How did that come about?

CD: I met up with him at a songwriting weekend and reconnected with him as a friend, so I invited him to the studio. He's a very talented young man and one of the funniest people on earth. It was always good to have a storyteller in the band because it kept up the spirit. He was also a great mimic.

The beauty of this song is in Glenn's vocal and his arrangement, which is tremendous. Kevin's drumming was also outstanding. On tour he grabbed hold of the baton from Pete Thomas and ran full-steam ahead into the final lap of the band. His drumming was very imaginative.

This is a similarly wistful lyric to 'Electric Trains'.

GT: 'Walk Away' falls into the same category to me as 'Some Fantastic Place', 'Cold Shoulder', 'The Truth' and 'Walk A Straight Line', because they were songs of experience written in a way that Squeeze songs hadn't been written before.

The song touches on how people grow up and that it's not only genes, but the baggage you carry around with you when you grow up that continues into your own parenthood. To encapsulate this within a song in the way Chris managed was fantastic. When I got a lyric like that my job was to carry it musically and not deflect from the lyric.

CD: It's a very passionate lyric about the father-son relationship and the point in your life when you become like your dad. Sometimes I find myself sitting like my dad would have sat or picking my fingers the way he did, or resting my hand on the side of my chin in the same way. When you're younger you don't want to be like your father, but as you get older you have respect for him and say, 'Yeah, he was a great bloke.' It's a very powerful song for me.

What was your relationship with your parents like?

CD: They were quite distant from me. My two brothers are much older. I was a bit of a last-minute addition, so I had a lot of time to myself. My mum and dad had already had two boys and probably thought, 'We've had enough here. We'll just let Chris get on and do what he wants.' So I would just sit and amuse myself, which is where my imagination comes from.

My parents were quite distant and didn't understand why I wanted to be a musician. They said that my musical career would never take off, but when I look at their attitude they had no tools to be any different because they took their information from their own parents. Ultimately their parents were Victorian people who thought that children should be seen and not heard, so they handed down a muted way of connecting with their children. It's difficult to rebel against that gene which is so strong in people. It's passed down inside you, a chemical almost that you can't dispel. Now that they have passed on I can see that properly, but I don't hold it against them in the slightest.

What I have learnt from that is how to deal with my children. I try to be as open with them as possible. When I went home after taking acid my father wanted to lock me up because he didn't know how to deal with it. I'd deal with that very differently if it was my son. Although I don't live with my children, which I'm sad about, I still hope that I can communicate with them at a better level than my parents did with me.

The lyric starts 'A black and white photograph/ Of me up the garden path'. It's interesting because I noticed there is a black and white photo of you as a child in your bathroom.

CD: That is a very important picture. The most important person in my life is that boy because he had nothing to worry about in his life. He was young. He did not understand fear, remorse, or heartache, or even what love was. He had an imagination that would go on for miles and miles.

The other interesting thing about that photograph is that I've got an ice cream in one hand and a toy bus in the other. That is a kid who is an addict and wants it all. He wants the bus for being a good boy and he wants the ice cream, also for being a good boy. That is exactly how my personality developed, from that photograph to 1992, when I went completely off the rails.

'THIS SUMMER'

GT: This was a little more complicated when I wrote it to the way it ended up and I'm glad we simplified it. It's one of those songs where I like the way it sounds but it feels a little bit fluffy to me and lightweight.

CD: The lyric was influenced by Blur, who were big at the time. They were a big inspiration to me and I spent some time listening to their lyrics and how jolly they could be.

GT: We were put into an embarrassing position where A&M labelled us the 'Godfathers Of Britpop'. That was a description that made it look to me like we were desperate to latch on to the coat-tails of something successful. I can understand why A&M did that, to make the younger audience aware of us, but I think if I was at that age there's nothing that would put me off more than someone trying to desperately latch onto a bandwagon. Then again, how else do you sell a band that's as old as us which hasn't had any success for a long time? It must have been hard.

Do you think you were much of an influence to the Britpop bands?

GT: We had a fair amount of influence on some of them. Blur and Elastica praised us at the time and occasionally we had bands telling us they liked us. There was a track on *Woodface* by Crowded House, where the first two bars were blatantly from 'Another Nail In My Heart'. Rather than get upset about it we took it as a tip of the hat, which was nice.

CD: We made another fantastic video for this, featuring John Thomson from *The Fast Show*. It was filmed down at Eastbourne where we got up to jolly pranks on the beach and on the pier, hitting each other with plastic hammers and being daft.

'GOT TO ME'

This was a song written by Keith. Did you feel disassociated from this one?

CD: I suppose so. People would say to me, 'What is this song doing on your album?' but because we were very much a democracy and wanted to facilitate Keith, the song stayed on the album. Glenn was very vocal about it staying on the record and stuck up for Keith. I don't hold any disparaging feelings towards Keith for having this on the record. It was just my parental feelings towards Squeeze's songwriting at the time.

GT: Keith was put in a really unpleasant situation of being told by A&M that he couldn't sing. I thought it was a lovely song and I was glad for Keith to have a song on the album, but we were told he couldn't sing it himself and that I had to do it instead. I wish we'd stood our ground.

'LONG FACE'

GT: Chris recorded his vocal separately from me – when I was out of the studio, which is obviously how he felt more comfortable – but with great results.

CD: Some people have said I sound like Robbie Robertson on this, but I don't think I'm singing properly. It sounds like I'm being buggered.

That's very funny. I don't know if your fans will be able to listen to this in the same way again.

CD: Then I should point out that it may sound like being buggered, but I'm not. I can't tell from experience either.

It was a track without a lyric and at the last minute I came up with one in the studio. It reminds me of a song on the first album, 'Hesitation (Rool Britannia)', because it has that same sort of rhythm and guitar riff.

GT: Yet again I was trying to get dance music into a Squeeze song and this time it worked. We were working on the mixes with Mark 'Spike' Stent, and his background is in dance music. He ended up working with Madonna. This was one of about four songs on this album that had the same chord sequence, one of which was 'Heaven Knows'.

'I WANT YOU'

CD: If I did a musical about alcoholism this is one of the songs that would be in it. It could follow 'Cold Shoulder' in a musical easily. The underlying snake-like sound of the song gives it a vicious edge. The lyric is not about anyone in particular. It's just from my imagination.

GT: This is another song that came out of 'Heaven Knows'. If I'd had my way this would have been the single, instead of 'Heaven Knows', because I think it's a beautiful song and one that is about something, as opposed to something about nothing. Our stuff was getting more personal and soulful in that sense of the word, which is something Squeeze never did in the '70s or '80s, and why I'm so proud of our evolution.

CD: By this stage of our career Glenn's vocals were becoming almost surreal in their brilliance. Towards the end of this song his voice is absolutely remarkable.

The song has a great climb to it, starting off quietly on acoustic guitar and then building into a crescendo. Was this your intention?

GT: Yes it was. Myself and Pete Smith worked long and hard on the production to make it sound atmospheric.

'DAPHNE'

This is my favourite on the album.

CD: Mine too. It was written in a traffic jam going through the Blackwall Tunnel, on my way to a recording session with Aimee Mann. The character Daphne is based on Aimee.

Why do you say she is being ridiculous in the chorus?

CD: That was her catchphrase. She was always saying, 'Don't be ridiculous.' Aimee is a great musician and songwriter, and a wickedly funny girl.

The line 'All that you want is here' sounds like you are suggesting a relationship.

CD: That's what I was hoping. I make no bones about it. I was having delusions of grandeur. I never had a relationship with her but I have always found her attractive in lots of different ways. She is very witty as well as being a great songwriter and I'm attracted to people like that.

Aimee is happily married and I was married as well, to Heidi, so it wasn't as if anything was going to happen. But flirtation isn't a bad thing. Looking at the menu is OK, as long as you know that you can't have everything at once.

GT: I love the lyric to 'Daphne', although I didn't know what it was about. Anyone who can put Nana Maskouri into a lyric is a genius.

It's quite a simple tune.

GT: Yes. I was using my acoustic guitars at the time, having started falling in love with playing the guitar again after a few years of shying away from it. Throughout my career I've had an ongoing love of music that changes from major to minor keys in a short space of time. I really like the mood it evokes.

'LOST FOR WORDS'

CD: I was listening to this the other day and thought it sounded like a Beach Boys song. Lyrically it is an observation, and not personal at all. I remember not liking it at all at the time, but it was good for tempo and had an intricate production.

GT: This was a song liked mostly by me, and if Chris had still been drinking he would have gone down the pub, so probably he sat and played on his computer. We had a problem about using the title. It was originally called 'Abandoned Words' but there was a song with that name that Elvis [Costello] had worked on, so Chris wanted to change it.

I like 'Lost For Words' musically because it's one of the odder songs on the album. I hold a flag up for those moments because I think they were an important part of what we did together.

'GREAT ESCAPE'

This is quite heavy musically.

GT: It's probably the heaviest song that Squeeze ever did and is another alcohol-influenced song about the negative side of drinking. It's brutal and straightforward in its lyric.

CD: I wrote this driving along the A21 on the Dictaphone having just listened to *Woman's Hour* on Radio 4. They were discussing men and women in violent relationships, which had become quite a common theme throughout my writing. The lyric was a lot more vicious than this originally, and we toned it down, but it's still pretty horrible.

The woman is raped by her alcoholic husband.

CD: That's right. It was originally called 'Rape', which Glenn didn't think was a good title for a song, so I changed it to 'The Great Escape'. Lyrically it's a great story. I remember writing it in the same way as I wrote 'Cold Shoulder'. It just came to me.

GT: My memory of this song is that myself, Keith and Kevin worked on the song musically, and that Chris didn't play a big part. I don't think Pete Smith liked the song either, so it was one I worked on pretty much alone and knocked into shape in the studio. I'm pleased with the way it came out because it wasn't typical of any kind of song we normally wrote.

'TEMPTATION FOR LOVE'

GT: I wrote this as a pseudo-George Michael dance track, which was not one of my finest moments as far as an idea for a song was concerned. I recorded a fantastically complicated demo for it, with loads of keyboard parts and backing vocals, but we stripped it down. It all boiled down to the guitar part which Hayter Beretta did a wonderful job on.

Who was he?

GT: He's someone who Chris had met on a songwriting weekend and ended up playing with Simply Red for a while. He's a fantastic guitarist and played it really simply. Instead of it being on eight keyboards as it was originally, it was just Hayter on guitar and sounded much better for it.

I topped off the song with my Mini Moog, that I bought with my first royalty cheque, and still use today. The Moog lines remind me of Stevie Wonder and, again, this is another song quite different from anything Squeeze had ever done before, which I'm quite proud of. I think *Some Fantastic Place* is a better album because the songs overall are superior, but what I like about *Ridiculous* is that we were pushing out in lots of different directions.

Glenn sang the vocals in a duet with Cathy Dennis. Tell me about her.

CD: Paul Toogood was going out with Cathy at the time and I think he suggested bringing her in. Her duet with Glenn was wonderful. I remember listening to this in the control room, and the vocals were so brilliant and portrayed the lyric in such a real way, that I found myself crying. It sounded as if they were reading lines from a script and it really moved me.

What can you tell me about your lyric?

CD: When you're in a strong relationship with somebody and you are tempted by a bit on the side, it's a very difficult emotion to deal with. I used to say to myself that I wouldn't act on these impulses until another lifetime. I wouldn't sleep outside a relationship these days. I'm very clear about that. Nevertheless, you do get temptations, especially on the road when there are lots of free women around, but you have just got to try and contain yourself.

'Sound Asleep'

CD: It was great when Glenn and I sang together. This song has a great sound and could have been on the *Difford And Tilbrook* album in some ways.

A lot of Glenn's trinkets are on this. He loves all those little bits of architecture in his songs. If he can get a tin whistle on a track, which he has bought in a hippy shop, he will.

The song is about being alone and vulnerable.

CD: Yes, although I don't remember much about writing this song. What I do know was that the vocals were quite difficult to sing. Glenn and Pete had to show a lot of patience until I got it right. Glenn is such a soulful singer that his vocals are very difficult to trace over.

GT: This isn't the greatest song on the album but it's musically reasonably dark, with quite a straightforward chord sequence. It has an unusual sound, with the pizzicato string line, the repeats through it and the drum machine. There's what I would call a claustrophobic intensity about it, which sounds slightly pretentious, but seems to have worked.

'Fingertips'

GT: I always felt Chris was having a pop at me with this song, especially lines like 'I only wish I had the power to cut you free from me.' I thought that at the time and I still think it now. It wasn't particularly nice. Having said that, I really like the song and I'm big enough to take it on the chin, and it has a lovely mood to it.

The way that Kevin played on the drums gave a lovely mood to the song and Keith played double bass on this, while I was on keyboards. It was influenced by the mood of the first Portishead album. The guy who was their agent was sharing a flat with Suzanne, who by this stage was my girlfriend. He sat us down and played the record and I thought it was fantastic. Strangely enough Chris was into that as well. Many times our musical tastes did not coincide but we both really liked Portishead and this song was a great framework for Chris's voice.

CD: Glenn's got the lyric all wrong. It's a song about all the parameters of addiction and how they affect you. When I used to sing this in the band it used to choke me up because of what it was about. I was in the first two years of recovery when I wrote it.

I played a big part in the writing of the music and certainly the ambience of the song. We recorded this in one take. I felt like I had almost 100 per cent ownership of this track because it was about my struggle with addiction. It was a wonderful moment when I walked out of the studio after we'd finished this track. I had to take a walk and reflect on how powerful that moment had been and wonder where it had come from.

It was one of those rare magical moments you get in a studio when cutting a song where everyone plays together as a complete unit.

***

THE RECORDING of *Ridiculous* heralded the continued renaissance of second period Squeeze. From the slipshod *Cosi Fan Tutti Frutti*, a whole ten years beforehand, the band had steadily improved their output on each subsequent album, until reaching their ultimate creative peak with 1993's *Some Fantastic Place*. Despite having such a hard act to follow, *Ridiculous* barely dipped below the standard of its predecessor and even saw Squeeze enjoy some belated chart action.

'This Summer' reached a respectable Number 36 in the UK charts in September 1995 and arguably might have gone higher had A&M had the foresight to release the seasonal single earlier than the autumn. Indeed, the following August a remixed version of the song managed to scale four places higher in the charts. In between those two hits came the release of 'Heaven Knows', which surprisingly reached 27, the band's second-highest chart placement in 16 years.

This unexpected success was a double-edged sword in Glenn's eyes. He felt that A&M were, in marketing terms, only prepared to push the boat out for the band's more middle-of-the-road sounding tracks. 'This album followed the trend that was set on *Play,* whereby songs that were released as singles were probably our weakest, with the exception of "Electric Trains". "This Summer" sounded okay but it was a very average song. If we could have released something of the importance or the emotional pull of "Walk Away" we would have been in a stronger position but A&M didn't believe in those songs.'

Glenn believes that the people who were by then running A&M were ultra-conservative by nature and attempting to push Squeeze away from musical experimentation, albeit with limited success. 'A&M wanted us to have a fairly traditional sound, like on "This Summer" and "Heaven Knows", and distrusted anything that was more experimental. They regarded us doing anything different in the way that people would look at Kenneth Williams trying to do Shakespeare or Christopher Lee branching into comedy. It was hard for us as a band to be in the face of that kind of opposition.'

Indicative of A&M's growing lack of faith in Squeeze was the label's decision not to release the album in America. With A&M undergoing major internal changes, a number of those people within the company who had championed Squeeze found themselves out of jobs, to be replaced by young bucks who had little interest in the 'Godfathers Of Britpop'.

'Everything started to change in the industry at this time and the whole chemistry between us and A&M changed,' complains Chris. 'It felt like buying a really nice ice cream when we started making this record, only to find that within minutes it had begun to melt all over our hands before we'd been able to enjoy it.'

Sensing an opportunity to make some money, Miles Copeland stepped in to offer the band a US distribution deal. Arriving at a gig in the States, Copeland was curtly informed that Glenn had no desire to see him backstage, but Chris agreed to go back into the auditorium after the show to meet him. Copeland's message was blunt: if the band wouldn't allow him to distribute the record then nobody else would be interested and the album would therefore stay on the shelf. Pragmatism was the order of the day and Glenn reluctantly agreed to sign the deal on offer. In the event, the album sold reasonably well across the States, so both sides ended up happy, despite Glenn's feelings of disgust that the band had seemingly supped with the devil yet again.

Unbeknown to Glenn and Chris, *Ridiculous* would mark the beginning of the end for Squeeze. A series of questionable line-up changes, yet another dismissal by a record label, and finally some over-hasty writing and recording, resulted in the damp squib that was *Domino*. It would also lead to a near-terminal rupturing of Glenn and Chris's songwriting partnership.

14 *Domino*

THE YEAR 1997 was a bleak one for Squeeze. Yet another manager bit the dust, when Paul Toogood departed for pastures new. The band had refused Toogood's initial advice to hire an accountant, and after his departure were subsequently hit with an unpaid tax bill of more than £30,000.

Chris retains sympathy for Toogood, whom he believes always retained the best of motives when dealing with Squeeze's affairs. He explains, 'When we first met with Paul, he said, "I urge you to get an accountant but if you want to save money we can do it in house." We made the decision collectively to do it in-house, and at the end of the day it cost us a fortune because the person accounting for Paul messed up. It was nothing malicious.'

Glenn, on the other hand, was distraught to find that the relative success Squeeze had enjoyed with *Ridiculous* was in fact masking financial failure. He says, 'We were left saddled with this huge unpaid tax bill which we only discovered a year later. That really nailed for me any desire to continue in that commercial world.'

When A&M failed to renew the band's recording contract, Glenn, disillusioned by the band's attempts at commercial success, saw this as a liberating opportunity and suggested to Chris that they establish their own independent label. Believing that the band could finally break free from the creative constraints of a record company, the singer thought the band should accept that Squeeze's days in the big time were over and reduce their focus on commercial success.

Glenn says, 'I'd had enough of record companies by this stage and wouldn't have signed another deal, whoever offered it, because another deal would just represent more of the same. I was very enthusiastic about producing music on our own label, on a smaller scale and without spending so much money.'

The more conservative Chris was less convinced by this logic and initially resisted the move to go independent. 'Having the secure rug of a record company pulled from under us by A&M was wounding, especially after making such a great record. I was very nervous of starting out on our own label and worried about who was going to pay for the PR and stuff like that.'

With no offers from record companies on the table, Chris eventually accepted the need to release an independent album, but declined the offer to go into partnership with Glenn on a label. The result was that Glenn formed Quixotic Records with his girlfriend Suzanne Hunt.

'I'd kept on and on at Chris about setting up our own company, but he just wasn't interested at all, which was very disappointing for me. I felt it was the only way forward for us, so I went ahead without him.'

Chris admits that at this stage, his enthusiasm for Squeeze's future was beginning to wane. 'Glenn already had his own recording studio and was now setting up his own record company, and I did not feel part of it, so I started to spiral into depression. I found the whole situation very difficult.'

Having set up the company, Glenn got to work quickly, using 45RPM as a base to produce an album by his good friend Nick Harper, entitled *Smithereens*. Squeeze's first release on Quixotic was the single 'Down In The Valley', recorded with the Charlton Athletic football team to mark their appearance in the Football League Division Play-Off Final against Sunderland in May 1998. Glenn, a season-ticket holder at Charlton, jumped at the chance of working with men he watched from the stands every other Saturday.

'It was great to get the team into the studio. I was more nervous having them in the studio than anyone else I'd ever worked with. Players like Danny Mills, Mark Kinsella and Richard Rufus were there and we recorded it as a traditional football singalong, with these blokes standing around the microphone not really sure of what was going on. It was great fun.'

Chris had little interest in The Beautiful Game but came up with a typically quirky Difford lyric, of which he remains affectionate. 'It's a good lyric, although it's a Difford And Tilbrook song, as opposed to a football song.'

By the summer of 1998, three years had passed since the release of *Ridiculous*, and thoughts turned to recording an album. There would be yet another shake-up of personnel. Kevin Wilkinson received his marching orders and was replaced by former Del Amitri drummer Ash Soan, while a gobsmacked Keith also found himself surplus to requirements after making seven albums with Glenn and Chris. The latter recalls that Keith had been pushing for more of a say in the songwriting stakes, which was out of the question, while Glenn believes simply that the band needed an injection of new energy. Keith's replacement was Hilaire Penda, an exotic black jazz player who sported dreadlocks.

Glenn had decided to concentrate his energies on playing guitar and producing the record. So, the band decided to revert to being a five-piece, hiring Chris Holland on keyboards to complete their radical new line-up. Strikingly similar in looks to older brother Jools, Chris was a talented pianist and a popular figure in Squeeze history, having performed briefly on *Cosi Fan Tutti Frutti*. Glenn had known Chris since the pianist was five years old and remembers 'an annoying little kid rushing around and getting in our way when Jools and I were rehearsing'.

In retrospect, both Glenn and Chris believe that such extensive surgery to the band was a mistake. 'Ash is a great drummer and very inventive, whereas Hilaire's playing is slightly more complicated,' says Glenn. 'He comes from a jazz background so was a bit over-inventive sometimes. He was fascinating to work with and great to play with live. Was this line-up right for Squeeze? No, I don't think it was.' Adding his typically cryptic two-penn'orth Chris adds, 'That line-up was an airfix model of what Squeeze had been.'

With Glenn taking up full production duties, the band decamped to Chris's studios for a week to lay down the backing tracks before returning to 45RPM for a further five weeks to work on overdubs. This surprisingly short timescale was a precondition of Chris's involvement in making the record.

According to Glenn, 'We embarked on *Domino* under some strict conditions from Chris. He did not want the thing to go on and on, which I had a tendency to do, but then again I've always thought that you can't put a time on getting a record right.'

Although the band had recorded *East Side Story* in 1981 under similar conditions, Glenn believes that it was almost impossible to repeat successfully such a feat this time around. 'You can make a good record quickly if it's done in an atmosphere in which everyone is feeling creative, and you have an external producer taking care of the technical things. As well as playing guitar, arranging and singing, I was producing the whole record and had to spend a lot of time editing.

'Chris seemed to be of the view that I just spent hours farting around to no particular purpose. Myself and the engineer, Neil Amor, did everything we could to get it finished, but we reached the point where there was no more time to work and we had to go with what we had. That is an insane way to make a record. We should have respected our own work more at that point and I feel like it was Chris who didn't because he imposed the small amount of time we had to make it.'

The decision to record an album in six weeks with a brand new line-up was indeed foolhardy and the studio rush job was glaringly obvious to the discerning listener. As Glenn himself would remark, '*Domino* was not really a dignified exit for Squeeze. It's a pity we had to go out on that note.'

Following on from the glorious albums *Some Fantastic Place* and *Ridiculous*, *Domino* is at best a patchy piece of work and both songwriters regard its content with similar disdain to their debut album of 20 years earlier.

The widening gulf between Glenn and Chris over which route the band should be taking was making life uncomfortable for their fellow passengers. However, Squeeze's co-drivers had grown increasingly weary of travelling on the same route and willfully ignored the pitfalls on the junction ahead. It was now just a matter of time before the wheels fell off. Within a few months Squeeze would be no more.

***

'PLAY ON'

GT: I don't think I finished writing the tune properly for this and the chorus is a bit weird towards the end. In a way it's a microcosm of the album as a whole in that parts of the song are good, and if I'd had more time I would have made it sound better. I can be somewhat slow when I'm working and without the benefit of time I was forced to go with my first instinct.

Jessica Rowan is playing recorder.

GT: Jessica is a friend of mine. I'd tried to use the old ochorena from 'Stranger Than The Stranger On The Shore', but it hadn't worked so I asked Jessica in to play recorder.

It's a great lyric, tackling that adolescent rock 'n' roll wannabe, but also slightly sour. It has a jaded and cynical element to it, which I didn't like much. I suspected that in the less cynical parts Chris was looking at his son Riley, who is in his own band with Laurie Latham's son.

CD: It could well be about Riley, but only subconsciously because I'd never considered that before. Riley is in a band and doing very well.

It is interesting that you refer to touring as a disease.

CD: It is a disease. You get addicted to it and you don't want to stop. I am less addicted now than Glenn. He is totally engrossed and immersed in the admiration he gets from playing live. Some philosophers say that playing live is like playing to your mother, and that the way your audience reacts is the way your mother reacted to you as a child. The theory is that if you do a bad gig and you're annoyed, you're actually pissed off with your relationship with your mother.

That's a bit deep. Do you think there's anything in that?

CD: Yes, a lot. When I play I see the audience as parental figures. What I have to do is not react and not be offended as if they were my parents.

Glenn is far more of an entertainer than me. If there are two people in the room he will happily pick up his guitar and play. There's nothing wrong with that, but there is a lot of complexity to a person like that. It's the same with people like Kylie Minogue, who have a narcissistic nature which makes them perform. That's how they get their drug.

I played with Jools the other night, who performs all year round and makes loads of money. There's part of me that thinks he's only doing it for the money, but another part of me thinks he's addicted to the reaction he gets from an audience.

'BONKERS'

CD: This is utter rubbish. I had to write the lyric at the last minute for this and even the vocal is quite half-hearted. It's a reflection of how the record is for me.

GT: Funnily enough I think it's an inspired vocal performance. Chris did some pretty wild singing on this, which was out of character and not at all what I expected. I loved the way that he turned up that day and did something surprising.

I cut up this track quite a lot and turned some of the drum parts into loops.

Some of the imagery of the lyric makes me laugh, like 'The size of her breasts/ Like woodpecker's nests,' even though I'm not quite sure what that means.

'WHAT'S WRONG WITH THIS PICTURE?'

CD: The title is very apt. It explains a lot about the band relationship. The song reminds me of a Difford And Tilbrook-period track, like 'On My Mind Tonight'. Lyrically it's not one of my proudest moments, but then there aren't many here.

GT: This song is the product of not putting enough time into work. It just sounds lazy and the song itself is not something I would want to be remembered for.

Were you aware at the time that it wasn't very good?

GT: When you're working on something you invest everything you can to make it as good as possible. Bearing that in mind this track sounds as good as it possibly could, given that the song itself isn't up to much. Chris was writing a lot of different lyrics for film scores and other musicians, so he was giving Squeeze a bit of his attention, but not enough. A lyric like this is a product of the small amount of TLC Chris was giving his writing for Squeeze.

'DOMINO'

GT: 'Domino' is an old song that we hadn't been able to use on *Ridiculous*. The lyric is good and the song showcases this band line-up very well. It's quite sparky and has a light feel to it, although the chorus is a bit stark. It's one of the most successful tracks on the album.

The verses are straightforward and there's a lot of room for playing. It clicked very quickly in the studio and this was the first or second take we did.

CD: The lyric was my owning up to my bad behaviour. It's what people in recovery call Step Four, when you write down everything in your life which has gone wrong for you and share it with somebody else.

I originally sang this in the studio and the song was much slower. It had a dark groove to it, which Ash and Hilaire really liked. It fitted my voice, but for some reason the song was sped up and Glenn sang it, so my version never got to see the light of day. It was such a personal lyric that it was bizarre that Glenn should sing it. I was a bit upset about that.

Did you speak up about it at the time?

CD: No, I had reverted to the old Chris who sat at the back of the studio looking pissed off and letting Glenn get on with things. Glenn was at the helm and producing by himself, so in many ways, *Domino* was his solo album. There was no partnership in making that record. It was all about Glenn. If you listen to this album and to his solo albums it's very difficult to tell them apart.

I still play this song live because it's personal to me, so I'm glad that it was written.

'TO BE A DAD'

CD: When Glenn split up with his wife Jane, I was really upset for him. He had two lovely little boys and she took them to live in Australia. His sadness was visible and I really felt for him. Just talking about it now makes me feel really upset. I mean, splitting up is one thing but her taking the boys to the other side of the world must have been very hard for him to deal with.

I knew what he was going through because I'd been through losing my children myself, but not to the extent that he had.

GT: There are a couple of really nice lyrics on this album that I was grateful to Chris for writing. I didn't think 'To Be A Dad' was so much about me, because I thought he'd taken bits of what was happening to me and parts of his own history to make into a lyric.

I also thought it was interesting and brave to write about the parts of parenthood which can be terrifying, the relentlessness of it and the responsibility that comes with it. I thought it was a good thing to say in a song and he expressed it well.

'Without You Here' is more obviously related to my situation at the time.

'DONKEY TALK'

CD: I think in terms of my lyric writing, the last drop of dishwater had just gone down the plughole. I was starting to write lyrics which were similar to previous lyrics.

Glenn is brilliant at doing demos and his demos of this album are better than the album itself, this one in particular. Sometimes his demos didn't translate properly on to our records.

GT: This is another song that we didn't use for *Ridiculous* and was cut pretty much live in my studio. The lyric is about rabbiting on too much when you've taken cocaine.

This was a song in which Chris fully contributed, which wasn't happening much at this time. He came up with the guitar line and was fully involved throughout the recording. Unfortunately, it didn't happen enough but I was grateful that it did on this song.

Chris more than me needed someone to push him, and that person, for whatever reason, could never be me. If he felt he was pleasing someone then he would work more, but I don't think he was able to draw that out from himself at this time. There was no A&R person working on the record, and Chris had the vibe about him that it was all a bit of a waste of time. If you approach making a record like that it becomes a self-fulfilling prophesy.

'SLEEPING WITH A FRIEND'

This is similar to an earlier Squeeze song, 'I Learnt How To Pray'.

GT: Yes, it's about a similar subject matter and showed off the life and vigour of this particular line-up of Squeeze. Given more time and better material from Chris and I this line-up could have been really good.

Was it less sparky with Keith and Kevin in the band?

GT: We could probably rock more convincingly with Keith and Kevin, but with the *Domino* line-up there was a certain skip in the step of the band that we didn't have before. This came out on songs like 'Domino' and 'Sleeping With A Friend'.

Again it's a song originally written for *Ridiculous*.

'Without You Here'

GT: This was written by Chris about my situation at the time, which was horrific. It was the year when Ted and Louis and their mum moved to Australia. The lyric understood my position perfectly and was a very sweet thing for Chris to write.

I think it was potentially one of the best songs on the record but I wished I'd had a bit more time with it because it doesn't sound as good as it could. It's a lovely song.

What's lovely about it?

GT: It expresses exactly how I was feeling. My kids, who were then aged five and eight, were living on the other side of the planet and there was this great sense of dislocation that I felt when two people I loved were not going to be part of my life. I'd split up with Jane several years earlier but before they moved to Australia I was still able to see my boys regularly. Now I only see them intermittently because they live so far away.

'In The Morning'

CD: 'In The Morning' was an idea I'd lifted from Suzanne Vega, being in New York and looking down the street and seeing all these things going on.

Do you like the song?

CD: Not at all.

GT: It's a shite lyric, I have to say. The tune is okay. It's a good performance by the band and the song sounds far better than it should have done. But overall it leaves me cold.

'A Moving Story'

CD: This is the story about two people in 'Up The Junction'.

'She moved from Clapham/ And didn't look back.'

CD: I thought it might be a good idea to revisit those characters, but in the end I don't think people gave a shit. I was trying to be inventive and it just didn't work.

GT: I haven't really got anything to say about this song.

I can tell that the pair of you dislike this album because you've both completely clammed up.

GT: The song is fine but it just sounds tired to me, like we are both going over old ground. It's not that bad a song but if you start retreading old ground there has to be something new that you are bringing to the table. I don't think there was anything new coming from either of us.

CD: I just found the whole recording process in Glenn's studio boring. It was driving me round the twist. It was so suffocating and unenjoyable that I just sat at the back saying nothing. I can only talk for myself but the spirit of Squeeze had been knocked out of me by losing a record deal and by Glenn producing the record on his own.

By that stage was it inevitable that the band was going to break up?

CD: Yes. The writing was on the wall but I couldn't read what it said.

'Little King'

This song has a real wall of guitar sound.

GT: Yeah. It's not one of my favourites, though. Chris had originally written a lyric to this which he tried to get past me called 'A Bitter Wind'. When I sang it sounded like 'A Bit Of Wind', which was Chris's joke, so I asked him to rewrite it. Perhaps 'A Bit Of Wind' should have been the name of the album.

What do you think of the song?

GT: I'm really lost for words, totally underwhelmed. We were both capable of better than this. I suppose it sounds okay. I will damn it with faint praise.

CD: This reminds me of 'First Thing Wrong' from our first album. It has a great guitar sound, a huge drum sound and a lot of attitude. To me, this was why you picked up a guitar in the first place. To play loud, not to mess about.

'SHORT BREAK'

CD: This is absolutely terrible. It's there just to make up the numbers, although hardcore fans love it for some bizarre reason. It's just excruciatingly bad. When I hear it I think, 'Tilbrook, for Christ's sake, get a grip, man.' Listening to that track shows why the curtain had to come down.

'Short Break' is quite an ironic title for the last song on the album considering the band was about to implode.

GT: I think Chris knew he was leaving, so he decided to call it that. The music was taken from a really old song we'd written and Chris wrote a new lyric, which sounds semi-detached. It's an interesting idea but Chris Holland has done a version on his own record which is far better than ours. I'm really sorry but this is another one that I'm lost for words over. There were just not enough good songs on this album.

The song has quite a strange ending, with the old-style Joanna playing in the corner and the record scratching.

GT: That was the most humorous part of the whole album, which is saying a lot. It still makes me laugh when I hear it.

***

AS THE dispiriting experience of recording *Domino* came to an end, Chris's personal demons were about to burst into view after a successful seven-year battle to keep them at bay. Deciding that he had overcome the worst of his addiction to alcohol, the lyricist had gradually stopped undertaking therapy, a decision that he believed proved costly. 'I stopped relying on the friendship of the people who had helped me get sober and wanted to go on my own, so I left the shoreline alone, which is the most dangerous thing to do as an addict. I ended up walking straight into the sea and taking water rapidly.'

Behind this cryptic analysis lay Chris's inexorable slide into a new form of addiction – compulsive buying. Rather than return to his previous habits of drinking and taking drugs, Chris began spending vast sums of money on random, often outlandish purchases.

'In therapy I was given the doughnut analogy. After an addict has stopped taking whatever they're addicted to, they may seek to fill the hole left in the doughnut with whatever they can get hold of. For instance, I bought ten computers, five short wave radios, six CD players, and numerous mobile phones. I spent all the money that was coming into the house. I even bought a Maserati, which was ludicrous because I was living on a farm.'

This compulsive buying caused a strain on Chris's marriage, with Heidi tearing her hair out at her husband's frittering away of his income. 'Heidi woke up one morning and pulled back the curtains, only to see my new Maserati outside. She went ballistic and said, "That's the school fees for a year gone." I was jeopardising my relationship with Heidi, but I couldn't see it at the time.'

After a low-key UK tour playing in pubs and small clubs, an increasingly dispirited Chris dropped a bombshell on his writing partner. In May 1999 the band were preparing for a lengthy tour of the States, but Chris was becoming increasingly unhappy about making the trip. He recalls the growing sense of doom that enveloped him as their departure date approached. 'The closer it became, I was saying to Heidi, "I don't want to do this," and she was saying, "You have to go through with it," because I'd spent all our money living in my fantasy world.'

With the flights booked for the following morning, Chris checked into a hotel with a view overlooking one of the runways at Heathrow. In a state of extreme anxiety he spent the evening pacing the room, unable to sleep. When morning came Chris could no longer bear the thought of going on the trip and, in a repeat of history, got a friend to call the airline to inform them he would not be accompanying the band to the US.

'I watched their plane take off and then got into my car and drove to a treatment centre because I desperately needed help. It might have seemed like a very selfish and destructive thing to do, because it was the end for the band and very nearly the end of my relationship with Heidi, but I was deeply depressed. I don't regret what I did, as I'm a much stronger person now because of it. Glenn probably is too, and maybe Heidi as well, so it all worked out.'

Left again to hold the baby, Glenn's sympathy for his errant partner was rapidly beginning to wither. 'I vowed that if Chris had problems then of course I was going to support him, but I also wasn't quite sure why he'd gone back in for treatment. I thought that not turning up for the tour for a second time was an undignified place to leave me. I was perfectly able to explain to our crowds why Chris was not there, but it felt like I was being left as the last person standing in the band.

'I think Chris had been edging out of the band for a while. My suspicion is that he wanted to do the more lucrative UK tour and then walk away. At some point he definitely wanted to do some dates that were more financially lucrative, which I thought was pretty insulting.'

After the band's return to Britain, Chris, by now in difficult financial straits, enquired about his share of the US tour revenue. This time around Glenn was not prepared to hand over any money. 'When Chris asked for a share of the tour money I felt very strongly that he should get lost. I don't know what he thinks now but I still feel he was taking the piss. I'll support anyone in the right circumstances but not if they're being unfair. You might be in a bad way but you don't pick and choose which gigs you want to do. It felt like Chris was saying he didn't mind the profitable part of the English tour, but when it became more of a slog in America he didn't really fancy it.'

Chris defends his standpoint robustly. 'I asked for my share because the name Squeeze was used to promote the tour and I felt I owned 50 per cent of that name. People were going to gigs to listen to Squeeze, not to Glenn. The fact that I was not there was because I wasn't well and I felt I had a legitimate claim to my share.'

As for the accusation that he was only interested in performing at the more profitable shows, Chris is happy to accept this criticism. 'I didn't see the point in doing small gigs and taking out a band at huge expense for so little reward. We were doing every gig that was offered to us, even in dingy pubs. I thought, "You never see The Kinks in a pub," and I thought we should be playing similar venues to The Kinks. Glenn can tour round America for the rest of his life in a Winnebago until his tyres are all flat, but that's not what I want to do.'

In the depths of his personal crisis, Chris decided that he no longer wished to continue as a member of Squeeze. But he knew that finding the strength to inform Glenn in the midst of an all-encompassing depression was going to be difficult. In the event, Chris's departure came in a low-key meeting at The Priory centre, where he had invited Glenn to visit. The centre's rules indicated that Chris's counsellor should be present during this encounter, to observe their patient's behaviour.

At the meeting Chris summoned up the courage to tell Glenn their 25-year-old partnership was over. Glenn recalls, 'It was a completely non-confrontational meeting, although Chris was quite shaken up and finding it difficult to tell me that he wanted to leave the band. When he eventually managed to tell me, it was really upsetting.

'My opinion is that what had kept Chris going for the last few years was the feeling that success was around the corner, but that after *Ridiculous* it became obvious that this was very unlikely. I would have liked to have been successful again but the important thing for me was to make good music and enjoy that for itself. I don't think Chris was of the same view.'

Break-ups are rarely neat. One or both partners usually feel let down or abandoned, whatever the circumstances, particularly when so much emotional energy has been invested into a relationship. It is to Glenn and Chris's credit that rather than sit and stew on the ending of their working relationship, they began the next chapter of their working lives without the animosity that so many former musical partners allow to spill into public view.

It was inevitable, given the circumstances of their parting, that Chris and Glenn would initially give one another a wide berth as they sought to embark upon the next stage of their careers. Wisely, both men had too much respect for each other to attempt to snatch the legacy of the band for themselves, acknowledging that the Difford-Tilbrook partnership was equally weighted.

Yet beyond the politeness and mutual respect both men knew that life without the other would never be the same again.

15 This Could Be the Last Time

THE END of Squeeze might easily have degenerated into an unseemly public spat, but the sense of inviolable respect on both sides has meant that five years on from their break-up, Chris and Glenn have gradually rebuilt their friendship.

Through thick and thin the songwriters were almost Siamese-like in their closeness during their quarter-century-long partnership. Even during those dark days, and in some cases months, when Chris and Glenn could barely speak to each other, the pair stayed loyal and successfully prevented their bouts of personal enmity from reducing the quality of their output.

It must also be acknowledged that fractious songwriting partnerships have been at the centre of some of the best rock 'n' roll bands in history. Without the intense jealousy of the Lennon-McCartney partnership, would The Beatles have become the biggest band in the world? If the squabbles between Mick Jagger and Brian Jones, or Dave Gilmour and Roger Waters had never occurred, would The Rolling Stones or Pink Floyd have made the impact they did? Roger Daltrey and Pete Townshend have barely spoken a civil word for 25 years and yet The Who remain an electrifying stage presence. In the case of The Kinks and Oasis, both contain a pair of brothers who often find working together about as palatable as eating horse manure.

In some respects, therefore, it is remarkable that the Difford and Tilbrook partnership lasted as long as it did. Both men have markedly different personalities, Chris being the introverted, urbane wordsmith, and Glenn the extrovert, inventive, entertainer. With either man's tendency to put his partner's nose out of joint by a stray comment, the pair's long spells of poor communication may in fact have been a healthier option than if they had bickered constantly.

What is crystal clear is that both men have always respected intensely the complementary skills that the other brought to the table, and to this day they are fiercely loyal to the reputation of their former partner in crime. There has thus far been no war of words and no act of treachery from either camp.

Observing the two men in a room together tells its own story. The first time I met Glenn and Chris they greeted each other like long-lost brothers. They told stories, shared in-jokes, gently ribbed each other and at times seemed to finish each other's sentences.

As Chris himself observes, 'When I see Glenn now I don't have to ask any questions, which shows how close we are. I know instinctively what he's thinking. Apart from my brothers and children, he's the person I've been closest to during most of my life.'

Chris, now single after his divorce from Heidi, is a successful music manager, Marti Pellow and Bryan Ferry being the most notable artists to have been in the Difford stable. He also released a highly-regarded solo album, entitled *I Didn't Get Where I Am* in 2003, and is working on a follow-up with a variety of songwriting partners.

Glenn has also been busy, recording two critically-acclaimed albums, *The Incomplete Glenn Tilbrook* in 2001 and *Transatlantic Ping Pong* earlier this year. Accompanied by his backing band The Fluffers, Glenn tours Britain and America in one of two enormous motor homes that he keeps on either side of the Atlantic, relishing his freedom from the monotony of endless, uniformly-dull hotels. He is also happily married to Suzanne, who is also his manager, and indeed was Squeeze's last ever manager. The pair have a young son, Leon.

Despite the deterioration of their relationship in the 1990s there is no intrinsic reason why Glenn and Chris could not get back together. Yet whether we will ever see the reformation of the Difford-Tilbrook axis is far from certain.

For a start, both men have enjoyed their time apart and have discovered that they can write accomplished songs on their own, although the possibility of their solo work reaching the commercial heights of Squeeze is remote.

Of the two, Chris appears to be most agreeable to some form of reunion. 'If you put Squeeze back together we'd go straight into the Albert

Hall for a week, because it's a trade name that people are affectionate towards. That's why people buy Walkers Crisps, for their name. People became fans of ours when buying records meant something to them and those memories will forever stay with those people. A Chris Difford or a Glenn Tilbrook song, as good as they are, doesn't have the same resonance.'

Glenn is reluctant to reform Squeeze merely for the purpose of topping up his and Chris's savings accounts. 'I've always believed that the moment that money starts dictating to anybody what they do and how they approach their work then that's the kiss of death. I find the thought of a bunch of grumpy old blokes like us getting together on an '80s revival tour awful.'

The pair did make a brief appearance together at Glastonbury 2003 after Glenn came backstage to wish Chris good luck before his solo slot. Chris recalls, 'I asked Glenn if he would like to get up and sing with me, so he came up and we sang "Is That Love?" and "Hourglass". When he got up on the stage the atmosphere was electrifying. I can only describe it as like when you wake up at three in the morning with the largest erection on earth and look at the woman lying next to you, muttering "You're gonna get this." The audience went bananas and afterwards we were really excited that we'd played together.'

Despite this brief reunion Chris has resigned himself to the fact that Squeeze have probably played their last gig, even though the pair regularly receive lucrative offers to play one-off shows. 'My honest opinion is that it won't happen because we're two very different people, much more so than when we first met. Glenn would take a lot of persuading because I think I really burnt his fingers in our relationship and by leaving the band in the way I did. Glenn is the type of person who burns bridges when relationships go wrong and I don't believe he would rebuild that bridge back to me.'

Although seemingly unwilling to cash in on the extraordinary appetite of modern-day music fans for '70s and '80s reunion tours, Glenn says he might be open to working with Chris on other projects, so long as they had artistic credibility. Indeed, the pair wrote a song together for Glenn's recent solo album, entitled 'Where I Can Be Your Friend'.

He explains, 'Although I can't think of anything that would make me want to go back, if a project was suggested that I believed in then I would consider it. Circumstances can always change, and Chris and I are gradually getting closer again. I know that Chris would like the band to get together again but I do feel wary because of my experiences during the final years of Squeeze.'

One potential way of reuniting their writing partnership would be by working on another musical together. The staging of *Labelled With Love* gave them almost as much pleasure as making records and touring, and Glenn admits that co-writing a second show is a possibility. "I think if Chris and I were to work together again a musical would be the most likely route, because it wouldn't involve being in each other's pockets. We could walk into doing a musical tomorrow and it would probably be more financially lucrative than what I'm doing now, but I still like making records and playing live enough to want those to be my primary focus.'

With a back catalogue of almost 200 recorded songs and 13 studio albums, Chris and Glenn's songwriting partnership is one of immense repute. Had the band never reformed in 1985, Squeeze, and in particular Messrs Difford and Tilbrook, would still have assured their place in rock history. The fact that they continued to record highly-crafted songs until the end of the '90s, in spite of the obvious fragility of their personal relationship, should make their followers eternally thankful.

Whether or not Chris and Glenn choose to rejoin forces for anything beyond the compiling of this book, the duo have left behind a permanent musical legacy. From the Blackheath sweet shop to Madison Square Garden and beyond, the two men have undergone a 30-year journey from wide-eyed teenagers to a place on the top table of British songwriters. It's been one hell of a ride.

Squeeze Discography

ALBUMS

Squeeze (A&M)
Release date: March 1978

Cool For Cats (A&M)
Release date: March 1979

Argybargy (A&M)
Release date: February 1980

East Side Story (A&M)
Release date: May 1981

Sweets From A Stranger (A&M)
Release date: May 1982

Singles – 45's And Under (A&M)**
Release date: November 1982

Cosi Fan Tutti Frutti (A&M)
Release date: August 1985

Babylon And On (A&M)
Release date: September 1987

Frank (A&M)
Release date: September 1989

A Round And A Bout (Deptford Fun City)++
Release date: March 1990

Play (Warners/Reprise)
Release date: July 1991

Greatest Hits (A&M)**
Release Date: April 1992

Some Fantastic Place (A&M)
Release date: September 1993

Ridiculous (A&M)
Release date: November 1995

*Excess Moderation***
Release date: November 1996

Domino (Quixotic)
Release date: November 1998

Up The Junction (Spectrum)**
Release date: August 2000

*Big Squeeze: The Very Best Of Squeeze***
Release date: June 2002

** compilation
++ live album

SINGLES

'Packet Of Three' (Deptford Fun City)
Release date: July 1977
Highest UK Chart Position: Did Not Chart

'Take Me I'm Yours' (A&M)
Release date: February 1978
Highest UK Chart Position: 19

'Bang Bang' (A&M)
Release date: May 1978
Highest UK Chart Position: 49

'Goodbye Girl' (A&M)
Release date: November 1978
Highest UK Chart Position: 63

'Cool For Cats' (A&M)
Release date: March 1979
Highest UK Chart Position: 2

'Up The Junction'
Release date: May 1979
Highest UK Chart Position: 2

'Slap And Tickle' (A&M)
Release date: August 1979
Highest UK Chart Position: 24

'Packet Of Three' (re-release) (Deptford Fun City)
Release date: November 1979
Highest UK Chart Position: Did Not Chart

'Christmas Day' (A&M)
Release date: November 1979
Highest UK Chart Position: Did Not Chart

'Another Nail In My Heart' (A&M)
Release date: February 1980
Highest UK Chart Position: 17

'Pulling Mussels (From The Shell)' (A&M)
Release date: May 1980
Highest UK Chart Position: 44

'Is That Love?' (A&M)
Release date: May 1981
Highest UK Chart Position: 35

'Tempted' (A&M)
Release date: July 1981
Highest UK Chart Position: 41

'Labelled With Love' (A&M)
Release date: September 1981
Highest UK Chart Position: 4

'Black Coffee In Bed' (A&M)
Release date: April 1982
Highest UK Chart Position: 51

'When The Hangover Strikes' (A&M)
Release date: July 1982
Highest UK Chart Position: Did Not Chart

'Annie Get Your Gun' (A&M)
Release date: October 1982
Highest UK Chart Position: 43

'Last Time Forever' (A&M)
Release date: June 1985
Highest UK Chart Position: 45

'No Place Like Home' (A&M)
Release date: June 1985
Highest UK Chart Position: Did Not Chart

'Heartbreaking World' (A&M)
Release date: October 1985
Highest UK Chart Position: Did Not Chart

'King George Street' (A&M)
Release date: April 1986
Highest UK Chart Position: Did Not Chart

'Hourglass' (A&M)
Release date: July 1987
Highest UK Chart Position: 16

'Trust Me To Open My Mouth' (A&M)
Release date: September 1987
Highest UK Chart Position: 72

'The Waiting Game' (A&M)
Release date: November 1987
Highest UK Chart Position: Did Not Chart

'853-5937' (A&M)
Release date: January 1988
Highest UK Chart Position: Did Not Chart

'Footprints' (A&M)
Release date: June 1988
Highest UK Chart Position: Did Not Chart

'If It's Love' (A&M)
Release date: September 1989
Highest UK Chart Position: Did Not Chart

'Love Circles' (A&M)
Release date: January 1990
Highest UK Chart Position: Did Not Chart

'Sunday Street' (Warner/Reprise)
Release date: July 1991
Highest UK Chart Position: Did Not Chart

'Satisfied' (Warner/Reprise)
Release date: November 1991
Highest UK Chart Position: Did Not Chart

'Cool For Cats' (re-release) (A&M)
Release date: April 1992
Highest UK Chart Position: 62

'Third Rail' (A&M)
Release date: July 1993
Highest UK Chart Position: 39

'Some Fantastic Place' (A&M)
Release date: August 1993
Highest UK Chart Position: 73

'Loving You Tonight' (A&M)
Release date: October 1993
Highest UK Chart Position: Did Not Chart

'Its Over' (A&M)
Release date: February 1994
Highest UK Chart Position: Did Not Chart

'This Summer' (A&M)
Release date: August 1995
Highest UK Chart Position: 36

'Electric Trains' (A&M)
Release date: October 1995
Highest UK Chart Position: 44

'Heaven Knows' (A&M)
Release date: May 1996
Highest UK Chart Position: 27

'This Summer' (remix) (A&M)
Release date: August 1996
Highest UK Chart Position: 32

'Down In The Valley' (Quixotic)
Release date: May 1998
Highest UK Chart Position: Did Not Chart

The Long Honeymoon Discography (Chris and Glenn)

SINGLES

'The Amazoon' (A&M)
Release date: 1983 (month unknown)
Highest UK Chart Position: Did Not Chart

Difford And Tilbrook Discography

ALBUMS

Difford And Tilbrook (A&M)
Release date: July 1984

SINGLES

'Love's Crashing Waves' (A&M)
Release date: June 1984
Highest UK Chart Position: 57

'Hope Fell Down' (A&M)
Release date: September 1984
Highest UK Chart Position: Did Not Chart

Lyrics

Strong In Reason

You get your trunks
Out of the drawer
You see yourself
As once before
Strong in reason
Strong in reason
The empty box
Lies on the chair
Another steroid
Grease your hair and you're
Strong in reason
Strong in reason

The sun-ray lamp
Is put away
There is no need
To be afraid
Strong in reason
Strong in reason

So fix yourself
Into a shape
Your audience
Is half awake and you're
Strong in reason
Strong in reason

The time has come
To flex your back
Another day
For you, meat-rack
Strong in reason

Strong in maker
Strong in arm
Strong with almost perfect charm
Strong intention
Strong in strength
Strong in almost every sense

Strong in reason
Strong in reason
Strong in reason
Strong in reason

And on the stage
The lights are green
It's one step forward
Now you've been seen
Strong in reason
Strong in reason

The right arm up
The left arm down
Open mouth
The vacant crowd
Strong in reason
Strong in reason

The chest of wax
Flips like a coin
Into the rhythm

Into the join
Strong in reason
Strong in reason

The ladies in
The comfortable seats
They look at you with
Eyes so deep 'cause they're
Strong in reason
Strong in reason

Well take a bow
Because you'll get the sack
I'm pleased to slag you off
Meat-rack
Strong in reason
Strong in reason

Strong in maker
Strong in arm
Strong with almost perfect charm
Strong intention
Strong in strength
Strong in almost every sense

Take Me I'm Yours

I've come across the desert
To greet you with a smile
My camel looks so tired
It's hardly worth my while
To tell you of my travels
Across the golden East
I see your preparations

Invite me first to feast
Take me I'm yours
Because dreams are made of this
Forever there'll be
A heaven in your kiss

Amusing belly dancers
Distract me from my wine
Across Tibetian mountains
Are memories of mine
I've stood some ghostly moments
With natives in the hills
Recorded here on paper
My chills and thrills and spills

It's really been some welcome
You never seem to change
A grape to tempt your leisure
Romantic gestures strange
My eagle flies tomorrow
It's a game I treasure dear
To seek the helpless future
My love at last I'm here

Slap And Tickle

She was frigid like a Bible
When she met her boyfriend Michael
He took her in his Zephyr
They sat like salt and pepper
Looking out across the city
From Lover's Leap is pretty
The lights they flick and flutter
He told her how he loved her

Next night he called for her
But Dad protected daughter
And told him she was poorly
A lie was told there surely
So Michael felt rejected
This wasn't quite expected
He drove off to his local
Where he felt anti-social

She cried all night at missing
The boy she could be kissing
While he was falling over
He drunk himself back sober
And went home in a taxi
And crashed out in the back seat
He slept just like a baby
Which he hadn't done just lately

He saw her in the morning
Out with his sister Pauline
She felt all shy and soppy
He acted cool and cocky
He said tonight at Charlie's
There's going to be a party
I'll meet you at half seven
She visualised the heaven

If you ever change your mind
Which you do from time to time
Never chew a pickle
With a little slap and tickle
You have to throw the stone
To get the pool to ripple

That night they danced together
It looked like love forever

He put his hand on her leg
You should have heard what she said
He tried again much later
It seemed to aggravate her
He drove home in silence
Avoiding all violence
She said let's watch the city
From Lover's Leap is pretty
I think I need the fresh air
She put a comb through her hair
Then while she turned to kiss him
And very nearly missed him
She put her hand on his leg
He felt her tongue in his head

If you ever change your mind
Which you do from time to time
Never chew a pickle
With a little slap and tickle
You have to throw the stone
To get the pool to ripple

Up The Junction

I never thought it would happen
With me and the girl from Clapham
Out on a windy common
That night I ain't forgotten
When she dealt out the rations
With some or other passions
I said you are a lady
Perhaps she said I may be
We moved into a basement
With thoughts of our engagement
We stayed in by the telly

Although the room was smelly
We spent our time just kissing
The Railway Arms we're missing
But love had got us hooked up
And all our time it took up

I got a job with Stanley
He said I'd come in handy
And started me on Monday
So I had a bath on Sunday
I worked eleven hours
And bought the girl some flowers
She said she'd seen a doctor
And nothing now could stop her

I worked all through the winter
The weather brass and bitter
I put away a tenner
Each week to make her better
And when the time was ready
We had to sell the telly
Late evenings by the fire
With little kicks inside her

This morning at 4:50
I took her rather nifty
Down to an incubator
Where thirty minutes later
She gave birth to a daughter
Within a year a walker
She looked just like her mother
If there could be another

And now she's two years older
Her mother's with a soldier
She left me when my drinking

Became a proper stinging
The devil came and took me
From bar to street to bookie
No more nights by the telly
No more nights nappies smelling

Alone here in the kitchen
I feel there's something missing
I'd beg for some forgiveness
But begging's not my business
And she won't write a letter
Although I always tell her
And so it's my assumption
I'm really up the junction

Slightly Drunk

Slightly drunk once again
All alone with my pen
I thought I'd write to you
How can I say how I feel?
Falling down on a deal
This last night with you
Is it the cold that makes me shake?
I just hope that I'm awake
I say alright I knew
(I knew)

I was wrong
You were right
(That's a line I cannot find)
I could not
Say goodbye
(To explain just why I lied)

Why's it always
Feel the same?
(Slightly drunk what you said to me)
I'm in love once again
(Can't fall in love without misery)

I'm pretty sad but so what?
I should be glad but I'm not
I'm confused once more
All tangled up in your love
Without it now so that's tough
My heart cries for

A little talk to anger me
Out on the road especially
Back to you once more
(Once more)

Slightly drunk once again
All alone without friends
Had it all, I know I lied
All my ends seem untied
I cannot say how I feel

Goodbye Girl

I met her in a poolroom
Her name I didn't catch
She looked like something special
The kind who'd understand
The room was almost spinning
She pulled another smile
She had the grace like pleasure
She had a certain style

Sunlight on the lino
Woke me with a shake
I looked around to find her but she'd gone
Goodbye Girl
Goodbye Girl
Goodbye Girl

She took me to her hotel
The room on the second floor
A kettle and two coffees
Her number on the door
She said I hardly know you
Agreed we kissed goodnight
I knew that in the morning
Somehow I'd wake to find

I lost my silver razor
My clubroom locker keys
The money in the waistcoat
It doesn't bother me
My wife has moved to Guernsey
So mug is not the word
If you ever see her
Say hello Goodbye Girl

Cool For Cats

The Indians send signals
From the rocks above the pass
The cowboys take positions
In the bushes and the grass
The squaw is with the Corporal
She is tied against the tree
She doesn't mind the language

It's the beating she don't need
She lets loose all the horses
When the Corporal is asleep
And he wakes to find the fire's dead
And arrows in his hats
And Davy Crockett rides around
And says it's cool for cats

The Sweeney's doing ninety
'Cos they've got the word to go
They get a gang of villains
In a shed up at Heathrow
They're counting out the fivers
When the handcuffs lock again
In and out of Wandsworth
With the numbers on their names
It's funny how their missus'
Always look the bleeding same
And meanwhile at the station
There's a couple of likely lads
Who swear like how's your father
And they're very cool for cats
They're cool for cats

To change the mood a little
I've been posing down the pub
On seeing my reflection
I'm looking slightly rough
I fancy this, I fancy that
I wanna be so flash
I give a little muscle
And I spend a little cash
But all I get is bitter and a nasty little rash
And by the time I'm sober
I've forgotten what I've had
And ev'rybody tells me that it's cool to be a cat

Cool for cats
Shake up at the disco
And I think I've got a pull
I ask her lots of questions
And she hangs on to the wall
I kiss her for the first time
And then I take her home
I'm invited in for coffee
And I give the dog a bone
She likes to go to discos
But she's never on her own
I said I'll see you later
And I give her some old chat
But it's not like that on the TV
When it's cool for cats
It's cool for cats

Pulling Mussels (From The Shell)

They do it down on Camber Sands
They do it at Waikiki
Lazing about the beach all day
At night the crickets creepy
Squinting faces at the sky
A Harold Robbins paperback
Surfers drop their boards and dry
And everybody wants a hat
But behind the chalet
My holiday's complete
And I feel like William Tell
Maid Marian on her tiptoed feet
Pulling mussels from a shell

Shrinking in the sea so cold

Topless ladies look away
A he-man in a sudden shower
Shelters from the rain
You wish you had a motor boat
To pose around the harbour bar
And when the sun goes off to bed
You hook it up behind the car

Two fat ladies window shop
Something for the mantelpiece
In for bingo all the nines
A panda for sweet little niece
The coach drivers stand about
Looking at a local map
About the boy he's gone away
Down to next door's caravan

Another Nail In My Heart

The case was pulled from under the bed
She made a call to a sympathetic friend
And made arrangements
The door was closed there was a note
I couldn't be bothered
Maybe I'll choke
No more engagements

With where have you been's
And faraway frowns
Trying to be good
By not being 'round
And here in the bar
The piano man's found
Another nail for my heart

That stupid old bug
That kills only love
I want to be good
Is that not enough

So play me the song
That makes it so tough
Another nail for my heart
Then play me that song
That makes it so tough
Another nail for my heart

I had excuses those little boy lies
That she computed by watching my eyes
And told me firmly

She couldn't stand it I'm bad on her heart
She dropped her makeup and I found the bar
Now it concerns me

I've had a bad time
Now love is resigned
I've been such a fool
I've loved and goodbyed

So here in the bar
The piano man's found
Another nail for my heart
And here in the bar
The piano man's found
Another nail for my heart

I Think I'm Go Go

Funny words I cannot read
Trams and boats where Strauss is street
Milky way and far out looks
On your bike and Anne Frank books
Down the disco it's clockworktime
Where's the humour where am I
This world's got smaller
I'm shaking lots of hands
Saying lots of things
That no one understands
You can shake my tree
But you won't get me
Where am I
I think I'm go go, go go, go go

Liquor store and rodeos
P I X and rock and roll
The freckled face the thin and fat
The drive-in films and drive-in macs
Strip and porno neon signs
Where's the building where am I

Buckingham Palace trains all late
Funny little men all out in the rain
Car front deals and after pubs
Tenth year plays and seedy clubs
Iffy people don't seem to mind
Where's the action where am I

Separate Beds

Tonight I take her from her parents
I came along to her rescue

Without a word about arrangements
She came along without a clue
So I said my love I want to take you
A place I have inside my head
And so it seemed I had to love you
With some cards and separate beds

Her mother didn't like me
She thought I was on drugs
My mother didn't like her
She'd never peel the spuds
So we took off together
And stayed at Mrs Smith's
Breakfast at half seven
Where you can view the cliffs

The moon was full and in our window
I could see her turning in her bed
I was loved but all in limbo
There was time to pass but not to spend
Soon I saw that this was silly
Spending all my wages on this peach
When we could sit so very pretty
And get our heads down out on the beach

Her father seemed to like me
I helped him fix his car
My father seemed to like her
And I couldn't see the harm
In going off together
To see the pier and lights
So we could be together
In separate beds tonight

If I Didn't Love You

If I didn't love you I'd hate you
Watching you play in the bath
A soap suds stickle back navy
A scrubbing brush landing craft
Your skin gets softer and warmer
I pat you down with a towel
Tonight it's love by the fire
My mind goes out on the prowl
If I, If I, If I, If I, If I

If I didn't love you I'd hate you
I'm playing your stereogram
Singles remind me of kisses
Albums remind me of plans
Tonight it's love by the fire
The wind plays over the coals
Passionate looks are my fancy
But you turn the look into stone

If I didn't love you
Would you sit and glow by the fire
If I didn't love you
Would you make me feel so
Maybe love me
Oh if I didn't love you

If I didn't love you I'd hate you
Cocoa mugs sit side by side
It's time to poke at the fire
But it's not tonight
Looks I find
Taking a bite on a biscuit
The record jumps on a scratch
Tonight it's love by the fire

The door of your love's on the latch

If I, if I, if I
Didn't, didn't, didn't
Love you, love you, love you

Vicky Verky

With her hair up in his fingers
The fish and chips smell lingers
Under amber streetlamps
She holds the law in her hands
The moistness of the damp night
Falls silent through the lamplight
Although she's only fourteen
She really knows her courting
And up the railway sidings
There's him and her
They're lying
Hand in hand they whisper
You're my missus and I'm your mister
The moon as white and virgin
And she was on the turning
Remember your first nibble
When best friends were so little

They really trooped the colours
When walking with each other
And all her mates would giggle
As ladylike she'd wiggle
All along the high street
They'd splash out on an ice cream
He'd sometimes really treat her
But he'd done his mother's meter

Well he went off to Borstal
He said that he was forced to
Rob the flats of Hi Fi's
Cuz she was ill
And she would cry
Each morning she got sicker
Her mother sometimes hit her
If she'd have known the story
She would have been so sorry

He received a letter and admitted it
There was nothing else to do but get rid of it
Lonely in his dormitory
He'd sit and stare
If this is for real
And is it really fair

Summer came so they went
Down to the coast in his tent
She cooked upon his primus
And sampled local cider
She told him in his rucksack
I think I want that chance back
To be perhaps the one who
Will forever love you

Tempted

I bought a toothbrush, some toothpaste
A flannel for my face
Pyjamas, a hairbrush
New shoes and a case
I said to my reflection
Let's get out of this place

Past the church and the steeple
The laundry on the hill
Billboards and the buildings
Memories of it still
Keep calling and calling
But forget it all
I know I will

Tempted by the fruit of another
Tempted but the truth is discovered
What's been going on
Now that you have gone
There's no other
Tempted by the fruit of another
Tempted but the truth is discovered

I'm at the car park, the airport
The baggage carousel
The people keep on crowding
I'm wishing I was well
I said it's no occasion
It's no story I could tell

At my bedside empty pocket
A foot without a sock
Your body gets much closer
I fumble for the clock
Alarmed by the seduction
I wish that it would stop

I bought a novel, some perfume
A fortune all for you
But it's not my conscience
That hates to be untrue
I asked of my reflection
Tell me what is there to do

Piccadilly

She's not a picture above somebody's fire
She sits in a towel with a purple hair dryer,
She waits to get even with me.
She hooks up her cupcakes and puts on her jumper
Explains that she'll be late to a worrying mother,
She meets me in Piccadilly.
A begging folk singer stands tall by the entrance
His song relays worlds of most good intentions,
A fiver a ten p in his hat for collection.

She talks about office she talks about dresses
She's seen one she fancies her smile is impressing,
So maybe I'll treat her someday.
We queue among strangers and strange conversation
Love's on the lips of all forms of engagements,
All queuing to see tonight's play.

A man behind me talks to his young lady
He's happy that she is expecting his baby,
His wife won't be pleased but she's not been round lately.

The girl was so dreadful we left in a hurry
We escaped in the rain for an Indian curry,
At the candle lit Taj Mahal.
My lips to a napkin I called for a taxi
The invite of eyes made it tense but relaxed me,
My mind took a devious role.

The cab took us home through a night I'd not noticed
The neon club lights of adult films and Trini Lopez,
My arm around love but my acting was her best.

We crept like two thieves from the kettle to the fire
We kissed to the sound of the silence that we'd hired,

Now captured, your love in my arms.
A door opened slightly a voice spoke in worry
Mum went to bed without wind of the curry,
Our secret love made its advance.

Like Adam and Eve we took bite on the apple
Loose change in my pocket it started to rattle,
Heart like a gun was just half of the battle.

Someone Else's Bell

We talk about each other
On our wrap around couch,
And live out all the romance
In our little town house.
I never fit the shower
And she never sews the threads,
And so we find our feelings
In other people's beds.
And if the grass seems greener,
But it turns out to be blue
The garden of Eden isn't quite the place for you.
Don't be surprised if I'm gone under the spell,
Of some other witches' wand
Ringing someone else's bell.

Meeting on the motorway
Your lover boy blue,
Steaming up the windows
With your last breath of youth.
Don't you think I see it
Your handbag's full of notes,
I'm feeling like the punch line
In someone's private joke.

Our eyes don't seem to contact
Never much to say,
Except perhaps excuse me
Or pass me the ashtray.
I see him waiting for you
As you go off to work,
I'm left to draw conclusions
While I button up my shirt.

Woman's World

The crown of the kingdom is given to the woman
The kingdom of the kitchen where she says she shouldn't,
There on the stainless steel her cigarettes and matches
Whistles to the radio to every hook she catches,
But the frowns
Eider downs,
Tie her down
But she likes to wear the crown of the kingdom.
She like the recipes a touch of oriental
Steaming up the windows burning egg on metal,
Sees in a catalogue a shiny new appliance
Another role swallowed by the wonders of science,
Lobster hands
Omelette pans,
Understand
How the crown can stick like jam in her kingdom.

He's been so busy and she's been neglected,
The problem is computed and always it's rejected,
Out of her heart I catch a spark,
And being smart
The crown is left out in the dark now there's no kingdom.

Fed up with the glory she abdicates her title
Sitting at a bar stool she gives her day's recital,
The family watch in horror
As she staggers up the hallway
Makes herself a sandwich
As they're looking through the doorway,
She goes to bed
Leg by leg,
Nothing's said
There's no crown upon her head there's no kingdom.

Press the button on the toaster
It's a woman's world,
Tuck the sheets in on the bed
It's a woman's world,
Take your apron from your holster
It's a woman's world,
Shoot the crown off of your head
It's a woman's world.

Is That Love?

You've left my ring by the soap,
Now is that love?
You cleaned me out you could say broke,
Now is that love?
The better better better it gets
The more these girls forget
That that is love.
You won't get dressed you walk about,
Now is that, is that
A teasing glance has pushed me out,
Now is that, is that
The tougher tougher tougher it gets

The more my lips frequent
Now that is love.

Beat me up with your letters, your walk out notes,
Funny how you still find me right here at home.
Legs up with a book and a drink,
Now is that love that's making you think.

You've called my bluff I'm not so hot,
Now is that love
My assets froze while yours have dropped,
Now is that, is that
It's the cupid cupid cupid disguise
That more or less survived
Now that is love.

Beat me up with your letters, your walk out notes,
Funny how you still find me right here at home.
Legs up with a book and a drink,
Now is that love that's making you think.

You've made my bed the finger points
Now is that, is that love
The more you more you more you cool down
The easier love is found
Now that is love.

LABELLED WITH LOVE

She unscrews the top of a new whiskey bottle
And shuffles about in her candle lit hovel,
Like some kind of witch with blue fingers in mittens
She smells like the cat and the neighbours she sickens,
The black and white TV has long seen a picture

The cross on the wall is a permanent fixture,
The postman delivers the final reminders
She sells off her silver and poodles in China.
Drinks to remember, I me and myself
And winds up the clock
And knocks dust from the shelf
Home is a love that I miss very much
So the past has been bottled and labelled with love.

During the war time an American pilot
Made every air raid a time of excitement,
She moved to his prairie and married the Texan
She learnt from a distance how love was a lesson,
He became drinker and she became mother
She knew that one day she'd be one or the other,
He ate himself older, drunk himself dizzy
Proud of her features, she kept herself pretty.

He like a cowboy died drunk in his slumber
Out on the porch in the middle of summer,
She crossed the ocean back home to her family
But they had retired to roads that were sandy,
She moved home alone without friends or relations
Lived in a world full of age reservation,
On moth eaten armchairs she'd say that she'd sod all
The friends who had left her to drink from the bottle.

When The Hangover Strikes

When the hangover strikes
And I open my post
And the coffee is on
And I'm burning my toast
I let the battle commence

I see a sun in the trees
And a draught at the door
With my head in my lap
There's a day to explore
But I'm left without sense
As the hangover strikes
And I turn on the tap
But the water's too loud
And I'm caged by the fact
That the battle's not lost
Is it the hair of the dog
Or the Baa of a Lamb
In a sheepish attempt
To be half of the man
That I might be or was

When the hangover strikes
And a mirror reveals
That it's Midnight or bust
And a drink does appeal
Now the battle is won
So the cure of the can
Pours its heart out on me
Though I'm feeling locked up
But I can't find the key
Well no damage was done

Poor poor poor, poor shaken one
Pour pour pour, pour me another one

Black Coffee In Bed

There's a stain on my notebook
Where your coffee cup was
And there's ash in the pages
Now I've got myself lost
I was writing to tell you
That my feelings tonight
Are a stain on my notebook
That rings your goodbye
With the way that you left me
I can hardly contain
The hurt and the anger
And the joy of the pain
Now knowing I am single
They'll be fire in my eyes
And a stain on my notebook
For a new love tonight

From the lips without passion
To the lips with a kiss
There's nothing of your love
That I'll ever miss
The stain on my notebook
Remain all that's left
Of the memory of late nights
And coffee in bed

Now she's gone
And I'm back on the beat
A stain on my notebook
Says nothing to me
Now she's gone
And I'm out with a friend
With lips full of passion
And coffee in bed

King George Street

She left in the middle of the night with the kids
Wrapped in a blanket with a packet of crisps
Heading for her mother's on another estate
The kids looked up at the light and the rain
In the middle of the night such adventures made
For two little kids staying up late
It was rainy and windy as winter was bleak
At four in the morning on King George Street
She couldn't get to sleep where on Earth had he gone
The door opened wide and the light went on
He was drunk as a lord with a tyre mark hat
Falling in the hall on top of the cat
Singing 'Viva Espana' to a crying wife
He took a swing at the shade on the light
They were knocking on the doors dressed like refugees
In the pouring rain on King George Street

She won't have that behaviour in her house any more
He's got to sober up or get kicked out of the door
Down on the corner the kids at his feet
As daddy comes home on King George Street

They stood around the kettle and watched as it brewed
Sneezing into hankies hands all blue
The next evening he came around to the house
With a bunch of flowers they locked him out
He peered through the window
Mouthed words through the air
Her lips to a cup she saw him out there
The kids came running but were they happy to see
Their daddy back home on King George Street

LAST TIME FOREVER

Did you ever hear the words
That said love would end I read them tonight
Mistakes I can't defend
I didn't stop to think
And I upset her
I said good night tonight the last time forever
I think of her tonight
She keeps me from my sleep but what can I do
With all these memories
I used to be so shy
And hide my temper
I'll say good night tonight the last time forever

It all went wrong when I grew jealous
I didn't realise my strength
Could take the life of one so happy
Together we were known as good friends

Did you ever read the words
That said I love you I read them tonight
But what good can they do
I regret what I have done
It wasn't clever
I said good night tonight the last time forever

NO PLACE LIKE HOME

I'm faced with the facts
And a fist full of threats
I stand quite amused
At the end of the bed
I have no defence

For what I have said
As a handful of love
Whacks me right round the head
She's growling and stalking
And grabs from a pile
A book that she throws
And it missed by a mile
I'm holding a pillow
And as naked as sin
I'm backed to a corner
With a wastepaper bin
Then up on the mattress
There's no place to go
I'm guilty yes guilty
But there's no place like home

I rewind the hours
To see what went wrong
I plead for forgiveness
And I'm hit like a gong
It seems that I'm guilty
Of smiling too long
When recalling lovers
That now are long gone
I'm guilty you're guilty
So let me be stoned
The past is the present
When there's no place like home

Off with the shoes
And a whack round the head
Your ear rings like a phone
Some explanation
Might patch and mend
A love that's lost control
Now there's no place like home

Tough Love

There she sits in an empty room
The look on her face says it all
A bruise appears round a crying eye
As the tear drops sadly fall
He knocked her over he hit her
And told her she's stupid
He's high as a kite once again
She knows that tough love is needed
To save the love of her friend

There he sits in a freezing car
She's in her bed in the warm
The cold light of the morning sky
Finds him cramped and looking worn
He wanders inside on tiptoes
And brews up some coffee
He's shaking and sweating again
She knows that tough love is needed
To save the love of her friend

They talk it over but it's not easy
Sorting it out
She cannot take it when he tells lies
And sneaks off out of the room
Returning like somebody's lost balloon

Tea leaves sit in an empty cup
No expression on his face
The TV's showing commercials
He's back in her arms again
No more the drugs and the drinking
Her heart can stop sinking
Now that he's home once again
She knows that tough love is needed

To save the love of her friend

They talked it over for hours and hours and hours
'Til everything sounded the same
She knows it's tough love that she finds in her heart
To dissolve the pain

The Prisoner

He's taking her away
He's acting like a general
Generally his game is so familiar
He wants her to play
With a toaster and a kettle
While he spends his day
Miles from the prisoner
She reads the stars he reads the sun
No wonder his IQ is below 21

He's helping her to see
How happy she is looking
Take it that he'll be
No icing on her cake
O how happy she would be
If someone did the cooking
He's helping her to see
How a marriage can be baked

Baked like a cake but without the file
The tool that she needs to make her life worthwhile

She's not a prisoner alone doing time
To love and to cherish for all of her life
To have and to hold, to lock up inside

What can this man know about her heart
To love, 'til death do us part

He's looking everywhere
She is nowhere to be found
And suddenly he cares
His dinner's looking burnt
There's a smell in the air
There's a prisoner in town,
He sits down in his chair
His face fills with concern
Concerned that he might not eat tonight
She's broken out of jail and run for her life

Striking Matches

Striking matches and I'm smoking cigarettes
Putting on the kettle, playing a cassette
Folding up the papers rubbing my eyes
Thinking of all that had happened last night
The passion, the feelings that soaked in her love
And the pools of silence when kisses were sprung
Her love levitates me, I'm walking on air
Two feet from the carpet, I'll always be there
Oooh I'm striking matches it's morning again
I look in the mirror I still look the same
I'm striking matches it's morning again
I look in the mirror I go up in flames

Striking matches getting a flame on the stove
There's some of her in the teeth of my comb
Dirty clothes piled up on the bathroom floor
She's silently sleeping, I half close the door
I see her beauty laying on my bed

I'm warm from within me with what she has said
Her love is my balloon, I won't let it down
For ever and ever I'll always be proud.

I'm a director casting for a part
(Turn on the light)
It's for a soap set here right in my heart.
(Leave her alone)
Shuffle to the window shuffle to the door
(Don't wake her up)
She gets the part I don't want to see anymore
(Unplug the phone)

THE WAITING GAME

I heard the stomping of feet dancing
On the wooden floor upstairs
I wasn't in the mood for laughing
So I sat silent in my chair
There was someone missing I knew
Outside there fell the rain
Where had she gone, what could I do
I played the waiting game
The cigarette smoke was annoying
My mood was fit for a bath
A drink couldn't oil my expression
Nothing could make me laugh
I was worried out of my head
I was in such a state
What's keeping her, where has she gone
I played the waiting game

When you love someone
You worry when they're late

When you love someone
You know the time it takes
To play the waiting game

The music got louder and louder
From the wooden floor upstairs
I played with a handful of peanuts
When I saw her standing there
My mood leapt right out of the bath
She had got stuck in the rain
Her coat dripped on a hanger
Playing the waiting
I couldn't understand her
Playing the waiting
Seemed like I'd wait forever
Playing the waiting game

PEYTON PLACE

In Peyton Place my heart now beats
And floor boards creak where an angel sleeps
Her hair hung across her face
Like a bush hangs across a wall
She was short with a tidy smile
I could hear temptation call
From a fly in her ointment
To the big feather in her cap
It's a small world we discover
I had once worked for her dad
I was in gear making up stories
And we laughed at each other's tales
I watched her lips I wanted to kiss them
My train of thought went off the rails

In Peyton Place my heart now beats
And floor boards creak where an angel sleeps
In Peyton Place
I lie awake and hear the sound
That the angels make
In Peyton Place

The party was now ending
So she gave me a lift back home
Somehow I felt so nervous
She drove so slowly on the road
Next thing I knew she was in my arms
Her hair was all over my face
I brushed it aside she invited me in
Now my heart beats in Peyton Place

Her hair hung across her face like
A bush hangs across a wall

SLAUGHTERED, GUTTED AND HEARTBROKEN

Slaughtered, gutted and heartbroken
With no spirit or no soul
My emotions have been stolen
Love has left me with this hole
Now my heart's a deep dark cavern
Emptiness is all I feel
I'm the pig she tried to fatten
And now all I do is squeal
But things could be worse
Things could be very bad for me
O' my dear I find myself
A stitch short of a tapestry

Patience on the verge of breaking
I'm kicking cans around the street
Like a bad cold I need shaking
Like a fool I want to cheat
But to me she was an angel
And I went and let her down
The attraction was so fatal
That she kicked me off her cloud

The light was on there in her window
I saw her shadow moving around
I tried to stand on tip toes
Hoping that she might look down
I wanted so bad to call her
But I had to walk away
Slaughtered, gutted and heartbroken
Another diamond down the drain

She Doesn't Have To Shave

She was washing the dishes
When she burst into tears
It was the time of the month
She was up to her ears
I put my arms round her neck
I said sit down a while
Cry as much as you like
I'll do the dishes
Tell me what's on your mind
There's a boiling point
That you're bound to reach
When it's all your fault

And you're half asleep.
She's lucky she doesn't have to shave
I'm so lucky I'm not doubled up with pain

Her eyes were like pools
Filled with newly wed tears
She was sat doubled up
With her hands on her ears
I felt useless
I smiled and I shrugged
I was sweet as could be
As I poured her some milk
Here was my flower
That was ready to wilt

A fairy tale finish
We flaked out on the floor
It was *Match Of The Day*
On the TV what's more
I fell asleep at half time
We had had a right result
It was kisses and hugs
At the end of the day
She's the one that I love

LOVE CIRCLES

The first circle comes around
You don't want to leave her side
You're staying in and don't go out
You're having such a perfect time
You make your bed and you lie in it
And time is precious every minute
The next circle comes around

And so domestic you become
In your matching dressing gowns
You think your life time's just begun
You cut the cake but just the one slice
You're crawling back all through the night

Love circles up above
It waits until your love
Breaks down and weeps
Then it's out of your reach
Love circles up above
It waits for your love
Down on the floor
Then you're there in its claws
Love circles up above

The last circle comes around
You're making plans to fill your days
You're always wanting to stay out late
And you can feel love start to fade
You fall asleep or read a book
The phone goes back upon the hook

When I lay awake at night
And love can't be found
The first circle's on my mind
It goes round and round and round and round

MELODY MOTEL

He drove up to the motel
In his town and country car
He watched the working women
With the field hands from the farm
He walked into the lobby
With his pleased to see you smile
Scribbled on to the register
His fictitious name and smiled
The footsteps of a young girl
Came tapping along the hall
The outline of his features
Were shadowed on the wall
She stood a little nervous
Half lit by the neon light
That flashed in many colours
Through the darkness of the night

The skin on his face
Like a well worn saddle
Smiled as he said goodnight
At the melody motel
It was business as usual
As the girls wiped the tears from their eyes

His shirt lay by his bedside
His jeans down by his feet
She swallowed hard and mumbled
With the key between her teeth
On went the television
The picture flickering slow
Top cat in the alley way
As they sat there all alone

He drove back up his driveway

In his town and country car
His wife was cooking chicken
With a baby in her arms
The smell of home cooked dinner
Filled the air at home that night
Screaming Officer Dibble
In the TV's flickering light

Slumped in his favourite armchair
His face as grey as stone
His feet up on the table
Next to the chicken bones
He seemed to show no feelings
Picking corn out from his teeth
Police down at the motel
As the blood dried on the sheets

LETTING GO

She plaits her hair, I bite my nails
We balance love on the scales
I wind the clock and go to bed
Our love is hanging on a thread
She gets undressed, I undress too
The draft is cold in my bedroom
We cuddle up and say goodnight
It's all the love there is tonight.
I can't be brave enough
She cannot say what we're feeling
Day after day
We're going through the motions
We find it hard to let each other go

She boils the eggs, I make the tea
Outside the sun shines on the street
We're at that point where love has gone
The fuse is lit, it won't be long
I take a walk, she cleans the house
This is the end, I'm in no doubt
But neither one of us can show
The slightest sign of letting go

The Truth

I lied to you, I've cheated too
So what friend can I be
But still you stick through thick and thin
Hoping that you'll change me
I towed the line then fell behind
Our love began to wane
The pressure grew and then I knew
That things were not the same
The truth
It's the toughest thing to explain
The truth
Playing tricks with me again
When the truth has to be told
My blood runs hot and cold
The truth is not my middle name

You threw a rope attached with hope
Way down into the sea
Where lovers swim so deep within
The tides of mystery
For what it's worth I don't deserve
A girl as strong as you
You're worth much more than me I'm sure
Accept this as the truth

Walk A Straight Line

I need some help
Help to decide
Whether it's our love
That steps out of time
You say you need
Time on your own
Time to accept how
Our love has grown
And when you think about
All of the bad in me
Think about this too
How me and you could forever be

In need of help
Help to expand
With each other's minds
Together to plan
Time in our lives
Time on our own
So one day we'll see
Our love has grown

And when that day arrives
I don't know where we'll be
But I hope that trust
Can be for us
And you'll still love me

I need some help
Help to be found
When you are alone
I won't let you down
We all need time
Time on our own

So we can step back
And see how love's grown

And when I'm stepping back
I hope that I will see
That faith can play a part today
For both you and me

And if love needs help
And if love needs time
Give love the strength
To walk a straight line

WICKED AND CRUEL

I had the rug pulled from under my feet
But I didn't feel a thing
I can't believe the luck I seem to have
And the joy that good luck brings
When I die I'll return as a housefly
And land upon her wall
So I can see who she'll end up with
If it's anyone at all
Did I say that
How could anyone be so wicked and cruel
I sat and listened to the radio
A landscape of moving noise
She was busy looking through the curtains
Her nose in a distant void
Then I thought I would come back as a spider
Because she hates them so much
They get sprayed down the bathroom plughole
Can I expect the same touch

Maybe not then
Because beneath it all we're wicked and cruel

Shut up, listen to the radio

I can't help feeling I've been stepped on
She likes to kick like a mule
Did I say that
How could anyone be so wicked and cruel

If I come back as her would I love me
How could anyone be so wicked and cruel

She likes to think I'm a fool
Two fools in love
How could anyone be so wicked and cruel

THERE IS A VOICE

There is a voice within us all
That says destruct
Go to the wall
And you can't choose when this voice speaks
Deep in our souls
This voice will sleep
There is a voice within us all
That says destruct
And you will crawl
From your own pit into the deep
Where you will sink
Until it speaks

Each day is a night
Then your lifetime is gone

There is a voice inside us all
That says rebuild
And when it's called
All that is wrong can be put right
There in your soul
To change your life
Each day's a hope each day's a prayer
That I might build
And I'll repair
The parts in me that may have slipped
Deep in my soul
When I lose my grip

And there's ropes and chains
Slowing me as I walk
I feel hope through pain
As the road ahead forks
To the left and the right
To the right and the wrong

Some Fantastic Place

She gave to me her tenderness
Her friendship and her love
I see her face from time to time
There in the sky above
We grew up learning as we went
What a voyage our life could be
It took us through a wilderness
Into the calmest sea
Her smile could lift me from the pain
I often found within
She said some things I won't forget
She made a few bells ring

So simple her humility
Her beauty found in grace
Today she lives another life
In some fantastic place
She showed me how to raise a smile
Out of a bed of gloom
And in a garden sanctuary
A life began to bloom
She visualised a world ahead
And planned how it would be
She left behind the strongest love
That lives eternally
I have the hope that when it's time
For me to come her way
That she'll be there to show me round
Whenever comes that day
Her love was life and happiness
And in her steps I trace
The way to live a better life
In some fantastic place

Third Rail

As much as I love you
As much as I care
I just can't pretend that
The problem's not there
We know all the boundaries
From where we both stand
Our life has been happy
Without any plan
But now I feel sorrow
As friendship turns stale
Our love's still on track but

Without a third rail
The moon has come up now
The sun has gone down
A million or more times
Since you've been around
Our life still goes on but
It won't be the same
As when we're together
Love only knows pain
With words that are tender
Our love will prevail
But can our love go on
Without a third rail

White clouds appear like cotton wool
The wind bends trees to bow
As we farewell this love of ours
Like some old sacred cow
As sure as heaven's above us
And hell is down below
Without a third rail to drive us
We'll have no place to go

There's a lump in my throat
I'm choked as I say
Our love has reached twilight
Let's call it a day
We kiss on the platform
The doors slowly close
Like theatre curtains
Pulled after the show
We both know it's over
And somehow we've failed
Love's going in circles
Without a third rail

IT'S OVER

Hey wait a minute
That's not right
I didn't want this to cause a fight
All I'm saying is
Nothing new
Listen to me, believe it's true
What's there to hide, it baffles me
Throw out those thoughts of jealousy
So don't you cry and hold your head
It's over
So wait a minute
Let me explain
Out of the blue she called again
To offer me
A peaceful meal
So we can talk see how we feel
It's nothing more than face to face
So trust in me I know my place
I know it's hard to let me go
It's over
All over

Have confidence
Have faith
There is no attraction there
And believe me
This way
I can wash her from my hair

Hey wait a minute
What's going on
I'm coming home where I belong
It's nothing more than face to face
Give me the time to pack my case

I know it's hard to let me go
It's over

What's there to hide it baffles me
Why should you waste your energy
But I won't leave if you're not sure
It's over
It's all over

Loving You Tonight

The full moon's glowing
Blood red in the sky
It hangs like fire
On this winter's night
I sit on feelings
That hang in suspense
Nothing in my life makes sense
A question mark hangs with the stars up above
As I'm driving home to the one that I love
Sometimes I can't see the trees for the wood
Loving you tonight feels good
The moonlight changes
From red into white
It sits on tree tops
Asleep for the night
I see the signpost
The road slowly bends
Nothing in my life makes sense
A flashing tail light speeds across the sky
My head's cooking trouble as thoughts seem to fry
The last temptation was misunderstood
Loving you tonight feels good

I'm faced with the ultimate truth
What if I see things don't improve
I know they could
Loving you tonight feels good

The sun is rising
There's mist all around
She sleeps beside me
And I feel so proud
Am I in heaven
With her by my side
This is how love feels tonight

COLD SHOULDER

My head was stuck in the cat flap on the door
Where I could see her walking on the kitchen floor
Down on my knees
Just like a dog
Begging for scraps that she said she hadn't got
She took her pen she poked me in the eye
As through the lock I looked to see my world inside
I kicked and swore
Void of all brain
I couldn't see that I was the one to blame

Cold shoulder
Like a slaughtered cow in a butcher's fridge
Cold shoulder
She had laid the plans where we built our bridge
To a better life
Cold shoulder

I had been chased by a hairbrush that she threw
Life was blurred when the hand of fate came into view
It smacked my face
I was released
I came back home where life became a feast

Cold shoulder
Like a slaughtered cow in a butcher's fridge
Cold shoulder
She had laid the plans where we built our bridge
To a better life
Cold shoulder
Then I fell over
Into a bush

Electric Trains

When I was crowned a mummy's boy by friends I didn't like
I made a meal of trips to school upon my father's bike
I used to sit between his legs, perched on a piece of wood
If it ever rained on us, I'd slip beneath his hood
And at home the radio was on
From Julie Andrews to Jerry Garcia
Life was all fun and games
I was out of my head and underneath my bed
Playing with electric trains

At home the stereo was on
My head was filled with rock
I played a willow cricket bat guitar
And soloed round the clock
My records stacked up in a pile
Collected from the charts
And *Top Of The Pops*

Kneeling with torchlight shining
Before me in my bed
My eyeballs stuck in *Reader's Wives*
Pubic hairs proudly counted everyday
Manhood took me slowly
Out into the milky way

I chased the girls and made them cry
My hair grew down my back
The passing of my teenage years
Were spent down in the sack
I played guitar and formed a band
I puked up all night long

As people came to sit and stare
While I raced through my songs
The sound of music passed by me
Just like the Grateful Dead

WALK AWAY

A black and white photograph
Of me up the garden path
Wrapped up in my football scarf
It sits here in my hand
And there mother smothered me
And how she would mother me
She knew how to suffer me
Like all mothers can
Now she is everywhere
The comb that runs through my hair
My posture on a chair
But that's not who I am
He ran from the arguments

And sat on the garden fence
And lived in the passing tense
That fell from her lips
He tended the house so well
And each time she rang his bell
He'd climb back from where he fell
And gathered his wits
Now I fear the mold is mine
A vibration shakes my spine
As I walk the crooked line
Reality hits

So let me walk free from you
You know that you want me to
Let me try something new
Let me walk away

If it's not one thing it's your mother
How I love her
How I love her
How I love her
But it's not so easy to say
Please won't you let me walk away
Let me walk away
Let me walk away

So let me walk on my own
And finish my ice cream cone
If we are to make it home
Then all will be well
Look see I'm a father now
I'm raising my own eyebrow
And being in my own row
And making life hell
This is me, see here I am
Doing the best that I can

This life has a subtle plan
But you couldn't tell

I Want You

You took all you could
And gave all you had
Knowing that I would have to understand
As you changed the locks
And threw out my socks
There was peace at hand
You sat in my chair
Your chin on your knees
I'm no longer there
And you look so pleased
I don't think that I know what to say
In my heart I love you anyway

I want you today

How can I score points
And win back your trust
Where our two hearts join
There's a sign of rust
From the tears you've cried
With the times I've lied
To the two of us
I don't think that I know what to say
In my heart I want you anyway

I can see the road behind me as I walk
I can feel the hurt that's burning as I talk

I can see the kids
As they play outside
I can read their lips
Their eyes open wide

Daphne

Daphne
Don't be ridiculous
This silence is killing us
Talk to me
Speaking with a loving tongue
Give life a sense of fun
Daphne
Don't be so cavalier
All that you want is here
Talk to me
Speak with your pretty eyes
Not without compromise

If you're used to a life of farces
Playing games of judge and jury
You know when you're wearing those glasses
You look like Nana Mouskouri

Daphne
Laugh and take silly time
Leave sadness way behind
Talk to me
Tell jokes and belly laugh
Don't cut your life in half

Daphne
Shelley wrote verse for you

He would have wanted to
Talk to me
Saying I must be thick
Love is a lunatic

If you're used to a life of farces
Playing games of judge and jury
You know when you're wearing those glasses
You look like Nana Mouskouri
So you can be adjourned
Daphne I'm so concerned

Daphne
Don't be ridiculous
This silence is killing us
Talk to me

Great Escape

Sitting there at home, he arrived home late
With no more blood cells to inebriate
He lunged at her there, she fell from the couch
He grabbed her body as he pulled her down
She was screaming no, kicking out at him
But he weighed a ton, she could never win
He fell down on her like a sack of snakes
Tears fell from her face as she cried and cried
When there's hope, when there's fear
What is there to say that he might hear
You turn him down with no mistake
Now you're leaving, the great escape

She ran from the room out of their back door
Leaving him to sleep on the front room floor

And she walked that night to the town hall square
She knew it was through and she didn't care
She stood up to him, he looked down on her
He shot the message and the messenger
When he woke he was sick with all the shame
Tears fell from his face as she cried and cried

She arrived back home, he was on his knees
Begging with his heart please come back to me

To Be A Dad

I lost the children
But they can be found
Home in a red house just across town
Sitting in boxes
Of opened up toys
Watching *The Simpsons*
And making some noise
I lost the children
But they're in great hands
When I cook the dinners
Right out of tin cans
I lost the children
And I have to pay
Some heavy duty on life everyday
Cupboards need filling
With deadlines to meet
Here in my cheque book
My fountain pen weeps
I should be thankful
And thankful am I
I went to the cleaners
And came back with my life

For a moment it all looked so grim
It looked like I would not get a thing
For a moment it all looked so sad
But now it's so good to be a dad

I lost the children
They haven't lost me
We're still together and happy to be
Out in the summer
On beaches in parks
Home in the winter and up with the larks
I should be thankful
And thankful am I
I went to the cleaners
And came back with my life

From pushchairs to games of football
My back was against every wall
For a moment it all looked so sad
But now it's so good to be a dad

For a moment it all looked so grim
It looked like I would not get a thing
For a moment it all looked so sad
But now it's so good to be a dad

I lost the children
They haven't lost me

Without You Here

I feel so empty
As the plane takes off
I see the ground below
I know that one day
It won't be long
That you will also know
Just how it feels
To leave you now, a hollow shell
A broken bow
I feel so empty high up in the air
Where heaven's meant to be
The distance gets me
When I'm on my own
Without you here with me

My world is turning
But it's upside down
Now you're so far away
While you are learning
How this world spins round
I'm in some other day
What can I do
But give my heart
From far away
A distant spark

I feel a challenge
For both you and I
That's how it has to be
In life there's balance
I hope time will fly
Without you here with me

What I am hoping for

As life moves on
And we reach finer years
We won't be thinking
Of the time that's gone
Or wading through our tears
We'll smile as one
And speak with pride
How life has swung
Back on our side

I feel tomorrow
Can't come by too soon
To bring you back to see
That love will follow
Like the red balloon
And you'll come home to me
I want you here with me

Index

Song credits

TEMPTED Words and Music by Christopher Difford and Glenn Tilbrook
© 1981, Reproduced by permission of EMI Music Publishing Ltd, London WC2H 0QY

PICCADILLY Words and Music by Christopher Difford and Glenn Tilbrook
© 1981, Reproduced by permission of EMI Music Publishing Ltd, London WC2H 0QY

SOMEONE ELSE'S BELL Words and Music by Christopher Difford and Glenn Tilbrook
© 1981, Reproduced by permission of EMI Music Publishing Ltd, London WC2H 0QY

WOMAN'S WORLD Words and Music by Christopher Difford and Glenn Tilbrook
© 1981, Reproduced by permission of EMI Music Publishing Ltd, London WC2H 0QY

IS THAT LOVE Words and Music by Christopher Difford and Glenn Tilbrook
© 1981, Reproduced by permission of EMI Music Publishing Ltd, London WC2H 0QY

LABELLED WITH LOVE Words and Music by Christopher Difford and Glenn Tilbrook
© 1981, Reproduced by permission of EMI Music Publishing Ltd, London WC2H 0QY

WHEN THE HANGOVER STRIKES Words and Music by Christopher Difford and Glenn Tilbrook © 1982, Reproduced by permission of EMI Music Publishing Ltd, London WC2H 0QY

BLACK COFFEE IN BED Words and Music by Christopher Difford and Glenn Tilbrook
© 1982, Reproduced by permission of EMI Music Publishing Ltd, London WC2H 0QY

KING GEORGE STREET Words and Music by Christopher Difford and Glenn Tilbrook
© 1985, Reproduced by permission of EMI Virgin Music Ltd, London WC2H 0QY

LAST TIME FOREVER Words and Music by Christopher Difford and Glenn Tilbrook
© 1985, Reproduced by permission of EMI Virgin Music Ltd, London WC2H 0QY

NO PLACE LIKE HOME Words and Music by Christopher Difford and Glenn Tilbrook
© 1983, Reproduced by permission of EMI Virgin Music Ltd, London WC2H 0QY

TOUGH LOVE Words and Music by Christopher Difford and Glenn Tilbrook
© 1987, Reproduced by permission of EMI Virgin Music Ltd, London WC2H 0QY

THE PRISONER Words and Music by Christopher Difford and Glenn Tilbrook
© 1987, Reproduced by permission of EMI Virgin Music Ltd, London WC2H 0QY

STRIKING MATCHES Words and Music by Christopher Difford and Glenn Tilbrook © 1987, Reproduced by permission of EMI Virgin Music Publishing Ltd, London WC2H 0QY

THE WAITING GAME Words and Music by Christopher Difford and Glenn Tilbrook © 1986, Reproduced by permission of EMI Virgin Music Ltd, London WC2H 0QY

PEYTON PLACE Words and Music by Christopher Difford and Glenn Tilbrook © 1988, Reproduced by permission of EMI Virgin Music Ltd, London WC2H 0QY

SLAUGHTERED GUTTED AND HEARTBROKEN Words and Music by Christopher Difford and Glenn Tilbrook © 1988, Reproduced by permission of EMI Virgin Music Ltd, London WC2H 0QY

SHE DOESN'T HAVE TO SHAVE Words and Music by Christopher Difford and Glenn Tilbrook © 1988, Reproduced by permission of EMI Virgin Music Ltd, London WC2H 0QY

LOVE CIRCLES Words and Music by Christopher Difford and Glenn Tilbrook © 1988, Reproduced by permission of EMI Virgin Music Ltd, London WC2H 0QY

MELODY MOTEL Words and Music by Christopher Difford and Glenn Tilbrook © 1988, Reproduced by permission of EMI Virgin Music Ltd, London WC2H 0QY

LETTING GO Words and Music by Christopher Difford and Glenn Tilbrook © 1991, Reproduced by permission of EMI Virgin Music Ltd, London WC2H 0QY

THE TRUTH Words and Music by Christopher Difford and Glenn Tilbrook © 1991, Reproduced by permission of EMI Virgin Music Ltd, London WC2H 0QY

WALK A STRAIGHT LINE Words and Music by Christopher Difford and Glenn Tilbrook © 1991, Reproduced by permission of EMI Virgin Music Ltd, London WC2H 0QY

WICKED AND CRUEL Words and Music by Christopher Difford and Glenn Tilbrook © 1991, Reproduced by permission of EMI Virgin Music Ltd, London WC2H 0QY

THERE IS A VOICE Words and Music by Christopher Difford and Glenn Tilbrook © 1991, Reproduced by permission of EMI Virgin Music Ltd, London WC2H 0QY

SOME FANTASTIC PLACE Words and Music by Christopher Difford and Glenn Tilbrook © 1993, Reproduced by permission of EMI Virgin Music Ltd, London WC2H 0QY

THIRD RAIL Words and Music by Christopher Difford and Glenn Tilbrook © 1993, Reproduced by permission of EMI Virgin Music Ltd, London WC2H 0QY

LOVING YOU TONIGHT Words and Music by Christopher Difford and Glenn Tilbrook © 1993, Reproduced by permission of EMI Virgin Music Ltd, London WC2H 0QY

IT'S OVER Words and Music by Christopher Difford and Glenn Tilbrook
© 1993, Reproduced by permission of EMI Virgin Music Ltd, London WC2H 0QY

COLD SHOULDER Words and Music by Christopher Difford and Glenn Tilbrook
© 1993, Reproduced by permission of EMI Virgin Music Ltd, London WC2H 0QY

ELECTRIC TRAINS Words and Music by Christopher Difford and Glenn Tilbrook
© 1995, Reproduced by permission of EMI Virgin Music Ltd, London WC2H 0QY

WALK AWAY Words and Music by Christopher Difford and Glenn Tilbrook
© 1995, Reproduced by permission of EMI Virgin Music Ltd, London WC2H 0QY

I WANT YOU Words and Music by Christopher Difford and Glenn Tilbrook
© 1995, Reproduced by permission of EMI Virgin Music Ltd, London WC2H 0QY

DAPHNE Words and Music by Christopher Difford and Glenn Tilbrook
© 1995, Reproduced by permission of EMI Virgin Music Ltd, London WC2H 0QY

GREAT ESCAPE Words and Music by Christopher Difford and Glenn Tilbrook
© 1995, Reproduced by permission of EMI Virgin Music Ltd, London WC2H 0QY

TO BE A DAD Words and Music by Christopher Difford and Glenn Tilbrook
© 1998, Reproduced by permission of EMI Virgin Music Ltd, London WC2H 0QY

WITHOUT YOU HERE Words and Music by Christopher Difford and Glenn Tilbrook
© 1998, Reproduced by permission of EMI Virgin Music Ltd, London WC2H 0QY

STRONG IN REASON Words and Music by Chris Difford and Glenn Tilbrook
© 1978 JAVEBERRY MUSIC LTD. All Rights Controlled and Administered by RONDOR MUSIC (LONDON) LTD. All Rights Reserved Used by Permission.

TAKE ME I'M YOURS Words and Music by Chris Difford and Glenn Tilbrook
© 1978 JAVEBERRY MUSIC LTD. All Rights Controlled and Administered by RONDOR MUSIC (LONDON) LTD. All Rights Reserved. Used by Permission.

SLAP AND TICKLE Words and Music by Chris Difford and Glenn Tilbrook
© 1979 JAVEBERRY MUSIC LTD. All Rights Controlled and Administered by RONDOR MUSIC (LONDON) LTD. All Rights Reserved. Used by Permission.

UP THE JUNCTION Words and Music by Chris Difford and Glenn Tilbrook
© 1979 JAVEBERRY MUSIC LTD. All Rights Controlled and Administered by RONDOR MUSIC (LONDON) LTD. All Rights Reserved. Used by Permission.

SLIGHTLY DRUNK Words and Music by Chris Difford and Glenn Tilbrook
© 1979 JAVEBERRY MUSIC LTD. All Rights Controlled and Administered by RONDOR MUSIC (LONDON) LTD. All Rights Reserved. Used by Permission.

GOODBYE GIRL Words and Music by Chris Difford and Glenn Tilbrook © 1979 JAVEBERRY MUSIC LTD. All Rights Controlled and Administered by RONDOR MUSIC (LONDON) LTD. All Rights Reserved. Used by Permission.

COOL FOR CATS Words and Music by Chris Difford and Glenn Tilbrook © 1979 JAVEBERRY MUSIC LTD. All Rights Controlled and Administered by RONDOR MUSIC (LONDON) LTD. All Rights Reserved. Used by Permission.

PULLING MUSSELS (FROM THE SHELL) Words and Music by Chris Difford and Glenn Tilbrook. © 1980 JAVEBERRY MUSIC LTD. All Rights Controlled and Administered by RONDOR MUSIC (LONDON) LTD. All Rights Reserved. Used by Permission.

ANOTHER NAIL IN MY HEART Words and Music by Chris Difford and Glenn Tilbrook. © 1980, 1988 JAVEBERRY MUSIC LTD. All Rights Controlled and Administered by RONDOR MUSIC (LONDON) LTD. All Rights Reserved. Used by Permission.

SEPARATE BEDS Words and Music by Chris Difford and Glenn Tilbrook © 1980 JAVEBERRY MUSIC LTD. All Rights Controlled and Administered by RONDOR MUSIC (LONDON) LTD. All Rights Reserved. Used by Permission.

I THINK I'M GO GO Words and Music by Chris Difford and Glenn Tilbrook © 1980 JAVEBERRY MUSIC LTD. All Rights Controlled and Administered by RONDOR MUSIC (LONDON) LTD. All Rights Reserved. Used by Permission.

IF I DIDN'T LOVE YOU Words and Music by Chris Difford and Glenn Tilbrook © 1980 JAVEBERRY MUSIC LTD. All Rights Controlled and Administered by RONDOR MUSIC (LONDON) LTD. All Rights Reserved. Used by Permission.

VICKY VERKY Words and Music by Chris Difford and Glenn Tilbrook © 1980 JAVEBERRY MUSIC LTD. All Rights Controlled and Administered by RONDOR MUSIC (LONDON) LTD. All Rights Reserved. Used by Permission.